Praise for Maureen's Writing:

"Maureen's empathy for the human spirit peppered with humor, makes her a refreshing delight to read and at the same time thought provoking." **Alison Barker**, San Diego

"One of the things I like about Maureen's writing is that it makes me want to converse with someone about what I've read – very thought-provoking! I also love to read things I get a good laugh from and Maureen is certainly in that category!" **Laura Meyer**

"Some of her writing stops me in my tracks. Maureen and Erma Bombeck are one and the same." **Linda Stafford**

"This book is a source of wisdom and humor written in a wonderfully natural way. Anyone can relate. Guaranteed to produce a chuckle, a heartfelt tear or a gem of insight and wisdom. Once you start, it is impossible not to keep reading." **Norman Nickle**

"Just when I think she can't reach any more soul depth, she does." **Nancy Wills**

"I absolutely loved this. Powerful, engaging, tender and inspiring." **Dr. Gary Hauck**

"Maureen has such valuable insight and writes so down-to-earth, logical, funny and wonderfully. She is a gifted writer. I love this book." **Barb Steffee**

"Maureen writes so beautifully. You feel like you are there with her. A big talent." **Harriette Cook**

"Maureen's writing is genuine, honest and filled with emotion and strong messages. It also often makes me laugh out loud." **Beverly Geyer**

"I enjoyed this - some of it is fun, some sad, some informative, some enlightening, some thought provoking, some just entertaining." **Kathy Kline**

"Even when Maureen takes a more serious note, there is always a chuckle in there somewhere, sometimes a hoot." **Kathy O'Donald**

"Maureen's writing is filled with humor and down to earth story telling. She entertains me and I relate to her messages." **Cathy Cornell**

Also by Maureen Burns

Forgiveness / A Gift You Give Yourself

Getting in Touch / Intimacy

Cara's Story (written with Cara Burns)

Run With Your Dreams

Looking and Laughing at Life

Maureen Burns

To Mick all the
Laughter of the
sunshine of the
soul

Maureen
Burns

First Printing   November 2009

ISBN: 0- 9613084-8-6

Published by:
Empey Enterprises
Greenville, Michigan
maureenburns@maureenburns.com

This book is dedicated to my Aunt Mary Empey -

You have encouraged, loved, supported and
guided me through my adult life.
You are one of the greatest gifts God has given me.
I love you dearly.
This is for you.

In Memory of Nelda Cushman - A dear, dear friend with whom I looked and laughed at life for 35 years - she left a big hole in my world.

Acknowledgements: A gazillion thanks ...

To my daughter, Colleen, who patiently and skillfully edits my writings, advises me, comes up with ideas and even squelches ones she doesn't think I should print. I wouldn't want to do this without her.

To my son, Dan, and daughter, Cara, who sat at breakfast on our vacation and excitedly encouraged me to do this book.

To my daughter, Donna, who calls to tell me specific things she likes in each article.

To my daughter-in-law, Ann-Drea, who took me aside and said, "Just do it!"

To my husband, Don, who encourages me, laughs with me and puts up with me.

To my sweet grandsons, Danny and Louie, who give me so much to write about.

To Julie Stafford Fowler and Rob Stafford who excitedly got me on this road and to Mary Stek for her wonderful creativity.

To my wonderful friends who are constant fodder for ideas, silliness, seriousness, comments, advice and critiques. Without them, I truly wouldn't have much to write about. They water my well.

To all the people who read me and take the time to comment, email, write and call me. I am more than touched by your kindness, your caring, your thoughts and your wonderful encouragement.

Contents

Life and Laughter

Remember When…

On the Road Again

Weather or Not

The Stage of Life

Insights and Inspirations

He Who Laughs…Lasts

For the Health of it

Spirituality and Philosophy

America, America

For Your Reading Pleasure

Relevant Recipes

Life and Laughter

Work Like a Dog

The other day I heard someone say they were working like a dog. I thought - whose dog? They certainly weren't talking about my dog. My dog's idea of work is a word with 3 letters in it, but it's not j-o-b, it's n-a-p.

His work consists of nappin' in the mornin', nappin' in the evenin', and nappin' at suppertime. The only thing my dog likes better than nappin' is more nappin'. And, then, of course, he is really excited each night when it's time to go to bed. He gets us all tucked in – that is kind of his work, I guess – and then he goes to bed. He's gotta get a good nights rest as he has all that work to do again tomorrow. He will sleep in as long as we do. He will sleep in so long that he misses his morning nap. How crazy is that?

Sometimes I wonder what he thinks about the weekend. Does he realize his workweek is over and it is time for him to rest?

As if my dog's life isn't soft enough, he loves to use a pillow. His head is so heavy, you know. Could be half a pound or so.

I found some cheap dog beds and now have them all over the house. I didn't think he'd know what to do with them, as he'd never seen one before. He tore it out of the bag and crawled right in. My husband and I just watched him, amazed. When he got all tucked in and curled into a ball, he looked up at us and we gasped, "He's gifted." How did he know that was for him and how did he know what to do with it? He is so happy to have the dog beds all over. Constantly napping on hard floors was such a bummer.

The only thing my dog likes better than a nap is a nap in the sun. When my dog hears me sing, "The sun will come out tomorrow" - He gets excited. That is good news for a dog. He can find a sliver of sunshine and bask in it for hours. He's like a CSI sleuth as he searches for any elusive sunny ray in our home.

I shouldn't sound like my dog is a bum and doesn't do anything. He has stuff to do. Each morning he searches for his toys and begs us to play with him. This playing hones his good work qualities: vision, persistence, positive attitude and communication skills. Communication isn't that easy for a dog. I mean they can't talk with words and they can't use their paws very well to help them talk.

Vision is hard for dogs too. They only see black and white and have no concept of time.

Persistence is one of his best skills. He doesn't give up easily once he wants something. For example, treats, more dinner, to go outside. And he is quite a good example of positive attitude. He rarely gets negative, unless he is looking at a cat or some critter.

My dog lives a pretty stress free life. No cell phone, no blackberry, no computer, no email, no newspapers (except to tear all over the house). He has no calendar, no planner. But he is not goal-less by any means. Oh, no, he has goals all right. His goals are defined and he is determined to go after them. His goals are quite simple. He wants to go wherever I go and be as physically close to me as he can. He also has a goal of sitting at the table with us. This is one he usually achieves. Now that the kids are gone, it is easy and routine to pull up a chair for the dog to sit with us. Doesn't everyone do that?

Dogs are the best. They give us lots of great lessons, but that's another column someday. Whoever said that dog is man's best friend was right on. And then there's all that adoration. Who else adores us like our dog? That may be the doggonedest best thing of all.

Look, Nina, Look

I am a regular at the grocery store. When I walk in the door, I often look at my watch and decide how many minutes it will take me, at the least, and then rush through the store as fast as I can to achieve that goal. You can imagine how little I notice as I go. I am on a mission. I know where stuff is. I go for it full throttle.

Compare that to shopping the other day with my two grand boys. Danny is three and a half and Louie is one and a half.

First, we have a big debate over whether we can have a video cart. I do not agree and stuff their little bodies into my regular cart. The tot is quite happy. The big boy is not so happy as he is wedged in looking through the bars. He can deal with it, I think. We are on a quick mission, after all.

Second, they *need* cookies. I ask the bakery manager if they have sample cookies. They do and we roll off quite happily with extra cookies for our "mission".

I am almost past the fresh meats when I hear screams, "lobsters". I guess I have previously noticed the lobsters in the tank, but not much. When I am looking for lobster, it is usually in the frozen chowder aisle.

We "ooh" and "ahh" over the lobsters as they crawl around the tank. It is really quite a sight and makes my chowder thoughts seem not so yummy.

I drag the boys away, even though they wish they could spend more time in lobster awe.

We enter the baking aisle and are moving fast. I am really rolling now and can almost see my mission accomplished. Then I hear little Louie yelling, "stish". I think - Why, oh, why, did I leave the diaper in the car? What am I going to do now? But before I think any further, I realize they are both yelling now and it is not for what I thought. They want to see *fish*, and they want it now.

We move to the very large fish tank and spend quite a bit of time. The fish are a variety of sizes and colors and kinds. The boys love all of them. Danny even knows their species. To me they are all just fish.

We then see dwarf guinea pigs. I think they are creepy mice, but Danny assures me they are delightful pets.

Then there are all the birds. They are colorful and chirpy. Some talk. Some ruffle their feathers. It is wonderful. I ponder if I have made a wrong turn and ended up at John Ball Park by mistake.

However, this joyful time does not go on forever. I end up remembering that we are on a mission and off we go . . . to the boys' wails and woe.

I have only one thing left to get and it is over by toys. As you can imagine, this is up their alley. The boys are full of joy and excitement as we meander down the toy aisles. This is so not my usual way of shopping.

We end up at the checkout. They both help load the groceries on the runner. They talk to the checker and introduce themselves, ask her name and other friendly questions. They seem to really enjoy this, as does the checker.

Danny gleefully signs the visa machine. I always sign it but never with glee. As we begin to leave the store, loaded for bear and clipping right along, Louie begins to yell, "Balloon". I look and, sure enough, balloons are all around the area. I don't get them one. They are thrilled just to see them.

But, alas, one more joy awaits us. Right by the door is an old brown horse. I have pennies and it is our lucky day. They ride with gusto, each taking their turn. It looks like so much fun. I almost want to hop on myself. Luckily, I manage to hold on to my senses.

As we wander out into the parking lot and their big car seats, I wonder at how much different this one stop shopping experience was compared to my normal run. I wonder at all the joy I miss when I time myself and rush to get through. I wonder at what else I am missing out on in life. When we take a moment to look at the world through the eyes of little children, it is amazing what we notice. Even at the grocery store.

Hunting Tales

Recently I asked a few women at the coffee house if they thought hunting was a hobby. They gave a resounding, "Yes". But it didn't stop there. The stories they told made the place rock with laughter.

One lovely lady said, "The mailman brings stuff from Cabela's for months, boxes and boxes. I don't even ask." She went on, "I tried to help once by washing their hunting clothes and putting them in the dryer. My husband nearly killed himself trying to stop me. 'The deer will smell us. They have to be scent free,' he yelped. Each year I beg him. 'Just let me buy a side of beef instead.' He never agrees. It's weird. They even paint milk cartons to go to the bathroom in – something about that scent free deal."

Another lady piped up. "My husband got a brand new snowmobile suit to hunt in. He was out hunting the first day and went to the bathroom outdoors. Later he smelled this bad odor. Turned out he had done his jobby job in his hood and hadn't realized it." She added, "One time he was out hunting and did his job under a tree only to realize that there was a hunter sitting above him on a branch, holding his gun and quietly watching."

"One year he spent $5000 to go to Colorado to hunt, another $2000 for a guide. Finally they saw an enormous elk. My husband was so excited. He shot it but hit the horns. He was left with only splinters to mount. It cost another $800 to ship the nasty head and meat home."

Once this conversation got started, the ladies could hardly talk fast enough. One shared, "They take so many groceries, they need a trailer to haul them. And then there's the beer. You could forget your gun, but don't forget your beer."

A lady pastor commented, "I think the woods is a place of worship." She had apparently gone hunting herself once, for duck. The duck had hit a tree and dropped dead. "Easy catch," she said.

My friend, Terry, has been hunting with the same buddies for over 20 years. His wife wrote me this. "They actually have a lodge on a lake in Michigan. Each year their planning becomes more elaborate. The main plan is about what they will eat and drink. They never ever pack a gun. One year they had the nerve to go "deer hunting" in Nassau. Their gourmet meals would put Martha Stewart to shame. The wine list would impress any five star restaurant. They begin planning in August. The actual hunting weekend is always done on November 15, which is when real hunters do their thing. One year they did go on the 15th of November. They caused a huge ruckus and bothered all the other hunters. They were so loud and having so much fun with their grills and wine, no one could hunt near them."

I received a few more stories from other wives, but the rest of them I couldn't print.

I saw the play, *Escanaba in da Moonlight* and still remember the raucous performances. It is one funny play and I'm sure you'd like it. I loved it. It just happens to coincide with this topic. And, after hearing the above women describe their husbands hunting hobbies, I think the play may be more realistic than we would like to think.

Would women behave like this? No, we have other things that we do that are weird. We wouldn't do this wild hunting thing. But then again, I have a sister-in-law who goes to tennis camp each summer with her girlfriends. They go for a few days and have a ball. They never pack a racket or play tennis.

*Note: Names have been omitted to protect the innocent.

The Stew of Life

Recent visits to our wonderful Farmer's Market have gotten me into the fall cooking mode. Seeing the enticing variety of squash, peppers, potatoes, etc. leaves me itching to make all those fall dishes – stuffed peppers and cabbage, chili, homemade bread, stew.

I have two favorite stew recipes. One is the stew* with wine and soup that bakes for hours. Mine came from Nancy Fox, a dear artist friend we lost to cancer. I have it in her handwriting, which makes it even more special. Our other favorite stew* cooks in a pumpkin in the oven and is a visual and tasty delight. That recipe comes from our friend, Sharon, and is a showstopper. You definitely feel like Martha Stewart when you prepare this keeper.

Stew always seems like a good metaphor for life. If I make my stew and only put in onions and gravy, it is lame. If I make it and only put in potatoes, it is bland. If I make it and leave out the carrots, it is not as beautiful. If I leave out the peas, it is missing something, and on and on. It is only when we put in all the variety that we get this delectable dish full of flavor and uniqueness.

When I think of how uniqueness and variety add to the spice of life, I find many examples – movies, TV shows, books, plays, music. We all gravitate towards different choices, and thus, our experiences, tastes and discussions can be richer. A friend suggests something we wouldn't think of on our own and our life gets broader when we try it. Even if we don't like it, we have grown. I remember telling our friend, Gary, that he would just love the CD, *Graceland* by Paul Simon. Our whole family loves it and knows the words to the entire disc. It won the Grammy for best album of the year. Gary hated it and still laughingly reminds me of it.

Suggestions we get from other people bring new things into our realm, things we might never find or try on our own. Some we like. Some we don't. The value is in experiencing different things in this grand potpourri of life.

I am in a scrabble group, ages range from 30s to 70s. It is a richer group because of the wide age range. We are all better for it.

Last year we went to the local ecumenical thanksgiving service held outside in downtown Greenville. It was moving to see the different pastors and choirs, to hear the different prayers. It is impossible to have an ecumenical service if there is only one faith or one church. It is the variety of the different congregations that makes it such a special blessing.

It would be an empty athletic roster if we were all on the same team. There would be no World Series, no Super Bowl, and no March Madness.

Where would we go to vacation if the world was all just like here? No deserts, no glaciers, no palm trees. No difference in cultures. No need for National Geographic or travel channels. No fun. Many of the best marriages and friendships are between opposites, each bringing their own unique flavor to the relationships.

Ah, yes, the spice and variety of life. When Auntie Mame said, "Life is a banquet and so many people are starving," I don't think she was talking about food. Life is a rich stew indeed, and mighty tasty for each of us when we try and experience it in different ways.

Before I close, let me give you one more favorite stew recipe. If you have an elephant in your freezer and a big crowd coming for a fall gathering, here is a superb recipe for Elephant Stew. I found it in the newspaper many years ago and still have the yellowed dog-eared copy.

Elephant Stew

1 medium sized elephant
1 ton of salt
½ ton of pepper
200 bushels of carrots
500 bushels of potatoes
3000 sprigs of parsley
1500 gallons brown gravy

Cut elephant into bite sized pieces (this will take about 2 months). Cut vegetables into cubes (another 2 months). Place meat in pan and cover with the gravy. Simmer 4 weeks. Shovel in salt and pepper. Stir. Simmer 4 more weeks. Garnish with parsley. I like to toss in a few peas for color.

This will serve 3800 people, but if you expect more, you can add 2 small rabbits. Beware, though. Most folks don't like to find a hare in their stew.

*See chapter 15 for the recipes.

Ticky Tacky Thingamajig

"What was this mean?" That question was from our friend, Tony, who is Lebanese, lived in Greece for over 20 years and has now lived in the United States for 12 years. Tony is charming, handsome and bright. He speaks 30 languages and 50 dialects. The new one he is studying is Mandarin, the main language of China. Most languages make sense when you learn them. English, on the other hand, has lots of things that do not make sense. We take understanding these words for granted. We grew up with them and to us they are common. But for poor Tony, brilliant as he is, they are a mystery.

We go on with our conversation. "What was this mean … willy nilly?" I have to think about that. I look it up and it is willy-nilly. I thought it was two words. I actually have never seen it in print before. It even has a definition: whether one likes it or not.

"I am making a list of these words," he said. "They are crazy and make no sense. I can't figure them out. How about boogie woogie? Thing-a-majig? Pigglywiggly? Hanky panky?"

I try to explain, "Boogie woogie is a dance. Thing-a-majig is like a thing-a-mabob." That doesn't seem to help.

I get my dictionary. Boogie-woogie is a specific way of playing jazz, often on the piano. So I guess it is not a dance, well kind of. Thingamajig is something you can't think of the name of, like thingamabob. That helps. Pigglywiggly is a grocery store in Southern states, but as a word, it is not in the dictionary. Hanky-panky is one every American knows easily.

It means naughty. I am surprised as I look these odd words up and find they are all one word, not two as I had thought.

Tony doesn't stop. His list is long. "How about namby pamby, wishy washy, itsy bitsy?" Turns out namby-pamby means weak, as does wishy-washy. Itsy bitsy brings to mind a teeny weenie bikini but Tony doesn't know that song nor has he heard of teeny weenie.

When I look, I spell teeny weenie wrong. It is teeny-weeny and means the same as teensy-weensy. It also means the same as itsy-bitsy and itty-bitty. They all mean tiny.

Tony adds that in French, there is one word for each verb. It is simple. There is nothing like this mumbo jumbo. I added the mumbo jumbo part. When I look it up it means meaningless language. It may be meaningless but one has to admit, it is colorful and fun.

Tony has more: topsy-turvy, ticky tacky, upsie daisie and hotsie totsie. "What they mean?"

Well, of course, topsy-turvy means upside down. To my surprise, ticky tacky, upsie daisie and hotsie tootsie are not in my dictionary. I give Tony my meager definitions: Ticky tacky means tacky; upsie daisie means get up and hotsie tootsie means vavavoom. He looks at me quizzically. "Is vavavoom like driving a car fast?" My, this is complicated.

Tony has more questions. "Hurly-burly, hustle bustle, dilly-dally, neck and neck"?

Hurly-burly means a commotion. Neck and neck means running even in a race. Hustle bustle and dilly-dally are not in the book. I explain they mean fast and slow. To just say fast and slow would sure be a lot easier on the person studying our language.

Tony is nearly spent. "I have one more," he says. "What is hokey pokey"?

I tell him it is a song but I wonder to myself, "What if the hokey pokey is what it's all about?"

This has been a fun conversation. The evening has drawn to a close. I tell Tony, "It is going to get cold soon. Can you handle that?"

He says, "Ah, yes, I just need to get some ear muffins."

I look at his wife. She quietly says to me, "I know it is wrong. I should have corrected him long ago, but it is so cute."

I agree and the vision of Tony in his ear muffins warms me all the way home. I might add that we did not dilly-dally but sat neck and neck as we drove our thingamajig through the hustle bustle of the night. And I'm not going to mention any hanky-panky.

Cacophony of Cell Phones

I'm waiting to get on a plane right now. It seems everyone around me is on their cell phones, many nearly screaming.

The woman behind me can be heard in the next concourse. The man next to me is yelling post office numbers and delivery dates. The man on my other side is talking money, loudly. I assume his extra volume is to be sure we all hear him.

The guy in front of me just keeps looking at me and rolling his eyes.

I get on the plane. People all over are chatting on their cell phones with zeal. It's like it's the last chat of their lives.

The woman I mentioned above, the one, who could be heard across two concourses, can now be heard across the entire plane. As I jot these notes the man next to me is dialing. The lady behind me is on hold. It goes on and on.

Recently I saw some young kids on bikes. I am guessing they were fourth-graders. Three of them were on cell phones. It sure looked strange to me, sort of like ice cream and anchovies. Small bikes and cell phones just don't seem to go together, but I guess they do.

It seems no one can be quiet anymore. Being with friends on your bikes isn't enough. We also need to be chatting with other friends at the same time.

Getting on a plane is no longer a solitary adventure. It now consists of you and the person at the other end of your phone line.

Now we have a latecomer - Sort of a surfer kind of dude. Flip-flops and a Jimmy Buffet look. Even though no one is in the aisle he is having a hard time finding his seat. He's so engrossed in his very loud conversation. It consists of "cool, dude, man, whatever, bro." It lets us all know he's a wild and crazy guy.

It seems most of these airplane conversations end with, "I'll call you as soon as I land." I'm sure that's a given.

Not long ago, I was having lunch at a restaurant. Two guys were having lunch together at the table next to me. They were both on their cell phones the entire time. They didn't even look at each other. I'm sure they were having a great time; it just didn't look like it.

The cell phone isn't what I hate. What I hate is having to listen to everyone else's conversations. Why do they have to talk so loud? Do they assume everyone wants to hear their every word? Or don't they even think?

When I use my cell phone in public places I try hard to talk discreetly and not bother others. I realize sometimes this doesn't work, but I do try.

I was at our local movie theater and a guy actually made a call during the previews.

"Hey, I'm at the movies. Yeah," he bellowed. When he finished that call, he made another. I thought the blackness of the movie theater was safe - Obviously not so.

On a trip to Grand Rapids I forgot my cell phone and had to make a call. I felt lost. I stopped at several places that used to have phone booths. Until then I hadn't realized that, like Oldsmobiles, phone booths are nearly extinct. When I asked folks if I could use their phone, they looked at me like I'd asked to spit in their food.

Cell phones are clearly what's happenin' now. They are here to stay. They are often a blessing.

I wonder, am I just crabby? Why is it that all this cell phone cacophony seems so irritating to me?

Perhaps there is a new pill to lessen the effects of all the cell phone craziness. If there is, I probably need a scrip - and pronto.

Good thing I have my cell phone. I can call my doctor as soon as we land.

Taking a Trip is a Trip

Vacation time. Spring Break. Let's get away. All these things have a nice ring to them but sometimes the getting there makes one wonder. Is the gettin' really worth the goin'?

There's all that stuff to tend to before you go: the mail, the newspapers, the yard, the house, the phone, the job. Oh, yeah, and the dog. Our dog is quite neurotic and needs lots of attention. He also has seizures and needs lots of TLC. This calls for very special care when he is left.

For some odd reason, I always feel I should leave my house clean when I go. I never feel that way when I am home. In fact, rarely does that notion ever enter my mind when I am home? So, there is all that to do. And, of course, the laundry has to be all done.

I also like to have work in order. Things I have put off for ages will get done under the gun of going away for a couple of days. I really need to go away more frequently just to accomplish things.

Years ago, my dear friend, Nancy Hammond told me about her packing list. She was always wise and organized. She even had lists to accommodate different kinds of trips.

So I made a packing list and have used it faithfully ever since. It has not, however, made for no errors in our packing.

Once we took our kids for a holiday weekend to a motel with a pool. We drove through a horrible blizzard. When we arrived we realized we had not packed our bathing suits. We ended up borrowing suits from relatives in that city. Thank goodness.

Once we went to Traverse City and left an entire suitcase at home. We had to have it UPS'd to us. That wasn't as bad as my friend, though. She and her husband drove from Port Huron to Traverse City for a weeklong visit. He left all of her bags at home and ended up buying her a whole new wardrobe and everything else she needed. She was pretty happy about that turn of events.

Still worse was another friend. He just so happens to be a judge, which even makes it more amusing, somehow. He pulled his car up to the door at Kent County Airport and unloaded his family and bags. They went in and flew off to the Bahamas for a week. The next day he was sitting in church there and remembered… He had left his car sitting right at the entrance, running. Luckily, someone at the airport took care of it for him. That remains one of my favorite stories.

Speaking of leaving things and taking off - My sister in law and friends visited once, they all brought their kids and we had a fun day. We waved them off as they drove away. We came back into our house and there sat Tony, their son, watching our TV. We had nothing to do but wait. No cell phones. Can you imagine?

They got half way to Grand Rapids and the kids were fighting in the back. My sister in law yelled at Tony to stop it. His brother replied, "Tony didn't do it. He's not here." Screech. U-turn.

If you add all the hassle of getting ready to go on a trip and combine it with all the hassle of returning home, it is something to consider. Usually we feel like we need a vacation from our vacation. It always takes me awhile to get going in work, routine and our normal life again. I think if we added up the time prepping for a trip and the time it takes to regroup after a trip, the time spent would be longer than the trip.

However, there is nothing like getting away, right? Ahhhh…

Lovin' the Lattes

My daughter, Colleen, walks into a Starbucks and orders a tall hazelnut latte with skim milk; very light syrup and no whipped cream or toppings. The barrister looks at her rather disgustedly and says, "So, basically, you want coffee with cream."

"Well, I *guess*," she says, "But I still want you to charge me $3.75."

What is it that has made so many of us become coffee drink addicts? Not that there's anything wrong with that

It's been a journey.

A few years ago, in order to enjoy a special java, one had to visit a big city like Seattle or New York. Then, around 1997 Starbucks arrived in the Detroit area.

A couple years later, Grand Rapids sprouted coffee shops. We quickly followed and now Monday through Saturday they are bustling with happy folks getting their daily jolt of java. Locals are giddy with caffeine excitement.

Why do we love it so? It is not just about the coffee. Though, I must confess that many days it is the thought of a morning latte that gets my body out of bed in the morning.

Coffee shops have a loyal following of both men and women who love the ambiance. They have the atmosphere of an Italian café where everyone knows your name. We love the banter behind the counter and appreciate the cheer and friendliness served with our coffee.

We love the smell. Starbucks is considering adding more food. One of their dilemmas is wanting the customer to always smell coffee, not food, when they walk in the door. And, ahh, it does smell good. Even those who hate coffee love the smell of a fresh cup brewing.

Folks fill the coffee shop to do a lot more than drink coffee. They meet for business, prayer, chat, book clubs, dates, after exercise, computer work, reading, solitude. Sermons and speeches are written there. Bills are paid there. It is a come-all-do-all kinda place. Oh, and don't forget you can buy gifts, books, music, food and coffee beans. And, if you aren't part of the coffee crowd, there are lots of other beverages to float your boat.

For many of us, embedded in our TV memories, are visions of Niles and Frasier ordering coffee. Coffee shops have a language of their own and this jargon has become mainstream America.

Half-caff. Grande. Venti. Tall. Macchiato. Mocha. Café Den Da. Double tall skinny decaf foamless no whip. Medium decaf skinny latte. Mocha breve. Soy venti. Dirty Chai. Small skinny dry cap. Half shot. Full shot. Small extra hot skinny no whip. Sugar free non-fat medium no foam. Medium light syrup no whip. Skim cap extra foam two shots sugar free sweet.

Time Magazine says there are 87,000 drink combinations available at Starbucks. I am guessing this is true for most coffee shops. I only have about ten in my repertoire and I normally order the same one each day. I like my ritual. I have worked with Julie, the barrister, to get it just right. I am hooked.

Here are some funny orders from her archives.

"I want that cold thing."

"Remember last fall you made me that one thing with caramel?"

"I want whatever that thing is my wife drinks." The barrister wonders, who is your wife?

"Just surprise me, but I don't like caramel or chocolate or hazelnut or macadamia, etc."

"Make me what that one girl makes me."

"I don't like coffee."

And lastly, "What do you have that doesn't taste coffeeish?"

Ah, yes, we love our coffee drinks, whatever they might be. We are aware that there is a large mark up on the product, but we don't care. It is so much bigger than that to us. It is, as the credit card companies say, "Priceless".

But, I suppose we should also beware. We shant overdo or we could act like Kramer on Seinfeld when he got free coffee for life. Who could forget his shaky crazy hyped up shenanigans?

There is a good test, though. You know you have had too much coffee when you have walked twenty miles on your treadmill and then notice it is not plugged in.

Change Your Clocks . . . If You Can

"What's that beeping?" is an oft-asked question at our house. For my husband, the beeping is like an extremely irritating chalkboard screech. Personally, I guess I hear the beeps but they're like background music – way, way back. I hear them but I don't pay much attention. Half the time though, I guess I don't really hear them at all. Until I smell the burning. Then I remember. "Oh, darn, the oven."

It is common in my house for two or three timers to be going off at once. Let me explain. First, I love to cook and that often calls for lots of delicate timing techniques. Secondly, I use timers for all kinds of odd reasons: to remind me to put the laundry in the dryer; to remind me to call someone; to remind me to do all kinds of things.

One challenge with the timers is to actually hear the beep and respond. A bigger challenge is to remember what I set the darn thing for. I wonder - Why'd I set this?

I ask, "Do you know why I set this? Hmmm." No one ever knows, and that usually includes me. But sometimes the answer comes quickly, sometimes not so quickly and sometimes not at all. Beep. Beep. Beep....

To add to this cacophony, my cell phone is usually on low battery so it beeps all the time too. Now do you see why my husband gets irritated? Are you irritated just reading about this craziness? Can anyone relate? Beep. Beep.

And then along comes the time change and there are all the clocks to deal with. I seem to have a serious disability when it comes to clock setting. When it is time for daylight savings time, I remember "spring forward, fall back". I am aware which day we need to do it. I just don't know how to reset all the clocks in my life.

Luckily my mate does this for me. What a guy. My hero, for sure! He resets every single clock in the house. He doesn't even need to be asked. He just gets up and does it silently and surely. You can set your watch by him.

But not my watch! My watch I often end up taking to the jeweler to reset. This is not due to my stupidity. It is due to the fact that I have fake nails and I can't get them to work the thingamabob that resets my watch. It's not easy being me.

And then there is the car clock to deal with. I have been known to stop at the car dealer to beg them to change the clock for me. They are always kind and do it. They want my business.

Sometimes my kids come home and change the car clock for me. But then I have to deal with all the shame. I'm a grown woman. I'm a college grad. I should be able to handle this timer and clock stuff. What's wrong with me?

My daughter assures me, "You can do it. You just don't want to." I'm not sure it is really assurance. It borders on scolding. How right she is, though. I really don't want to do it. I prefer to have someone else reset all my clocks.

Sports Illustrated summed it up for me. "These are the souls that time men's tries."

Of course they were talking about the official timers at track meets. But I think it sums up my dilemma just right. Tick Tock. Beep. Beep.

Thief! Thief!

Last weekend we had friends visiting from Seattle. I stopped at the store to grab some fresh bread. It sounded like a quick easy task. Hah!

My friend, Norm decided to go in with me. At the time this sounded okay. We quickly picked out our bread and rushed to the automated self-serve checkout line. Norm had never seen such a thing before, but he was all about helping me. He's a very nice guy.

It began. "Scan your first Item."

I did. No problem. But then the machine kept yelling at me. "Return item to the bagging area. Return item to the bagging area. Return item to the bagging area."

I looked over at my helper. He had taken the bag off the rack and was unsuccessfully trying to open it. The plastic was determined not to separate but he tried and tried, as he held the bread in his hand.

"Return item to the bagging area. Return item to the bagging area." There was no respite from the machine, which kept giving us the command.

Tensions began to rise. People began to look.

"Norm," I said, "You've got to put the bread in the bag and put the bag back on the frame."

He looked at me confused. He was determined to open that plastic bag.

Now let me add here that Norm is highly educated. He is a world traveler, a mountain climber, a counselor and fluently speaks two languages. He is no dumb guy, for sure.

But this checking out scenario was getting him good. Finally the attendant came to our rescue. With her expert assistance, he was soon able to get the bag open, put the bread in it and replace it in the proper place. Whew. Then we thought we were almost done. Wrong.

The machine continued. "Which payment do you prefer?"

I decided to pay with cash. How easy is that? It turns out not very. My dollars were a bit bent and soon I was too. Over and over we tried to feed the money monster to no avail. At last we got it to eat. We thought we were ready to go but then the machine began chanting at me again. "Replace the items on the counter. Replace the items on the counter. Replace the items on the counter."

It sounded like it was yelling, "Thief. Thief. Help. Get the police. Thief. Thief."

It wouldn't quit. Once again, heads turned, tensions mounted. Actually the tensions hadn't even eased yet. Who would have guessed we would have this much of an ordeal just buying a small loaf of bread?

I looked over and my helper had now taken the bread in the bag and was holding it. To him it seemed like the right thing to do, especially as we were in a hurry. But, of course, those of us who shop there regularly know that you cannot do that. In fact, it is a great big NO, NO. You must leave your things on the rack until they tell you that you can take them, and then, only then, may you take them off the rack.

Norm did not understand. He said, "In Seattle we don't have this kind of stuff. We just go get our bread and pay the man for it." Ah, for the easy days before modern conveniences.

After word: The bread was excellent and after a bit of Sangria we forgot the frustration and tension of the whole ordeal.

Mental note: Perhaps next time baking my own bread would be quicker and easier.

Celebrate Good Times . . . Come On!

If you have been to a wedding reception in your life, you have likely heard the Kool and the Gang song lyrics, "Celebrate good times, come on!" It is a mover and shaker song, designed to get the crowd going. Though I don't really care for the song, I love the concept. I think we all need to celebrate good times. Come on.

Today was a two-year anniversary of my exercise class. We celebrated with a good ole party of food, laughs, conversation and bunco. Everyone had a great time and it felt good to pause and reflect on something we all share and enjoy.

In December my husband surprised me with dinner at the Winter Inn to celebrate the 42nd year of our engagement. It is wonderful to celebrate wedding anniversaries. It is also special to celebrate first dates and engagements, especially one so long ago.

My kids always had half birthday celebrations. They got to choose the dinner and receive one gift. I remember one of them telling my friend,

Bonnie, how their Dad was older than her. He was 32 and a half. When you are a kid, a year is a long time. Why not celebrate birthdays in two parts?

I also gave my kids a birthday party every year. Children are young for such a short time. Who said they should have only a couple birthday parties? Why not one a year? Who cares? Celebrate good times. Come on.

Adults often have birthday parties starting at 21, 30, 40 and 50. I really haven't noticed anyone having a party for their sixtieth. Then along comes 70 and the parties pick up again: 70, 80, 90, 100, woo-hoo.

People celebrate their high school and college reunions. That's good. But there are all kinds of groups we could celebrate reunions with. A friend of mine has reunions with her elementary classmates. I like to have reunions with people I used to work with. There are always special bonds we share with different groups in our lives. Reunions are so good for the spirit.

I remember when one of my children got a D and we had a family party. Someone asked why we were excited about a D. "Because it wasn't an F," I replied. Progress is certainly good cause for celebration.

People are used to bridal and baby showers. My friends and I have always thought we should have a shower after being married 30 years. That's when everything you own looks yucky and worn out. Wouldn't it be wonderful to have a shower then?

When people celebrate they do so with parties and festivities. They honor and commemorate. An unknown quote I found said, "Support wildlife. Throw a party."

Ellen DeGeneres said, "Stuffed deer heads on walls are bad enough, but it's worse when they are wearing dark glasses and have streamers and ornaments in their antlers because then you know they were enjoying themselves at a party when they were shot."

When I look back at my life of celebrations, one sticks in my mind as an extra special blessing. The memory warms my heart. My friend, Rita, found out she had cancer and was given three months to live.

Rita and I were roommates when we were single in Grand Rapids. We lived with about twelve other girls. Through the years we had never all been together. I hosted a tea party to celebrate Rita. They came from all over, even out of state.

Rita came in with her bare head covered with a lovely scarf. We gathered around the table, prayed, ate, laughed, talked and had tea. In the midst of it all, Rita ripped her scarf off and shared her very personal cancer journey.

Rita had gotten very ill after her diagnosis and we weren't sure she would make the party. She rallied, came, felt great and enjoyed every second. When she got home, her illness took over and she died not long after. Not all of us got to the funeral, but that really didn't matter. We had done our celebrating with her, in all her glory. It was one of the most special afternoons I have experienced. Death was knocking on the door. No one would open it. We weren't done celebrating yet. When the day was over we all knew we had celebrated a very, very special event. Life - while it was still here.

Think for a bit and I'm guessing you will come up with some mighty fine reasons in your life to party. Go ahead. You deserve it. And so do the people you care about.

Celebrate good times, come on!

Mourning Morning

It should be a simple thing. People do it every day. You would think it would get easier after one has done it for more than a half a century. (Boy, that's a depressing thought!)

For me personally, it still takes all I've got. Against every force within me, I do it. I grit my teeth and make it happen. I am talking about getting up in the morning, of course.

Did you ever wonder why morning and mourning are so close? I think it is because we are mourning our inability to stay in bed. Don't you agree? Why have we never realized that before?

There are clearly two kinds of people in the world – the morning people and the night owls. I guess I am an owl. I love the nighttime. I slug around in the morning, putting one foot in front of the other, but it takes effort. I am never perky or gleeful in the a.m.
Oh no, not me.

My dear sister-in-law, Rosie, leaves for work a little after eight each day. She gets up around six because she likes to take her time in the morning. She says she loves to linger over her coffee, enjoy her daily oatmeal, take it slow and easy, relishing every second. Man, I think that is so whacked. What the heck! She could be sleeping nearly two more hours and then rushing like crazy like the rest of us. That would make more sense, to me at least.

I should also say that Rosie goes to bed nine-ish each night. She relishes her early bedtime too. I would resent that. I would resent all the TV I would be missing. I would resent that wonderful nighttime laziness, the doin' what ya want when life quiets down.

We raised four children. No one in our house was ever an early bird. One daughter now likes to go to bed at 10 and we think that kind of behavior is odd. I mean, that's when the really good shows begin. She will say things like, "I feel better the next day when I get my rest." That's a bit much.

But, what if the rest of us went to bed earlier each night? Would the morning really be easier? Would we feel better for the first few hours after we rise? That's a hard pill to swallow.

I mope around in the early morning. About mid-afternoon I want a nap. I don't take one but I really, really want one. Okay, sometimes I do take one, but it is rare, I swear. About four p.m. I kick into high gear. Look out world. I am movin' and shakin' to get stuff done, faster than the speed of light, or something like that. I'm faster than the speed in the morning, at least.

They say that as we age we get up earlier. I do find that true. I wake up much earlier than I used to. I also wake up around 4 a.m. and lay there wide eyed with my brain rapidly engaged as I desperately try, try, try to get back to sleep. That is a delightful part of being my age and many of you will identify.

People seem to line up on one side or the other on this issue. They usually do not understand the other side and are often irritated by them. What would the world be like if we were all the same? What if we all stayed up enjoying until the cows came home? What if we all hated morning? What if we all got up very early for work, lingered and enjoyed before tottering off to work? Would work be different then?

We sleep about 1/3 of our life. Wow. Just think. If we put it end-to-end it would be a really big nap. But we don't do that. We take it a little at a time, our daily dose. And whether we are morning people or night owls, for each of us, our way is the right way and the rest of those other folks are just plain oddballs. Like Frank Sinatra sang, "I did it my way".

Vacation Exhaustion

What is it about a vacation that is so exhausting? Isn't it supposed to be time to refresh and renew us in mind, body and spirit? Wasn't that on the vacation brochure? Oh, wait; my vacation didn't have a brochure. If it had, I am sure it would have said that.

For a week or so before a vacation, there is a lot of planning, packing, primping, catching up, working hard to get away, working hard to do things you should do while you are on vacation, etc. This is very stressful. In fact, after just writing that sentence I feel like I need a vacation.

Vacation preps seem to go like this. Pack. Prepare. Rush. Rush. Do. Do. Ready. Set. Go.

And then you arrive on vacation and it goes like this. So tired. Tired. Still wound up a bit. But then on about day three, here it comes, relaxation. Ahh, now that feels mighty good. I needed that. Just what the doctor ordered.

The next day dawns. Oh, my goodness, we leave in a couple of days. Oh, no, we go home tomorrow. Pack. Pack. Clean up. Gear up. Travel. Drive. Drive. Drive. Unpack the car. Unpack the stuff. Do all the laundry. Get back into your life. Gear up, tomorrow is looming.

Back to reality. So, so tired. That vacation wore me out. I think I need another vacation.

Can anybody else relate to this madness? And yet we go. We never give up. We wear ourselves out looking for that elusive bit of relaxation and fun.

Each year, when my kids were being raised, I would make a big long list as soon as summer began. Then along would come mid-August and, whoa Nellie, where did the summer go? Wouldn't it be nice to have a bit of money each time you heard someone ask that question? But where does it go?

Summer begins full of plans and expectations. We are going to see all these places. We are going to do all these projects. We are going to go here and there. We are going to read, relax and enjoy. The days fly by. We keep busy every day, but somehow, when this time of year arrives, our lists are mostly undone; our summer plans are mostly put off until another year.

I think with our limited amount of hot, sunny weather in Michigan, we feel extra motivated to wring all we can out of those three measly summer months. But we never wring hard enough.

I like to think I am an optimist, though. I am not going to give up. I am going to try it one more time. Vacation, here we come.

P.S. Totally unrelated but very worthwhile: My daughter gave me the best blueberry crisp recipe. It is not too heavy, not too sweet and full of berries. Oh, and it is easy and fast. You may want to make it while you ponder your vacation routines. It is always better to ponder with a full tummy.

*See chapter 15 for recipe.

Wacky Warnings

Okay, we all know life is hard. We need to pay attention. We need to follow the rules. However, there are some really goofy rules.

The other day I picked up a prescription for my dog. It was a bag of pills. On the bag, in important looking letters, it said, "Do not give with grapefruit juice."

I don't know about you, but my dog never drinks grapefruit juice. Nor have I ever considered he might. Did they need to put that on the envelope?

Some of you have seen the breathing masks that folks wear for sleep apnea. They go over your face. Straps hold it on your head and surround your head in several places. This all connects to a huge hose that runs from the mask on the face and connects to a machine that feeds one moist air through the night. The machine is serious looking, kind of heavy and has a big read out area where it lists information, which is all lit up. You can tell this is not something to take lightly. The directions state, right at the top of the list: "Do not wear this in the bath tub." I swear this is true. Now I ask you, what kind of fool hooks himself all up, adjusts his mask, plugs it in and decides, "I think I'll take a bath now".

I asked others if they had any crazy directions to share. One noticed that hemorrhoid cream says, "For external use only". Uwwwwww. Who would look at that, smell it and think, "Yumm"?

Connie said her hair dryer read, "Do not use while sleeping." I called her and said, "Is this true?" I couldn't believe it. She assured me it was. Have any of you dried your hair with a hair dryer while you were sleeping? Not me. To go along with that one, I found another hair dryer warning that said, "Do not use while taking a shower." Are they serious? Come on.

Directions on a disposable razor list: "Do not use during an earthquake." An iron guides us with, "Warning. Do not iron clothing that is on your body." A curling iron lists, and I kid you not, "Do not insert into any bodily orifice." Hello!

On a bottle of children's cough syrup for age 2+ it says, "Do not consume alcohol or drive and do not take if you're pregnant or nursing." My 3 and 5-year-old grandsons rarely drink and drive and I don't think any of their little play date friends are pregnant.

Ronda said that on the box for suppositories it says, "Do not take orally." And a thermometer instructs, "Do not use orally after using rectally." I will not say more on that. I believe that one may be a good idea.

Continuing on, Jackie said she has a bottle of body lotion, which reads, "Prolonged use may cause irritation to urinary tract." It's just body lotion, for heaven's sake. We don't eat or drink it. We just apply it to our hands and legs. Gosh, I am so confused.

Hollie reminded me of the cup of coffee you get at the drive-thru. It reads, "Caution. Hot." And, of course, if it were cold you would not accept it. Right? Do I see lawsuit in here somewhere?

Mo said her lawn mower read, "Do not use to mow shrubs." She said you know that is because some idiot did it. I loved the visual I got of that in my mind. Think about it. Vroom. Vroom. To go along with this foolishness, a chain saw manual lists, "Warning! Do not attempt to stop blade with your hands."

A microwave oven warns, "Do not use for drying pets." Gives new meaning to Mulligan Stew. My dog's name is Mulligan.

Linda wondered about the written directions at the bank ATM for the Braille. Oh, yes, that's an odd one.

Kean said when you call the electric company to say your power is out, they tell you to go to your computer and report it on their website. Hey, wait a minute. What about all those who have computers that need electricity?

A couple folks mentioned directions that say, "Get in the left lane and turn right."

And, several, of course, mentioned that one about, "if you have a certain condition that lasts more than four hours, call your doctor." Hmmmmm.

I think my favorite in this inane collection is on a superman costume. "This costume does not enable you to fly."

I guess common sense isn't so common anymore.

Oh, the Games People Play

I raised four children and I remember when my first two left for college, I quit cooking. I thought, 'Why cook for only four people?'

When my last child left home, I remember thinking, 'Yippee-i-o-kay, now I can play games.'

First, I began a monthly Scrabble club. It involves eating, drinking, laughing and talking. Oh yeah, and Scrabble. I contacted the National Scrabble Association and brought all the rules to our first game. The group made a quick decision. "Let's forget the rules and just play." So we do. We have dictionaries, lists of two letter words and words without vowels, etc. We use whatever we want, whenever we want and take as long as we want to make our word. After our first game, we eat. After our second, we have dessert. It is a marvelous plan. Oh, and, of course, we have snacks along the way. We don't want to get faint.

Then I was talking to a friend in Chicago who mentioned her Bunco group. I immediately perked up and asked for details. As she explained it all, I felt like Tina Fey on *30 Rock*, "I want to go there".

I asked a fun friend, Patti, if she had ever heard of Bunco. Luckily she had and we immediately began a group. Bunco is a complicated dice game. You may not think it is all that complicated but you have to be very bright to handle all the details. You have to roll dice, count to six, and be able to eat, laugh, talk, drink and throw the dice all at once. It is quite an ordeal. We toss in a couple dollars for prizes at the end. None of us need prizes, but we really love prizes - so we all leave happy. Except for the eight who don't win. We play monthly. We talk, laugh, cry and lift each other up. We love Bunco. But it is not the game we love as much as the bond. And then there is that, "I feel lucky tonight", which really adds to the bliss.

Connie recently brought Mah Jongg to town. She taught a few gals who taught a few gals who taught a few gals and presto, there is now a long list of Mah Jongg players who will drop their busy lives in a second to sit and play Mah Jongg for hours. Mah Jongg is a Chinese tile game. It intimidated me at first but you quickly catch on. Mary says, "What I love about Mah Jongg is the relaxing ritual and clicking of the tiles." Oh, and did I mention the hostess always has a bunch of food so we graze through the afternoon to keep up our mental prowess?

There are solo games. Julie always has a crossword puzzle going. Sudoku is a number game. I thought I wouldn't be able to do it but a sister-in-law patiently showed me how and bought me a book for beginners. I moved on up the scale and am now one step above beginners. I thought it would be good for my husband and got him a book. He jumped on the bandwagon in a hurry and has now gone through several books and quickly moved on to the highest Mensa level. I think to myself, "So what!"

The bad thing about Sudoku is it is so addictive; you withdraw from the world and can hardly stop. Rosel told me her husband has nearly driven her crazy with it. Beware.

I see people in coffee shops playing Cribbage. Friends play that after every meal and keep a running game going. Which reminds me of my friends who played scrabble every night and kept a combined score to beat their best game rather than beating each other. How sweet is that?

Open one of your closets and you are likely to find boxes and boxes of games - Dominoes, Boggle, Pictionary, Trivial Pursuit. If you don't have any, you can always play Charades. Oh, and don't forget that old standby, Bingo. You really don't have to be Catholic to play it.

Places like Senior Centers and Legions have open card playing days. Euchre, Bridge, Texas Hold 'Em and others provide fun social times.

I play lively games of Uno, Candyland and Go Fish with my grandsons. We discuss how it isn't important whether you win or lose. "Winning is not important, right, Nina?" "Hmmmmmm."

So try it. Just because the economy is tight doesn't mean you can't have fun. Turn off the T.V. You don't need to watch that movie a second time. Look each other in the eye and play a game. I'm betting you'll find you'll win in more ways than one . . . and that's important, right?

Act or React

I watched an interview of the man who jumped into the New York City subway to save someone who had fallen in. He was an average man, doing average things. His children were with him. He told someone to watch them and then jumped into the subway, without hesitation. A train was coming. He saw it and still jumped. He cowered over the person in the subway pit, nose to nose, as tightly as two bodies can get. Two strangers staring into each other, as the roaring screeching train flew over them. Any movement would have caused their death.

Luckily, it all worked out. The trains were stopped. The power was turned off and both men survived. The next night David Letterman interviewed this hero. Dave asked him, "What made you do it?" He humbly answered, *"It was the right thing to do."* - As simple as that.

I have thought a lot about that. I am pretty sure I would not have reacted that way. I have ridden many subways. I have seen the big wells with signs warning of "electrocution" posted all around. First, I think if I jumped into the well, I could never get out without a hoist. Second, electrocution is definitely not on my list of things to do in this lifetime.

I think I would have more likely screamed, prayed for that doomed person and stood on the sidelines gawking. I am not proud of that, but I am pretty sure that is what I would have done.

The thing about situations like this is they come upon us without warning. We don't have time to think them through, make a sensible decision and act on it. We usually just act, react.

When our two oldest children were in college at Marquette University in Milwaukee, my husband and I were there for parents' weekend. We were on a very crowded city bus. Unbeknownst to us, it was the day that senior citizens got their state check. The bus stopped and several seniors crowded into the already full bus. I was sitting up front and my husband had been pushed to the back. As I sat there, a young man slipped his hand, which was wrapped in a silk scarf, into the pocket of a very elderly man standing in front of me. Without thinking, of course, I screamed, "Don't rob that old man." The thief looked me in the eye and my heart stopped. My husband said, he recognized my voice and thought, "she's gonna die". Just then the bus stopped and the thief escaped quickly with his hand full of the old man's money. The bus driver then informed us that this was a common occurrence as everyone knew the day the checks came in, making the senior citizens sitting ducks for predators.

I am not sure I reacted well. The man was still robbed and I could have been shot and killed. The thing is, these things happen on a dime, giving us no time to reflect. Rationality is never part of it. Reaction is the whole game, for better or worse.

Saying No to Crack

The other day I heard two words on National Public Radio that I never thought I would hear there: Butt Cleavage.

'Oh, no, they didn't say that!' I said to myself. But they had said it and it cracked me up. No pun intended.

I think of NPR as high level, intelligent, sophisticated even. I do not think of butt cleavage in that same way.

The program went on discussing how much butt cleavage could be put on newsstands. Seems like some stores won't carry magazines unless they have the right amount of cleavage showing, which to me would mean none. I guess they have their own standards.

So I go home and study up on butt cleavage. As you can imagine, there is a lot to learn. Or should I say, can you imagine?

Apparently butt cleavage is part of a new thing called "raunch culture". Butt, of course. Sorry, I couldn't help myself with that one.

It is called in many articles, "the newest fashion statement". Wow. I never thought of it as a fashion statement. Unless the statements are, "Heck no, I don't want to see your hiney. Thank you very much."

This has become such a big part of our society now that *Saturday Night Live* did a skit on butt cleavage advertising a new product called Neutrogena Coin Slot Cream. Uwwwww.

Butt cleavage seems to be a national epidemic. I don't know about your experiences, but for me, I have seen enough butt cleavage to last the rest of my life. It is cute on toddlers and babies. It is not cute on adults you don't know and sometimes don't even want to know.

In 2005 the American Dialect Society, which is a group of linguists, editors and academics, listed "butt cleavage" as the most creative word of the year. What a society! No wonder this turns up on National Public Radio and wherever we happen to glance.

The Sun, a British newspaper, declared an entire week in August 2001 as Bum Cleavage Week. I shudder to think of the festivities that went on in that celebration.

I probably shouldn't mention Joe the Plumber. I know it is a stereotype. I know many plumbers do not fill this bill. I have friends that are plumbers and their butt cleavage never leaps out at ya. But as I listened to this informative show on NPR, I thought they might be interviewing good ole Joe.

*Sidebar: It is listed that in America we call this phenomenon "plumber's butt" and in Australia they call it "plumber's crack". I call it disgusting. They go on in this information to say, "Because plumbers are particularly prone to this kind of mishap." I have thought of calling it a lot of things but mishap was never one of them, except the mishap of me seeing it. They go on further, "especially on occasions of careless bending over." I don't know about you, but for me, bending over is never careless, it is very deliberate, slow and carefully thought out.

So as I listen to this delightful and quite unbelievable discussion on NPR, I naturally expect they will be interviewing Joe the Plumber, but they do not. I then think that perhaps Jack Six Pack will be coming on. He does not show up either. It ends up being just a group of seemingly intelligent folks talking very seriously and most proper about butt cleavage.

Now I say to you, the economy is tanking. We are in two wars. America is full of major chaos. There is a lot happening here and the airwaves are discussing butt cleavage.

A while ago I was in a nice restaurant. The girl in my view whenever I had my head up had a long slot of butt cleavage. Now, I can eat just about anytime, anyplace and anything. But, watching that unwelcome sight, I couldn't eat. I also couldn't quit looking. I finally had to move tables. But by then, my appetite had done what the crack should have done, disappeared.

I know politicians keep talking about how our nation needs change. I think we need change in lots of ways and one change includes eliminating public butt cleavage from innocent viewers. Just like the newsstand that has standards on how much butt cleavage they will show, I want standards too. I want to eliminate it from my sight. I think we should all just boldly stand up and yell, "America, say no to crack".

It's a Computerized World After All

I'm going to come right out and admit it. I'm a baby boomer. Translation: I'm intimidated by my computer.

I always have an on-going list of computer things to ask my kids and/or have them show me or fix for me on my computer. Until they do so, I am stumped, handicapped even.

Don't think I haven't tried to learn this computer stuff on my own. I have taken lots and lots of classes, several from a very gifted, kind, helpful teacher. Can I give a shout out to Ms. Day? It really didn't help me very much. After a few minutes, it was all blah, blah, blah. I just couldn't take it in, no matter how much I tried. My intentions were stellar. My reality was a whole different story. I would take note after note. Then I would never look at them again. My computer class books sit in my "someday" pile.

I have had computer people say to me, "You can't hurt it." I never believe them. I'm sure I can. Yet my kids are no more intimidated by a computer than I was by a toaster.

For thanksgiving all of our children and grandchildren convened at our daughter's in Chicago for several days. I observed the computer action.

My daughter in-law was in charge of dinner on Wednesday. The pans were cooking, the food was all being prepped and in the middle of it all was her computer screen with her recipes.

Once we needed a phone number. It was immediately looked up on the computer. Why bother with a phone book?

They read the newspaper on the computer. They watched movies and TV shows on the computer. They played all kinds of music from the computer.

At one point, the TV was on and we all sat around watching it, sort of. Three sat on the sofa, each with a laptop in their lap. A fourth had a Blackberry in her hand. They all were doing something on them. TV was just background.

We wanted to communicate with extended family members. That was done by texting on mobile phones. Should we call them? Why? Texting is the way to go. For them, of course, not for me. I still have the odd notion that you call when you want to talk. How old am I, anyway?

One daughter and I spent a long time watching YouTube songs, more than I could have imagined. I mentioned I had never seen a certain interview. Within a second she had that playing for me.

One night we went to a restaurant. My grandson, who turned five this week, played a game on the computer the entire time. No one helped him. He knows what to do.

Recently a young Mom was telling me about her little girl. She went to show me a photo and reached into her purse. I assumed she was pulling out her billfold, but of course, she pulled out her mobile phone. What was I thinking?

One of my past jobs was selling World Book encyclopedias. Can you imagine? People used to go to hard cover books that were dated to get information. How archaic can you get?

I have a friend who had an exchange student a couple years ago. She thought it would be a terrific experience for her children. It really didn't work as she expected. The student spent most of her time in her room on her computer emailing her friends from home and never connected much with her host family.

My kids now do almost all of their shopping on the net and get free shipping for it all too. I'm afraid to shop online. What if someone took my credit card numbers? I prefer to shop by phone or in person. Of course, I have had my numbers stolen but it felt more comfortable.

As a baby boomer, my generation shaped the 20th century. As the net generation, my children and their children will shape the 21st century.

Yes, we're not in Kansas anymore, Mulligan. My dog's name is Mulligan. Toto wasn't real, you know. This clearly is not the old days, like 1997. In 1997 there was no Google, no Facebook, no Blackberry, no YouTube. Good Lord, what a different time it was. How did we do it? I suppose there are many sites to go to for information on what it was like then, but I don't need to do that. I remember it well.

Hobbies and Mental Illness – It's a Fine Line

Saw a fun quote the other day by Dave Barry. "There is a very fine line between hobby and mental illness." I had to laugh, thinking how true that often is. Just a little bit more. Just a little bit more. And soon we are over that edge.

I thought of one of my hobbies, scrapbooking. I would never have gotten into it, but my daughters gently pushed me. One sold scrapbooking materials and I went along with them for the ride, so to speak. It gave us lots of quality time together - Lots and lots. Scrapbooking would take our entire weekends, often late into the night. Backs would hurt. Necks would ache. No matter. The end result was worth it.

I began scrap booking by doing the year we got married, 1967. I am now doing 2008. I have filled 17 large albums and a few smaller ones. My husband is thrilled that I am doing this. I have a feeling he might not be quite so thrilled if he had any idea of the amount of money that has been sunk into it. One not only needs all the supplies, one also needs multiple containers to store it all in. Ka-ching. Ka-ching.

I have this idea that my scrapbooking is for the family, for the future, for the generations to come. But, in reality, I am not sure that any of them will ever care or even bother to go through all these books.

The other day I was with a friend sharing our recent vacations. She had said, "Bring your pictures." So I did. I showed up with over 200 stunning photos. She had a few. She said, "You take so many more pictures than I do. Isn't it redundant? I mean, one Christmas is like all the other Christmases. One birthday is like the past ones. Same people, just another year older."

I felt like - Oh, no, each picture is so worth it, so unique, such a treasure. But I keep thinking about her words. The birthdays probably do blur together. The Christmases have the same people, the same routines, the same decorations. You really can't tell one thanksgiving from the last, one Easter from the previous.

Am I teetering on the edge of that thin precipice between hobby and mental illness? Have I gone overboard? Is it really worth so much of my time and money? Will anybody else ever care about these photos?

But then I think to myself, 'What the heck! It's fun'. And that may be enough. We love to "ooh" and "ahh" over our photos and scrapbooks. We laugh at our dated hair-dos and clothes. We lovingly remember old décor, previous homes, past routines, even people. Photos end up being the visual images of our memories. Talk about value. That's pretty rich stuff.

Hobbies chronicle our past and our present. I used to love tennis. Now my knees don't. I used to sew. Now I am quite happy to buy ready made. I used to do crafty things. Now I am content to appreciate other people's crafty things.

Currently, I love dabbling in photography of nature. My photos are really quite good. I would love to do a show of them, but I am pretty sure I don't have the energy it would take to do that.

I still love to cook and try new recipes. Not long ago, my friend, Linda, said she had quit clipping recipes. I was stunned. What a concept. I couldn't even imagine. But now I'm rethinking it. Am I teetering on that edge again? I have two bushel baskets full of recipes to organize and try, plus a cupboard full of cookbooks, many of them quite new. I have a house full of magazines with recipes calling, "Clip me. Clip me." In my saner moments, which are rare, I think of how many years of cooking time I have left. I look at the bushels of recipes and I know I should stop myself. I am sure I have enough. I won't run out. I don't even cook that much, for heaven's sake. But, then again, I think, 'What the heck. It's fun.' And I keep on clipping.

There are so many hobbies one can have. Golf. Fishing. Hunting. Sewing. Gardening. Photography. Music. Sudoku. Reading. It goes on and on. Too many to list, for sure. Everyone has their own interests. I am always stunned to go into a magazine section and see the enormous variety of magazines about hobbies. It is mind blowing. It confirms that we all live such different lives and have so many different hobbies.

Hobbies don't mind being on our back burner of life. They don't mind sitting on the shelf, unused, dusty, neglected. They are even okay when you let go of them. They are just happy when we pay the least bit of attention to them.

Life can't be just work, routine chores and relationships. We need hobbies to add color to our lives. They bring satisfaction, growth, fun, people, experiences. Hobbies are good. They are the froth on my latte of life.

Even if no one ever looks at my scrapbooks and even if I never try all those recipes - What the heck. It's fun. Ka-ching. Ka-ching.

And the Oscar Goes to . . .

Tomorrow the hills will be alive with the sound of, "and the Oscar goes to…" The Annual Academy Awards will be presented. This may not interest some folks, but for others like me, it is the Super Bowl. Some years it is much ado about nothing. This year holds promise for a great show and several excellent movies to root for.

Movies are timeless and everyone has their own classics. Movies take us places and make history come to life. They make us laugh, cry, think, discuss. They help us understand different cultures, different lifestyles, plights people go through. Some are of little value. Many are treasures and become woven into the fabric of our life and language.

The other day I saw my friend, Jim, running around the lake. When I stopped to say hi, he started singing the *Rocky* theme and doing the *Rocky* moves. He didn't have to tell me what he was singing. Who wouldn't know?

Who doesn't get chills when they think of Jack Nicholson beating the door in with an axe saying, "Here's Johnny"?

Anyone who didn't cry when *Old Yeller* died probably didn't see the movie.

Remember Brando saying, "I coulda been a contender"?
And was it him who gave us the lasting impression of "*Stella*"!

Christmases come and go, but not without Jimmy Stewart in *It's a Wonderful Life* and more recently, a 24 hour TV marathon of *Christmas Story*.

Grease was the word. I love the music. I love John Travolta. My daughter, Cara, and I have forever sung the songs from *Grease* together, each having our parts. As we drive down the road we can howl with the best of dogs!

Beaches with Bette Midler, I assumed was going to be a comedy. I took my dear friend, Linda to brighten her up. She was recently widowed. We cried through the whole movie. I remember her comment when I took her home. "Thanks a LOT, Maureen." Some brightening! With friends like that, who needs enemies! Luckily she has a great sense of humor and we still laugh about it.

My Dr. told me he heard his first swear word in *Gone with the Wind*. Ah, there was a great movie (and book!). Who could forget Clark Gable telling Scarlet, "Frankly, my dear, I don't give a damn". I recently read that the studio really wanted him to say, 'I don't give a hoot'. Somehow that wouldn't have left the same lasting impression.

My friend, Nelda, took movie loving to a new level. She loved most movies but was "all about" the *Wizard of Oz*. She had an amazing collection of Oz memorabilia and even asked me to quote Oz in her eulogy.

Oz never did it for me. The *Sound of Music* is my fave. I saw it 18 times at the movies. I am not sure I should be proud of that. I can recite every word to every song and every word to the whole film's dialogue, before they say it. It spoke to me on many levels and has given me the quote that has been my lifetime anthem. "When God closes a door, he always opens a window." When was the last time we had a flick like that – nuns saving the day; kids hanging in trees; people whistling, dancing and running through the hills – and to top it off, a love story involving an entire family. They just don't make 'em like that anymore!

So, I don't know about you but for me, I plan to get in my comfy pajamas and comfy chair and tune in to the Academy Awards. I am gonna sit back, relax, and say to the TV, "Play it again, Sam."

To Be Back Home Again

"Hey, it's good to be back home, again," sang John Denver. And, boy, was he right.

We just returned from one of those *trips of a lifetime*. Sights were phenomenal and as pretty as they get. We had great fun. Great time. Great weather. Everything was perfect. We loved it!

It amazes me, then, that it is so exciting to come home. It feels like *ahhhhh*.

We slept well in all the beds, yet to crawl into our own feels like a soothing snuggle.

With all the breathtaking sights we saw, the sight of our own flowers in bloom and tomato's turning red on their vines is awesome.

After visiting the largest and most famous cathedrals, it is going to church the morning after our return that is like a hug. It is being back with our church "family" that lifts our souls. Praying and singing together. Holding hands as we pray the Our Father. Chatting with friends in the foyer after mass. Amen!

It is exciting to catch up with two weeks of newspapers and mail. During our time away we didn't use our phones, email. No TV or radio. No newspapers. We were really out of touch. Though it felt very good and relaxing to be out of the loop on things, getting back *into it* feels great.

Even though we had umpteen meals out, it is the digging back into our ole fridge and freezer, making the usual grocery store run – that really seem fitting. Sitting down to our own table turns out to be a delicacy, after all.

Talking with our friend, Elmer, yesterday, he said, "I just like being home. It is good to go away, but it is best to be back in my own surroundings."

Our friends went to California for five months over the winter. Their daughter told me they were so excited to get home. They really missed friends, home, the community.

This seems to be a universal phenomenon. We all need breaks and vacations. We all need to get away - The pause that refreshes. Yet it is when we get away that we appreciate home, work, people, routine. We may love being away. It may all be perfect, but the return is just as perfect.

When our plane landed, our two grandsons, holding a colorful bouquet of balloons, ran to greet us with giant hugs. Oh, yes, "It's the sweetest thing I know of…to be back home again."

The cost of the trip $$$. The cost of the grandson greeters…priceless.

Beauty School Dropout

Yesterday another one bit the dust. That is to say another local business closed its doors for the last time. However, this one was not due to hard times. This one was thriving with more business than they could handle.

Seems that doing hair and nails is hard work that leads to a milieu causing leg, back, joint problems and breathing difficulties. It is these kinds of obstacles that forced my wonderful hairdressers to close their salon and begin different career paths. They did not want to and their loyal customers did not want them to.

What makes hairdressers, barbers and nail technicians so special? They become cherished friends. Movies have been made about this phenomenon – *Shampoo, Barber Shop*, etc.

Think about it. Who do you sit across from, intimately facing each other, and talk nearly undisturbed on a regular basis. They give you nearly undivided attention. When you are in their chair, it is all about you. We like that.

Remember the phrase, "Only her hairdresser knows"? Hairdressers and barbers become counselors, pastors. They listen, support, encourage. They empathize, laugh and cry with you. As years go by we share births, deaths, graduations, weddings, vacations, retirements, moves, jobs, frustrations, joys, aging, health. These people are hard to replace.

For years I went to Carl and would go home and complain about my hair. My husband finally suggested that if I didn't like my hair, why didn't I try a new hairdresser? I looked at him in dismay and said, "Oh, I would never leave Carl. He's so much fun."

When Carl left, I went to Jeff for years. Same scenario. He was great fun and became a dear friend. When he moved to Florida, I was among many who were left high, dry and devastated. Lucky for me, I found Kathy. She has become a dear fun friend and caretaker of my lame coif and nails.

My husband goes to a barbershop downtown. I asked him to describe it. "It's all guys. They have TVs with sports going. They have periodicals men want to read - Sports Illustrated, The Detroit Free Press, Men's Health, Golf, Fishing. No fluffy ones."

"It is all ages, little boys to older men. Heads get shaved. Beards get trimmed. Even mullets and Mohawks need grooming."

Every once in awhile my husband will drop a nugget of news on me. I look at him and say, "Where'd you hear that?" It is often not from a newspaper, NPR or a TV news show but from, "The Barber Shop". And then, of course, we know it's true.

Places of hair are like the watering wells in olden days. You don't have to know folks to talk with 'em. People congregate. People talk. People enjoy. Oh, and some necessary work gets done. It is a win-win.

When I was in high school, I was the local hairdresser. I would ride my bike to neighbors and give perms, sets and haircuts. And without any training or expertise, I got paid for this. The women were clearly desperate. This fed my high school dream of becoming a beautician. As I look back, I was fortunate this dream didn't materialize. I don't have what it takes. My physical stamina would never have made it. This field of work is definitely harder than it looks. I bow to those who have made long careers out of it. They are tough cookies.

If you open your local phone book, there is nearly a full page of barbers and beauty salons. Everyone has their favorite. Whenever you walk in their doors, you hear a buzz of laughter and chat. These are happy places.

I always joke that I asked God for thick hair and thin hips and he got it mixed up. I am never very happy with my hair. I suppose it won't look that different no matter who cuts it. But my relationship side is taking a big hit and I am just one of many who will have a hole in my life with my local salon closed. They have been the epitome of good customer service. They have been dedicated professionals and dear friends. We wish them well. Gosh, endings bite.

Remember When...

Extinction of the Casserole

Oh where, oh where, has my casserole gone? Oh where, oh where, can it be?

The other day I went to buy four wedding and two shower gifts. Besides costing about the same as a small vacation, they took quite a bit of time and thought. What to get?

This process got me thinking about wedding gifts and wondering what others do in these situations. I asked a friend, who was about my age, "What do you give for wedding gifts?" This got us discussing gifts we had received when we got married. The first thing that came to our minds was casserole dishes. I got a variety of them. My grandma even gave me a silver one with a silver lid. I still have it in the basement. It is tarnished but treasured, and definitely not used anymore. As we laughed about casserole dishes we wondered… Where did they go? No one gets casserole dishes today. No one even mentions the word casserole today. Where, oh where, did it go?

I have always been amazed when someone says to me, "My husband won't eat casseroles." I always reply, "My husband will eat anything." And so will I. Well, I do hate one thing but I can never remember what that is. I think its radishes. But I can even eat those in a pinch.

Most of us grew up on casseroles. I bet there is not a Catholic out there that was not raised on tuna fish casserole as a Friday night staple. When did casseroles leave us? What was their demise? Was it Dr. Scarsdale? Dr. Atkins? Martha Stewart? Emeril?

I love to cook. I collect cookbooks. I subscribe to cooking magazines. I have collected recipes since I was a teenager and still have and use them. Each one reminds me of whom I got it from. I love that.

A couple years ago, I had some relatives for dinner. I made a casserole* from an old cookbook. They chowed down and yelled for more. My daughter said, "This is like one of those really bad for you dishes that tastes really good but you never make it anymore." That seems to sum up the ole casserole. They taste good. They may not be so good for you, depending on how you do them, and we don't make them much anymore, if at all.

I did a bit of detective work in my house today. I looked through my cookbooks, cooking magazines and recipes. One touted, "More than 120 best recipes of 2007", but not one single casserole.

It seems the casserole left us in the seventies. It has been replaced with new terms.

Pastas. Open any cookbook, magazine or menu and you will find recipes for pastas. They are condoned. So are bakes, tosses, warm salads, crustless pies, terrines, delights, noodles, strudels and things with things. For instance, ground sirloin with spiral whole-grain pasta. I don't know about you, folks, but in the old days we would have called it plain ole goulash. And loved it.

In my sleuthing, I did find a few cassoulets. I guess that is the new vogue word for casserole. But I have never seen any cassoulet dishes.

I loved making casseroles as my kids were growing up. I would open the fridge; haul out all the leftovers I could find. Toss them together; add a bit of something to glob it all together. And then the grand flourish – Cheese, lots and lots of cheese. This made for a nice topping or you could call it a mask for all the surprises inside.

Sometimes people get so picky about leftovers. As I said, my husband would eat anything, and perhaps I have taken advantage of that over the years. But we never wasted anything and, to quote Martha Stewart, "That's a good thing." Right?

*See Chapter 15 for recipe.

Disney Delights

When I was a kid, I used to run home from school to watch the Mickey Mouse Club on TV. Annette, Darlene, Jimmy all lit up my days.

Disney has been a part of the fabric of many of us. We grew up with it. Our kids grew up with it and our grandchildren are growing up with it. Luckily for us all, Disney continues to inspire and lift.

Let's get nostalgic for a minute. Remember when "a spoonful of sugar helped your medicine go dow-wown in the most delightful way?" When *Zip-a-Dee-Doo-Dah* made you feel better? "It's the truth. It's actual. Everything is satisfactual."

Can you say *Bibbidi-Bobbidi-Boo*? How about *Supercalifragilistic-expialidocious*? Faster. Faster. Now can you spell it? "Even though the sound of it is something quite atrocious" and even when you say it "you always sound precocious".

A funny memory I have is taking my son, Dan, to see *Bambi* in Spain. Seeing *Bambi* talking in Spanish was really odd. Everybody knows deer don't speak Spanish.

Last week I was teaching my three-year-old grandson, Danny, the Disney song *Davy Crockett*. He sang it a few times with gusto and then looked at me seriously and asked, "Nina, what is a great frontier?" I gotta confess. The first thing that came to my mind was - a really big shopping mall.

I decided not to confuse him with that because *it's a small world* after all. "A world of laughter, a world of tears. A world of hope and a world of fears." There's so much that we share that it's time we're aware, it's a small world after all."

Disney broadens our world. I had never heard of a nanny until we met Mary Poppins on screen. Who wouldn't want a nanny like her?

For generations, girls have wondered if *Someday my prince will come*. Later they wondered *Can you feel the love tonight*? Many lived happily ever after with the philosophy of "you've got a friend in me, yeah; you've got a friend in me."

So you say you don't want to go to work? Perhaps you should *whistle while you work*. "When there's too much to do, don't let it bother you. Put on that grin and start right in to whistle loud and long. Hi ho, hi ho, it's off to work you go."

We've all seen super sports stars who win the Olympics, Super Bowls, World Series. It seems within minutes of their win, they are on TV answering the question, "What are you going to do now?" And they enthusiastically reply, "I'm going to Disneyworld!"

When tourists visit the United States, Disneyworld is often at the top of their sights to see. Families celebrating their major anniversaries often go to Disneyworld or on the popular Disney cruises. Some folks we know have gone for their honeymoon.

We took our kids to Disneyworld and I saw a quote by Walt Disney that has been in my workspace ever since. "If you can dream it, you can do it." Love that.

Walt was an incredible visionary. He said, "We don't only aim for kids. Adults are only kids grown up anyway. I only hope we don't lose sight of one thing, that this was all started with a mouse."

May I close with one more Disney thought? *Hakuna Matata.* "It means no worries for the rest of your days. It's a problem free philosophy. Hakuna Matata."

Imagine This

John Lennon sang, "Imagine." I am good at imagining. I believe in it and use it. It has worked well for me. But there are now a lot of things in my life that I never imagined.

- I never imagined I would be excited to see the price of gasoline dip below $3.00 a gallon.

- I never imagined I would go to the post office and only get two postage letter stamps for a buck.

- I never imagined I would be able to predict rain because of the pain in my body.

- I never imagined how sweet a nap would become.

- I never imagined I would go to the store and be told, "Sorry, Lady, we don't sell VCRs anymore and haven't in a couple years." And think to myself, "What will I do with the tons of videos I use to tape and re-tape on?"

- I never imagined I would consider chocolate such a good friend.

- I never imagined vitamins and supplements would be one of my major food groups.

- I never imagined I would become an early riser.

- I never imagined I would have my chiropractor's phone number on speed dial.

- I never imagined when we arrived for a one-year job that we would live most of our adult lives here, and happily so.

- I never imagined I could own so many gifted dogs and love each one so deeply.

- I never imagined I would pay more for my mediocre car than we did for our first house.

- I never imagined I would go to as many funerals as parties. But then, a few of them turn into parties, especially the Irish ones.

- I never imagined I would see girls on the newspaper sports page almost as much as boys. How sweet it is.

- I never imagined I would see a woman, a man of some color, a Mormon, a Baptist minister – all running for president of the United States and nobody hardly mentioning any of these things. We've come a long way, baby.

As my mind began to roll with these thoughts, I decided to ask a couple others what they never imagined.

Mary, a teacher, "never imagined her doctors would be young enough to be her grandchildren".

Aunt Julie "never imagined I'd hear myself saying so often, 'I used to… sew, cook, play golf, dye my hair, have dinner guests and parties, make Christmas candies, etc…' I'm beginning to sound like an echo".

Brent in San Diego "never imagined I would someday consider my mother a genius".

He also "never imagined the term *my space* would be anything other than something you invade on a train".

Tara, a masseuse, "never imagined I could spend a whole day doing absolutely nothing and feel like I accomplished so much".

Dale, a retired teacher "never imagined I'd prefer to stay home on Friday nights".

Rudy in Tucson "never imagined I could or would pump my own gas".

Darci "never imagined half the Beatles would be dead and the Rolling Stones would still be alive".

Jodie "never imagined after being such a challenging child, that my parents would actually trust me as the administrator of their estate".

Beverly, full-time RVer, currently in Phoenix, "never imagined I would pay a dollar for a bottle of water and carry it wherever I went".

I guess I will close with one more of my own.

I never imagined I would go to a class reunion and see so many old people.

Crestfallen

I just ran into the store to get toothpaste and a couple of other items. Sounds easy enough, right? Not as easy as I had thought.

All I wanted was 2 tubes of Crest. That should have only taken a second. After all, I know right where the toothpaste was located.

I hurriedly whipped my cart into the toothpaste aisle and was astounded to see a gazillion, or so it seemed, kinds of Crest. Whitening expressions extreme herbal mint. Whitening expressions lemon ice. Whitening expressions refreshing vanilla mint. Whitening expressions cinnamon rush. I don't know about you, but I am pretty sure I don't want a cinnamon rush when I first wake up in the morning.

It goes on. Sensitivity whitening. Sensitivity extra-whitening. Nature's expressions citrus clean. Nature's expressions pure peppermint. Nature's expressions fresh mint. Nature's expressions mint and green tea extract. Dumb me! I thought plain ole mint was good enough, but alas, I see no plain ole mint.

I kept looking, feeling sort of glazed over, feeling more tired and weary by the second. Who knew this would be like an exam? Mega multiple choice.

Pro-health clean cinnamon. Pro-health clean mint. Pro-health clean night mint. Is night mint different than day mint? Guess so. But that is still not enough.

Extra white plus scope mint splash. Whitening plus scope mint fresh striped. Whitening plus scope cool peppermint. Whitening plus scope citrus splash. Whitening plus scope extreme mint explosion. Whitening plus scope extreme cinnamon ice. Extra whitening (because whitening isn't enough) clean mint. Multicare whitening. Multicare whitening fresh mint. Tartar protection whitening cool mint paste. Baking soda and peroxide whitening fresh mint. Tartar protection regular paste. Is this one the old regular Crest? Could it be? I am so confused and now so bleary eyed I need a nap.

And still there's more. I kid you not. Tartar protection fresh mint gel. Cavity protection regular paste. Cavity protection cool mint gel. You can't make this stuff up.

And if that isn't enough - If you still need one more choice. There is also Kids cavity protection sparklee fun. I am quite sure I do not want sparklee fun early in the morning. That would be way more fun than a gal should have.

When did this happen? How did it happen? Are the folks at Crest sitting around in some conference room, drinking margueritas and laughing trying to see who can come with one more kind of toothpaste? Are the mint growers of America lobbying Crest to make one more mint kind of toothpaste, please? Do other shoppers walk into the toothpaste aisle and really know which one they want? Am I the only one who is overwhelmed here?

Life is busy. We hardly have time to do what we need to do. We work hard to simplify our schedules. We try not to waste time. We try to cram one more thing into our hectic day - And then this.

Choice is good. In fact, it is our greatest power. But it is not always easy to make the right choice. For instance, once I saw a sign in front of a church that said, "If you are tired of sin, come in." Below it someone had scrawled, "If you're not, call 555-1229." Oh, what to do.

Good choices. Bad choices. Too many toothpaste choices. I ended up so utterly overwhelmed I just grabbed 2 boxes of some kind of crest. I didn't even know what it was. I just felt pressured to make a decision and get out of there. I am hoping I grabbed a mint one. I am also hoping it is the right mint one. What if I got the wrong mint one? What if I got whitening and I should have gotten extra whitening? What if I got tartar control but I need cavity protection? Should I have gotten pro-health, because who isn't pro-health? Should I have gotten the sparklee fun to use before I go to parties? But then again, after choosing the toothpaste I hardly have any energy left to actually brush my teeth. Perhaps next time I'll just go with Colgate.

The Treasure of Old Friends

"Make new friends, but keep the old. One is silver and the other gold." I believe that is an old girl scout song. It is also a true adage.

Yesterday we had old friends visit. We had been friends when we lived in Spain for two years, just before we moved here.

Our grown children were here and we all had a great visit. It was like a living history lesson. "Was the civil rights movement really during the Viet Nam war? I didn't realize that." "Did the country really care about the war?" "When was the Kent State shooting?" "How long did you have beards?" "Cambridge, where I live, is still full of people who look like that." There were lots and lots of comments and questions. Details of history put into perspective, stories full of laughter, memories and learning.

Hopefully, we all have friends like that. They bring our past into living color. They help us remember all we've been through and grown through. They loved us then and love us now. They appreciate our journey and we appreciate theirs.

Perhaps if we met now, we wouldn't have the same dear relationship. But given when it was made and where it was, it remains a treasure.

I remember once a lady said to me, "It is nice you have held on to so many of your old friends. So many people just let them slip through their hands."

I was honored with her comment. I also thought how right she was. Friends just slip, bit by bit, through our hands. I don't think we plan to let people go. It is just that life changes. It gets busy. It takes you in different directions. We get tired. We get distracted. We get older.

It isn't that we don't care about the old friends or wonder how they are. We still think of them fondly. But they are just a thing of the past, like our youth.

Keeping a relationship going with old friends can add such texture to the fabric of our lives. It can bring that to our children's lives and heritage, as well.

For people who remain where they grew up, this may be easier. For people who move and live in different places, this becomes more of a challenge.

A few days ago we went to a 60th wedding anniversary. I hadn't seen the couple, friends of my parents when I grew up, since I was a teenager. That was a while ago, for sure. When I saw them I started to cry. I am not sure why. So much emotion tied up into our memories, especially when they haven't been visited in a long, long time. We didn't stay long, nor did we visit a lot. But what a treat it was to touch base with them and their children. Some might call it a warm wonderful blast from the past.

Everyone knows aged things have great value – wine, antiques, coins, stamps, cheese. People are the same way. We are all here at this point in our lives today. We went through a journey to get here. It involved lots of challenges, joys, sorrows, growth and people.

What makes a difference in one person's life from another? I believe a huge part of that difference can be the people put in our path.

I have been very blessed to have wonderful, colorful, inspiring, faith-filled people put in my path. They have helped me become what I have grown into today, whatever that is, for better or worse. Without them, I can't imagine where my life would have gone.

Yes, keeping in touch with old friends is a treasure because it is keeping us in touch with who we were. That keeps us in touch with who we are and who we can become. When we do this it is truly golden. It is gold for our friends, for our selves and for our children. And don't we all love win-win situations.

The Way We Were

"Let me ask you three questions. Are you alive? Have you had any experiences? Can you communicate with others?" Thus began a class on writing your memoirs given by a delightful instructor.

It is an intimidating thought, writing one's memoirs. Who is able? Who wants to read them? What to say?

I am immediately reminded of memories others have shared that have meant a lot to me.

Last week, September 11th, our book club met to discuss a book about true happenings on September 11th, 2001. A lady came and shared her experiences. She had been in a plane leaving Newark, New Jersey, along with the first plane that hit the World Trade Center. As they flew over New York City, a man in the front of her plane actually witnessed the plane hit the towers. He assumed it was an accident. Shortly thereafter, her Minneapolis bound plane was grounded to Toronto, Canada, as all U.S. airspace was cleared. Her story of how they were told, how they reacted and how she spent the next two days was extremely touching.

It was the first time I had heard someone who had actually experienced this, tell it in her own words. Emotion filled her as she told it. We heard things we had never thought of or knew: the incredible silence at the Toronto airport as thousands of people moved around in a trance; the vulnerability of all; the aloneness of each person in the midst of so many. Her story will remain etched into our memories forever. It enriched us.

When my father in law was around 80, he verbally shared memories with one of his daughter's who recorded them on paper for the family. The one that especially struck us was his sharing of the first time electricity lit his farm. To us it had always been lit. We had never thought of it any other way.

"I came home. Mom was fixing supper with a lamp. I pushed a switch and the room was flooded with light – I couldn't believe the light! I ran to the barn and pushed the switch – it was the greatest thing that ever happened in this area. I could have sat right down and cried. It was such a sight!"

As he shared this, tears welled in his eyes at the memory. So did ours. That memory lives on in my heart often when I think about what that must have been like. It is hard to imagine in our lives of technology beyond comprehension that he lived in a time when there was no electricity to light the world or the farm.

The other day I was reading *Profiles in Courage* by John F. Kennedy. In the prologue, Bobby Kennedy said, "When President Kennedy was assassinated, his grandmother was alive. She had also been alive when President Abraham Lincoln had been assassinated."

Can you imagine the stories that lady had to share? We are such a young country. We have come a long way, baby, and in a very short time.

Not long ago I had lunch with a friend, Charlotte. We discussed many things from her life of 100 years; one was when women got the right to vote. She shared what it was like to live through that time. Most of us don't remember when women couldn't vote, yet it wasn't that long ago. Charlotte made history come alive for me. I treasure her memory.

Thomas Berger said, "Why do writers write? Because it isn't there."

Too often we look back regretfully after someone dies and think, "I wish I would have asked him about this or that. Now it is gone. They took the stories and memories with them."

How do we begin to record our memories? Are ours worthy of recording? If they were a part of your life, likely your children, grandchildren, friends and family would greatly treasure them.

As Barbra Streisand sang, "Memories, like the corners of my mind. Misty water colored memories, of the way we were."

Let thoughts of perfection go. You can always add and delete. Write the way you talk. Make it fun. Add the color of your life and personality. Share your experiences.

I took a class years ago and the instructor said, "Just get a lined notebook and begin to write." I think that is the hard part, to begin.

I'm a Musical Dinosaur

When did I become such a musical dinosaur? I used to be cool. Well, maybe not, but at least I knew about current music.

I remember when rock was young. When I was a kid, I wanted to grow up and be like our neighbor, Franny. She was the coolest Mom because she played rock and roll. She was my musical role model.

Recently I saw my role model. She was frail, on total oxygen and had a walker. I thought, she sure doesn't look like my rock and roll Franny. I am sure she looked at me and thought, she sure doesn't look like that teenage girl, Maureen.

I have a large eclectic CD collection. I think I am musically "with it" but I am wrong - Very, very wrong.

Recently I was reading one of my December *Time* magazines. I know it is May but I had saved it because I love all those Top Ten of the year lists, and reading those 5 months late is just fine. Also, I can skim past all those people running for president, as they are no longer news.

So, I am skimming the top ten of this and the top ten of that – all interesting, nothing earth shattering, and then I get to *Top Ten Albums of 2007*. I read it. I read it again. I wonder. Who are these people? Feist. LCD Soundsystem. Radiohead. Aly and AJ. Manu Chao. 50 Cent. I have heard of him and think he is a rap star. I have always agreed with the comedian who said they left the C off the front of the word rap.

The list goes on: Plain White T's, The Fratellis, Rihanna. I think she is like a younger Beyonce, but I'm not sure. And then number one, Amy Winehouse. I have heard of her.

Amy Winehouse was in the newspapers in January. I remember wondering who she was and why we cared that she was being picked up for drugs. She has big black hair and seems smeared with black eye make up and lots of tattoos. She wears black clothes and a big sad pout. My kids assured me she has a great voice.

She got the Grammy for best song of the year. At the Grammy Awards she sang it from England via satellite, as she wasn't allowed to enter the U.S. due to her "problems". When I heard her sing, I really did understand what my kids meant. Her big song, *Rehab*, is catchy and has a good beat. I give it a 7. It got locked in my brain for a few days and I was going around singing, "They tried to make me go to Rehab but I say, 'No, No, No'." The "No, No, No" part is quite empowering to sing as you clean house and run around town. Except for all the looks you get. I swear some of the lookers were considering shipping me to rehab but I kept giving them the evil eye and singing, "No, No, No."

So, back to my original dismay. When did I become a musical dinosaur? A couple years back I was teaching at Grand Valley State University. I used some songs in my classes. I remember students, in all sincerity, asking, "Who's John Denver? Who's Garth Brooks?"

"Who are these students?" I thought.

A couple years ago I suggested to our choir director that we do a concert of oldies. She said, "Whose oldies?" Everyone had a different take on what oldies were. Of course, I thought mine were the right oldies and theirs were wrong.

Music is an identifier. There's the big band era, the Frank Sinatra era, rock and roll, The Beatles, the 70s with Barry Manilow and Anne Murray. And the beat goes on.

These days I am thrilled to get a new Alison Krause or Emmy Lou Harris CD. I like the new Bob Dylan and think Bob Seger's latest was super and Josh Groban is sweet.

I have known folks lost in the fifties or lost in the eighties. I think I must have gotten musically lost in the last century. I don't think my musical prowess ever left the new years party for the new Millennium.

And that is how I became a musical dinosaur. However, being outdated isn't so bad. I am happy and I know the words to all the songs I like. In fact, I am going to the store today to get the new Van Morrison CD. I don't even care if he's not on the top ten. He's got a good beat and I'm giving him a 7.

On the Road Again

Driving Miss Crazy

Before you get married, no one ever thinks about what it will be like driving together after you become a mature couple. If they did, perhaps there would not be so many marriages.

One day as we were driving along, my husband said, "You know, when you start in, I am never sure if you are going to say, 'Don, you are driving too fast or Don, you are driving too slow.' Sometime you should just say, 'Don, you are driving really well'."

So now sometimes I do just say, "Don, you are driving really well." But I don't do that very often. What I do more often is feel panic that he is too close to the car in front of us or anxiety that he is going faster or slower than I think he should. He tolerates my comments. I tolerate his driving, but not well.

When I am driving, he has lots of advice on which route I should take. Oh, I forgot. I also give him lots of comments about the routes he should take too. I am always sure my routes are faster, more direct and with less traffic.

It is quite amazing that we go through the rest of our lives together without all this "advice". How do we get along on our own in other areas of living? And what is it that makes two normal – a relative term, I know – people act so critical once they get in an automobile?

In all honesty, I think I am more critical of his driving than he is of mine. I imagine that is because I drive better than him. However, I am guessing that may be different from his perspective.

We talked about this with our friends, David and Patti. Seems they don't have the same *car talk* that we have. Patti just has a pretend brake that she keeps pumping on and David asks her every once in awhile, "How's that brake working for you?" She assured us she would never say anything to him about his driving and that he is a wonderful driver. Don and I just looked at each other. We couldn't identify with them.

Is it a given that as couples grow seasoned in a marriage, they complain about each other's driving or are we just a couple of nuts?

I asked my friend, Donnie, if she and her husband complain about each other's driving. "Oh, yes," she exclaimed, "all the time. The only way we survive when I drive is I tell him to just close his eyes and take a nap."

A few years ago, my son said to me, "Did you ever notice how the cars going slower than you are fools and the cars going faster than you are maniacs?" I sure have. And it goes double when you are the passenger and your mate is the driver. If he drives slower than I would, he's a fool. If he drives faster, he's a maniac. To get along, he must drive the exact same speed I would. Actually, I could drive faster than I think he should because then I would be in control and that's really the important thing here.

We have many friends who get in big vehicles and spend the winter driving across the country. One couple sold their homes and bought a really big motor home in which they have lived and traveled for several years now. I get chills just thinking of it.

We discuss the possibility of doing things like that in our future. We don't discuss it very often. The thought of spending your sunset years, or whatever folks call them, in a big vehicle driving together – well, let's just say it doesn't sound very appealing to me. I can't imagine the stress it would cause. I don't think I would mind the small quarters or any of the rest of it. I just think the driving and driving and driving might take a big toll, and I don't mean at a booth.

All in all, I am pretty grateful that my spouse is so patient with me and my comments as he drives. He is really much nicer than I am in this regard and I must drive him crazy. I better be careful, though. I saw a sign outside a car dealer that said, "Come in and get a new car for your spouse. It'll be a great trade!" I just hope he hasn't seen it too.

Got Gas?

I am driving to a funeral today and realize my gas tank is on empty. I hate when that happens. When I have the time, it is okay, but when I am on the run and a bit late, it is a thorn in my side. Then there is the price of gas, which is another thorn.

I saw a semi with a sign on the back, "How's my gouging?" I may have read it wrong.

I can remember when I would pull in to Ray's gas station and the guys would run out, fill 'er up, wash my windows, check my tires and oil, take my money, and cheerfully chat with me. I loved it. Gas was cheap. We were all happy in la-la land. Little did we know what was ahead.

I also have a memory of being with my friend, Joan, at the gas station. We were on our way to the flea market and needed gas. It was the first time we had to pump our own. I remember us reading the signs telling us how to proceed. We got to number 1, "extinguish your cigarettes". We were zanily proud that we had immediately accomplished that. The fact that neither of us smoked was beside the point. Being able to do the first step made us feel successful. From there it got harder. Somehow we got our tank full, laughing at our new life skills as we went.

It seems like yesterday my friend, Gail, said, "They say gas will reach $1 a gallon." I remember thinking she was crazy. Of course gas wouldn't go that high. This was America, after all.

I pull up to the pump today overjoyed when I see gas is $2.86 a gallon. It is my lucky day. Wow. Perhaps I should buy a lottery ticket. Not long ago, gas was nearing $4 a gallon. Today's price is truly a bargain and a blessing. I hum contentedly all the way home.

However, when I get here I notice gas is $2.74. My "oh, happy day" ends in a hurry. I have just paid 12 cents a gallon more only a couple miles away. I think - Why me, Lord? What did I ever do? I quickly calculate. Even though it sounds like a lot per gallon, I realize I only overpaid $1.68 on my total fill up. That doesn't sound so bad.

Get a grip, I think. It is just the way it is. It is not like I have any choice here. As my friend, Linda, says, "This is the new normal." She wasn't referring to gasoline prices, but that thinking applies to so many things. This *is* the new normal and I don't like it.

When it is cheaper to get your car towed to work than to drive it, something is seriously wrong.

Jay Leno said, "Gas is so high in California that women in Malibu are thinking twice before running over their cheating husbands."

Jimmy Kimmel said, "It is nearly cheaper to buy a new car than to fill your gas tank." He further joked, "Oprah tried to give a car away to someone in her studio audience today and the woman spit in her face."

We joke about it. We hate it. We complain. We keep pumpin'. But not everyone does. Not everyone can.

An area woman, who is a nurse in Grand Rapids, recently shared that she may have to sleep in her car some nights because she cannot afford the gas to drive back and forth to work and she needs the job.

A local family of five is planning their family vacation. They have camped with a camper for several years. Now they figure it will take double the gas to pull the camper so they have decided they will have to camp in a tent instead.

Gas prices affect everything. More than we realize.

Recently I was in the post office complaining about the new stamp hike. The clerk looked at me and said, "It's because of gas. We can't afford to move the mail." That made sense to me. I quit complaining, paid up and shut up.

I realize we all live in our own world. We see gas prices the way they affect us personally. But, there is a larger picture, like shipping. Almost all products in our stores are shipped. In some ways, gas is involved with nearly everything.

I read ads that say beano can help with gas. I wish it could help with gasoline. All of this makes my stomach hurt. I am grateful that Pepto-Bismol is not what I run my car on. It is $123.20 a gallon. At that rate, gasoline is a bargain. Life is all about perspective.

Leisurely Driving Into Road Rage

There are a lot of dumb drivers on the road – You know there are. There are as many sleep deprived drivers as drivers who are not sleep deprived. There are a lot of careless drivers. There are a lot of drunk or drugged drivers.

And then there are all the distractions – kids, cell phones, text messaging, food, drink, cigarettes, etc… And all those "behaviors", like putting on make-up, reading newspapers and books, doing paperwork. I saw a man in Holland with a huge snake in his hands as he drove. I saw a lady driving in Jackson playing a violin. I kid you not. You can't make this stuff up.

What no one seems to be doing is giving full attention to their driving.

Combine that with the so-called "death trap" of certain area roads and we've got a problem. Oh, yeah, I forgot about all the deer, wild turkeys and other critters scampering across the road in front of us. What a picnic! And I don't mean for eating all this road kill.

Can anyone remember when folks would go for a "drive" on Sundays? They would get in the car and take a leisurely drive to nowhere in particular. Just for the sake of pleasure. Where did that go? People might go for a Sunday drive now, but for sure it won't be leisurely. If they do drive leisurely, other drivers will definitely be riding their bumper, passing them and giving that "sign".

Once we met a woman and she said, "You know that *Eagle* sign, you should give them that." I looked at her in dismay. "Do you mean the *bird*," I asked? She looked at me like, "Whatever."

Speaking of this well used American "sign" reminds me of our life in Spain. There are birds in Spain but there is no *bird* in Spain. That gesture means nothing to them. They have their own special gesture. Translated it means "your mother had bad milk". Our gesture means "up with people" or something like that.

Back to the road, and the rage. My friend had someone jump out of his car and yank his door open, pull him out of the car and begin to pound on him. Our friend's driving had ticked the guy off and so our friend had given him the "gesture".

I quit giving the gesture while driving. It's too dangerous. Some of those people are really crazy. You don't know what they'll do. I don't have time to be shot. I gotta get to my destination and I'm usually late.

Do you remember the cartoon of the Roadrunner? He was a wonderful peaceful dude until he got behind the wheel. Then he sprouted horns. The devil made him do it, I'm sure. I know a man like this - Very peaceful, gentle, non-aggressive – until he gets behind the wheel. Then, look out. Here come the horns.

In Texas I have been told they have a statewide philosophy of "friendly driving". If you are wanting to go faster than the guy ahead of you, he will sweetly pull over and let you pass, wishing you well as you go. What kind of a world is that?

The other day I was driving out of town and in front of me a slow poke was going 45 all the way. Several cars backed up behind me. Two cars in front of me passed the slowpoke, but when they shouldn't have, and both drove the oncoming cars off the road. At long last, I had a chance to safely pass. When I went to do so, the young woman behind me pulled out and took the shot instead. As she did, she gave me the *gesture* and screamed and swore at me. Immediately my heart rate quickened. I inched on down the road still behind the slow poke, now fuming over the woman's nasty behavior. About a minute later we both got to the light next to each other. I couldn't help myself. I looked at her. She looked at me. She screamed several obscenities and raged even more. My only sin had been being locked behind a slow poke with no safe chance to pass. I gave her a kinda *whatever* gesture back and went on my way. That was 10 days ago. Now if I can just quit thinking about it and if I can just get my heart rate back to normal, I'll be all right. Come Sunday, I might even go out and try a leisurely drive. Or maybe I'll just take a nap. Yeah, that's it - A nap, the best gesture of all.

Signs of the Times

Driving alone can be so boring. I drive alone a lot for my work.

As I drive I see people busily doing things. Of course, there is always the usual. People eating, people on their phones. People reading newspapers opened up over the steering wheel. I see books opened up on the steering wheel too, as the driver reads and drives. I see people reading maps. I am quite sure I see people texting. This all means I see a lot of drivers only paying half attention to their driving. It also means I am paying attention to them. What a cycle.

Once as I was driving home, I saw a man I knew in the lane next to me. Sidled up to him all cozily tucked into his arm was a blonde. His wife was a brunette. He and I caught each other's eyes and I could see his reaction, "Caught!"

To keep myself perky as I drive, I look for fun signs to laugh at. I have decided it is mentally okay to laugh out loud when you are by yourself. In fact, I am sure it is a sign of superior mental health.

Just as you enter Indiana on Highway 69, there is a truck stop restaurant with a sign that has lights. It reads, "Eat here and get gas." I don't recommending stopping, but it is good for a laugh as you mosey on by.

As you enter Toledo, there is a tiny cemetery with a billboard on a hill that leans over it. It reads, "Marlboro Country." Nuff said!

I went to give a talk at a Holiday Inn. The marquis read, "Have your next affair here." I was confused and thought perhaps it was a political convention.

As we drove to Milwaukee once we saw a monastery that said, "Passionate Fathers of the Immaculate Conception". That just didn't seem right.

A man in one of my talks told me he had been in Arkansas and saw a sign in front of a building. "Veterinarian / Taxidermist. Either way you get your dog back." I didn't see that one. But as sick as it is, it makes me laugh every time I think of it.

Churches often offer great signs with food for thought. I saw one locally that said, "When they anger you, they control you." Wow. I don't mind if they anger me but I sure don't want them to control me. I think that sign changed my life. Really.

The first sign I ever saw and laughed at while driving was at a nearby church. The sign out front read, "Morning service – Jesus walks on water. Evening service – Search for Jesus." I always wondered if they realized how funny that was when they put it up.

Another church sign I like is, "Where will you be sitting in eternity? Smoking or non-smoking?" Yikes.

And what would driving be without some fun bumper stickers. Some of my favorites: "Due to recent cutbacks . . . the light at the end of the tunnel has been turned off!!!"

"The more people I meet, the more I like my dog."

And one of my all time favorites, "I wonder if you'd drive any better if that cell phone was up your butt!"

Car Wash Blues

Why is it so hard to keep one's car clean? The inside of the car, that is.

The other night we gave a friend a ride somewhere. The minute she got in, I was aware that you could barely see through my car windows. There was a thick smeary glaze of dog lick all over them. This, of course, comes from my dog licking the inside of the windows whenever he is left in the car, which is often. I think he needs some puppy Prozac to calm his nerves. He has lots of anxiety and licking my car windows is just one symptom.

When I get my car cleaned inside and out, I always have a strong will to keep it immaculate from then on. This dream lasts until I drive someplace for any length of time. The minute I travel any distance, the clean car glow begins to dim rapidly.

The other day I decided I absolutely have to get my car cleaned. I clear out all the stuff that lives in my car. That takes quite awhile. A lot of stuff considers my car home. Then I have to pick up all the obvious crud, which is all over the inside of my car.

Am I the only one who has enough crumbs in their car to feed a whole family of mice? Do anyone else's dash and cup holders have films of dust and gunk all over them?

Are there other folks that have actual litter in their car: debris from all kinds of things, bits of broken dog bones, straws, tissue remnants, stubs to remind me to pick up things, lids from take out drinks, sticks and stones enough to break some bones, a gaggle of pens, some which even work, and the occasional nuts and French fries I find under the seats. Does this mean I am not a neat and tidy person? Okay, Okay, I already knew the answer to that question. I think tidiness may be overrated. Then again, it sure would be nice to always get into a clean tidy car.

At the car wash they give me all kinds of options on which kind of wash I want. What I want and what I want to pay for are two different things. The hardest thing to decide is what kind of odor I want to have them put in the car. Clearly the odor I am used to is dog. Wet dog. Dry dog. Dog breath. Oh, yeah, and then there is the one – "Man, that dog stinks." None of these are on their menu of odors. They offer things like vanilla, mango, spring breeze and new car. I can't quite imagine the real smell of dog mixed with the phony smell of vanilla or mango. I go with the new car. I don't know if it is accurate. It has been such a long time since I had a new car.

While they clean my car I have to wait with the cashier, a very nice fellow. I ask him what kind of unusual stuff they see at the car wash. He looks at me with distrust and wonders why I want to know. When I tell him I may write a column about it for a newspaper, he has the fear of *60 Minutes* on his face. I try to schmooze him by saying I won't use his name or the name of the car wash. He begins to talk.

"We see it all," he begins. "During the holidays we get a lot of spilled food. A lot of crock pots tip over every year. One lady had her water break in her car. They rushed her to the hospital and then rushed the car over here to let us clean it. What a mess. Even worse was the guy who shot a deer and didn't have anything to tie it on top of his car. He decided to shove it into his wife's back seat and the deer bled out all over."

"Oh, and then there is the usual – vomit and feces." I decided I didn't want to hear anymore. All of a sudden I felt quite smug. My car has never had a deer bleed out in it. Nor has anyone done their duty in it. Who cares about a few nuts, fries, straws, etc.? My car isn't so bad after all.

Potshots and Potholes

Last night we drove home from Grand Rapids. We had some major decisions to make. Should we drive in the wrong lane and get hit by oncoming cars or should we drive in our own lane and fall into potholes the size of Rhode Island. Oh, what to do.

I swear some of these potholes would hide a good size cow and Michigan is full of thousands and thousands of them. Some crews are working ten-hour days and Saturdays to fill them.

As I drive around Michigan, I wonder why the right lanes seem to be the worst. I suppose they are more heavily traveled.

Driving these days is a bit like riding a ride at Cedar Point. Potholes slam us, shake us and destroy our cars. They also surprise us, as we often don't see them coming until we are airborne. Whee!

All this is hard on our vehicles. As we are wringing our hands with angst, auto repair shops are wringing their hands with glee. This is going to be a busy lucrative spring for them. Not so for the owners of the damaged vehicles.

We can send claims to the government. That will likely be as fruitful as shopping for ocean front property in Arizona. Yes, you can run to the government to get money to cover your damage. Yes, you can turn in legitimate auto repair bills, but you will likely not get any reimbursement for your woes. The majority of claims are denied. One reason is a little detail. The state must know about the pothole for over 30 days before your car was hurt and they must not have repaired it during those 30 days. Also, government budgets are tight. There is likely not enough to cover all the needed pothole repairs, let alone those of individual auto repair claims.

As we face pothole obstacle courses wherever we drive, we can look ahead to a nasty spring in this regard. This is a problem that is not going to go away quickly. When you talk to folks in the know, there is not a lot of optimism. This problem is going to stick around for a while.

I have heard that Michigan has only two seasons, winter and construction. Perhaps now we can have three - winter, construction and pothole season.

What can we do to take these pothole problems off our minds? We could start thinking more about our potbellies. We could ponder which politicians inhaled or did not inhale when they smoked pot. We could make ourselves a nice potpie or a tasty pot roast for dinner. If you choose not to cook, perhaps you could find a nice local potluck.

I suppose you think I am a crackpot so rather than take any more potshots at Michigan and our potholes; I will end this with a quote by Robert Byrne. "Winter is nature's way of saying - Up yours." I think he's right.

Weather or Not

Weather or Not

We can count on a lot of things in life. But one of those is definitely not the weather. Whether or not the weather will cooperate with our plans is totally up to Mother Nature, and lately, she seems to have quite an attitude.

A few days before Easter it was definitely spring. I think it even hit 80 degrees in some spots. Daffodils sprouting. Folks were walking about town. People sporting T-shirts, shorts and sandals. Spring energy permeating the area.

And then, along came Easter weekend with all the glory of snow, ice and freezing temps. The daffodils shriveled up in icy gloom, along with our spirits.

Is this kind of weather normal, we wonder? I suppose the question really is - What is normal when it comes to Michigan weather?

Our daughter came home from Boston at Christmas with snowshoes for us all. She could hardly wait to play in the snow. And, of course, as you remember . . . There was no snow the entire week of Christmas - Just a dirty shade of taupe in our great outdoors. It was certainly not the white Christmas of songs and holiday expectations.

As I write this, it is April 11. A severe storm has shut everything down in our area. Everything is heavily laden with snow, which has been coming down at an unbelievable rate for several hours. And friends, Jodie and Donnie, both told me they heard Christmas music on the radio today. As I describe this, there is a big fat Robin sitting on the snowy branch next to my window. Life is weird. I have heard of Christmas in July – but Christmas in May? Come on!

This past Thanksgiving was like summer. We all walked around the lake in sunshine and warmth, a rare turkey day treat.

Memorial Day, Labor Day and the Fourth of July are often holidays dampened by damp weather. We hope and plan for sun and heat but we get what we get and it is often not what we want.

And all the graduation open houses, tents, more folks invited than homes can hold, everyone holding their breath for good weather for their parties. For our daughter, Donna, we had a wonderful ice cream social in a tent outside. It was a great idea. But, old Mother Nature really dissed us with cold, cold temps. People stood around eating ice cream and trying not to freeze, so much for our great idea - Brrrr.

I am always in awe of folks who dare to plan an outdoor summer wedding in their backyard. I think it sounds lovely but I am not sure I could take the stress of worrying about it ahead of time.

Local Festivals are always up in the air. There are years where rain ruins booths and events. The hard part is we just plan and hope. We do our part and hope Mama Nature grants us a pardon or blessing.

There seems to be one thing that is a given with weather. You can always count on extremely hot days after the kids get in school. We may have a chilly rainy Labor Day and September, but October is sure to cook for a while. Like the cold weeks when the kids can't go out and play at recess, these are the times when teachers really earn their money, and lose their sanity.

But variety is the spice of life. We lived in Madrid, Spain, for two years and really missed the seasons. Our friends there had never seen snow or a colored leaf. They had never felt the joy of spring, which you can only appreciate if you have had the dark cold of winter.

And how would many people converse if they had no weather to talk about? A new study said weather is the number one conversation starter. It is easy and non-threatening.

One of the most glorious parts of weather is the rainbow. Each time you see one you know you have seen something special and lovely. A gift.

Mark Twain said, "It is best to read the weather forecast before praying for rain."

I guess my personal philosophy about weather has always been to not think or talk about it too much, because we have no control over it. It is absolutely out of our hands.

My favorite weather forecast, and the one I find to be the truest, comes from weatherman, comedian, George Carlin. "Weather forecast for tonight: dark."

The Unconstant Gardener

A couple of years ago there was a movie, *The Constant Gardener.* I am more like an unconstant gardener. I love gardening - Sort of. I mean I love the *idea* of gardening. I love the final product of gardening. Of course I never love *my* final product of gardening because it is never lovely. I am what you might call an appreciative gardener. Meaning I appreciate other people's gardens. I do not enjoy my own.

For me the most exciting part of gardening is going and buying all the annuals. I am especially good at the buying part. I really get carried away. I almost turn into another person as I buy the flowers. I am full of ideas for this and that and am sure it will all be just beautiful. However, by the time I get home from the nursery, I have forgotten most of my great ideas. I wander around looking at my purchases, thinking - Where was I going to put that? What was that for? Who can I hire to plant these suckers?

I usually get excited for gardening around the first of June and by July 4th that excitement is long gone. By July 4th, I hate the thought of gardening. I don't want to weed. I don't want to water. I don't want to fertilize. In fact, I don't even know how to fertilize.

Two years ago, I decided to really get *into* it. I got some Miracle-Gro and spent a couple of hours watering and fertilizing my garden. I was amazed it took so long. My arm was sore. I was bored. Nothing looked any different. I really prefer hobbies that show results right away - Like going to a movie. Watering a garden for ages, while being assaulted by bugs and being constantly on guard for snakes, does not seem like a joyful hobby to me.

A few days after I had fertilized my garden, I was feeling like Martha Stewart or some hotshot gardener. I don't know enough about gardening to even know who the Martha Stewart of gardening is. But I was feeling *all that,* for sure. Some friends were discussing their fertilizing experiences and how their water turned green as they fertilized. I said, "*What?* My water never turned green." Come to find out, I had watered for two hours without removing the seal from the bottle. I had read the directions and I had never noticed anything about removing seals. For someone like me, I need to have absolutely every step spelled out. I am not proud of this experience. I really should not share it. But fact is fact.

My friends and I had a good laugh over my stupidity. If you can't keep up, you might as well laugh at yourself while everyone else is.

I feel a lot of pressure with gardening. I don't know what is plant and what is weed. A friend shared how she had fertilized her weeds, thinking they were the plants. She had pulled the plants and let the weeds grow. And grow they did. Now there was a girl I could relate to.

I mean, how is one to know? Have you noticed how pretty some of the weeds are? Some of them even flower. It is so confusing.

I think gardening is just an extension of houseplants and I gave up on those years ago. At times people have given me lovely big houseplants and the pressure to keep them alive is nearly unbearable. I try so hard out of respect for the giver, but my best is never good enough. Sooner or later, they all die.

Jerry Seinfeld said, "I have no plants in my house. They won't live for me. Some of them don't even wait to die. They commit suicide." I wonder does he live in my house?

I hear from many people that gardening soothes their souls, lifts their spirits, and adds years of joy to their lives. For me, not so much. It irritates my soul, flattens my spirit and adds stress to my life. However, I do love to look. I love to visit gardens wherever I go. The Hershey Gardens in Pennsylvania. The Botanical Gardens in Phoenix. I photograph rolls and rolls of beautiful flowers. I truly enjoy garden tours. I "ooh" and "ahh" over the beauty of gardens, other's gardens.

I guess it is another reminder that it takes a village. Some in the village are gifted gardeners. Some are not. But what would a garden be if it did not have a grateful audience - And that, I am good at. My spirit and soul clap in glee as I admire the gardening delights of others. Without them, my world would be diminished. So I say, thank God for the constant gardeners. And thank God that does not have to be me.

Falling for Fall

Every year after Labor Day, I wonder. How does the earth know it is Labor Day? It must, as it immediately changes the Tuesday after Labor Day Weekend. The nights get earlier. The mornings get later. The weather gets cooler. Jackets come out. Leaves begin to turn. God's artistry is all over, a sight to behold.

Summer toys and furniture and clothes get put away. Furnaces get revved up.

Football begins. No matter if it's high school, college or professional, it has its own special excitement. Soccer and other fall sports pique interests as well.

Homecomings bring folks together. Beautiful young women and handsome men wear crowns and get cheered.

Halloween costumes and candy vie for our attention at the stores. Trick-or-Treaters knock at your door and adults pray it is good weather for them.

Fall festivals are all day treats. Some shine with music, food and art. Orchards can take a full day to explore and enjoy. At one our grandsons rode camels and donkeys, picked apples, jumped in air houses, rode hay wagons and on and on.

Rakes come out. Bonfires add appealing smells to the fall air. Cider is a favorite brew.

And then there are the pumpkins, mums and squash. People begin to think about making stew, pies and comfort food. I have a yummy Apple Custard Pie* recipe that will make you go, "mmmmmmm". I also have great recipes for Sharon's Pineapple Zucchini bread* and my daughter's Baked Apple Donuts*. All are fall delights. In fact, when Colleen was about 10, she won a cooking contest in the newspaper for those Apple Donuts.

As colors turn it is a perfect time to walk down streets and relish the lovely homes. Nature trails are another favorite just waiting to show you their fall splendor.

Soon we will be up to our eyeballs in snow, ice and grey days. We will be snuggling in for the long haul until spring. But for now, we can really enjoy this beautiful unique time of year. We lived in Spain for two years and there were no leaves turning color. Life just stayed hot and then it wasn't quite as hot and, before you knew it, it was hot again.

Summer gets too hot. Winter goes too long. Spring can be too short. We are truly blessed to live in Michigan and get to fall in love with fall again this year. Enjoy.

*Recipes in chapter 15.

We'll Sing in the Sunshine

We all know friends and family who go to Florida, Arizona, Texas, California or the like to bask in the sun during our long Michigan winter. As they are enjoying the sunshine, we are left to freeze our buns off. That is what I thought until recently.

One day last week I ran into the store for a quick grocery grab. It was freezing cold and I went in with my hat, gloves, parka and chilled to the bone. A funny thing happened. As I left, I didn't think of the cold anymore. I had been warmed by the many friendly encounters as I rushed through the store. Nothing had changed outside but something had definitely changed inside – of me, that is.

Come to find out, the sun isn't just a big yellow ball of heat in the distant sky. It is also the warmth in your heart and spirit generated by the caring friendliness of others.

We all know that we need to plug in an electric blanket to get warmth. I think we also need to plug into something for warmth within our heart and spirit.

We can plug ourselves into action within our community. I see dynamic guys like Al and Dan. They are both heavily plugged into helping with Habitat for Humanity. Al, Mary and others are also plugged into volunteering at local hospitals. Jesse works with students at the catholic school while Dotti mentors students at another elementary. Hilda and others cook food for the soup kitchen. I could go on and on and on. Volunteerism in our local communities seems to bring warm sunshine into people's lives. This works both for the one giving and the one receiving. What a heck of a deal that is. Everybody wins.

Then there is the warmth generated by friendliness as you visit local haunts. Stop in at the coffee shop and you will find a place where everybody knows your name. Well, maybe they don't, but they know your face and give you a, "Hey, how are you?" or a hug or a friendly comment of some kind. We go there for the caffeine to perk us up but find that even though we leave with a hot drink, it is more than the drink warming our heart on a cold day. It is the sunshine of friendship and fun.

I find exercise groups are like that. Mine just took a holiday break. When we returned to work out, quickly the exercise took second seat to the first seat of renewing friendships amid colorful chatter. Yes, we got a good work out but more than that, we were so aware of the bond we share of friendship, support, caring and laughter.

Going to church and standing outside afterwards basking in conversation with people becomes a definite breath of warm air. This is extended family. This is sunshine for the soul.

Years ago Debbie Boone sang a song, *You Light Up My Life*. It is true we all enjoy lighting up our life with warm sunshine. We love to get away and enjoy the heat. But, it is not the only way to get through winter. There is also warmth of a different kind if we take the time to relish each other. The friendly dry cleaner. Pearl at the post office. Veronica at the library. Alan who cleans windows. There is really no end to this list. Each community has its own. Each person has their own.

If we stop and take a moment to think about the folks we each come in contact with on our jaunts around our communities, the people we see as we do what we do in our lives, we will realize that sunshine is warming us each time we go out - The sunshine of friendly faces.

Gail Garnett sang one of my all time favorite songs, which went, "We'll sing in the sunshine. We'll laugh every day." Great words of wisdom as we plow through these cold wintry months. We can sing in the sunshine of each other. We can laugh together each day. We just have to take time to be aware it is an option. Not everyone gets to go south. We need to get sunshine where and how we can.

Big Blooms to Deadheads

What's with all the lying? Year after year it's the same thing. And I'm such a sucker.

You might even call me a fool, because I believe them, hook, line and sinker. They look me right in the eye. They look honest. I throw my good sense to the wind, what little is left at this point in my life, and give them my trust - And my credit card.

I am talking about the people who sell you all the flowers for your yard each year. Big liars. "This will bloom all summer." In my case, that's a week or two if I'm lucky.

"You can't kill it." Wanna bet?

"This one loves the partial sun." Maybe at their house but not at my house.

"All you need to do is dead head it." I feel like a dead head when they die within the month. Summer goes fast in my garden.

My gardening leaves a lot to be desired. You really can't even call it gardening. It is more like – buy 'em and weep. Oh, there is glory, but it is very short lived. I buy them with big blooms, bring them home and have about a good 48 hours, if the wind isn't big.

I hired a master gardener because clearly I am challenged in this area. She comes once in the beginning of the season, to "get me going". Somehow that never quite happens. She is bouncy, bubbly and works harder and faster than any person I have ever seen. Well, Tim the tile man fits into that category too. To be around them when they are in motion is to wear yourself out rapidly. The watching is so hard. It takes your breath away and your heart beats way too fast. You have to leave. You just can't take it.

Back to the gardener - She bustles around. Dirt flies. Stuff is pulled, propped and perked. She fertilizes, stakes, and on and on. The other day she paused to tell my husband and me the name of a plant. She couldn't remember it and it took her a long time to think of it. I wanted to interrupt her thoughts and say, "Fugeddabout it. We will not know what you are talking about anyway and you couldn't be talking to two people less likely to care about the name of that plant." Sadly, as bad as I am in the garden, my husband is worse. Don't judge us.

The gardener teaches me each year. I take voluminous notes on my legal pad and draw out things I need to remember. She leaves and it all mysteriously turns into Greek. What was this? What was that? I don't understand any of this. I have a few years of notes now and I have never been able to do anything with any of them.

She tells me inane things like. "Water. Fertilize. Do this. Do that. It's simple." My head is buzzing and I just wanna go inside. Can't I go inside, please?

This year we either had too much cold, too much rain or we were too busy. I don't remember, but it delayed the big buying of the garden plants. I didn't get them in until the first part of June. Then as the perky gardener drove away, she suggested that I get a few more to "make it pop".

I dragged myself back to the flower place and brought home some sorry looking specimens. By mid June most of the good-looking ones had already found loving homes.

I brought the suckers home and left them in the garage for days. Guilt finally took over and made me put them outside. Even though they clearly needed to be potted, I just plopped them out there in a cluster and let 'em lay. While out there, I noticed that everything else was screaming for water and dead heading. Nothing looked pretty anymore, including me. July 4th came and went. Why does this gardening stuff have to go on *forever*?

I wish I could be like my friend, Jeff. I was in his backyard the other day and felt like I had died and gone to heaven. It was so beautiful that Meijer Botanical Gardens better start worrying. I asked him once who gardened for him. He said, "Oh, I just like to do it." I don't understand that. These are feelings and skills that were definitely not in my gene pool.

I know some people who have artificial flowers in their yard. I used to scoff at them, but I gotta tell ya, they are looking better every time I think about them. No watering. No fertilizing. No guilt. I think I like it.

Weary Winter Wonderland

I've always wanted to go to Alaska but this winter is beginning to make me feel like I'm already there. I just called the TV meteorologist. Although very nice, he was not encouraging. As I write this on February 19, we have had about 85" of snow this year and it has been falling steadily for hours today. I just stopped to do an errand and a person said, "It is supposed to snow several inches today and tomorrow." - Just what I was hoping for.

Last year we had 83.3" of snow for the entire year. We are way ahead of ourselves and they expect us to end up in the top five snowiest winters since they began to record it way back in the 1800's. Whew. Pass the hot cocoa, please.

We live in a winter wonderland but I am beginning to lose my wonder. In our last forty days, we have only had two days without snowflakes.

I remember the big snowstorms of the 70's and I remember snowstorms during the month of April. This could get very tedious. Oh, wait, it already is.

What to do in all this white stuff? Tower Mountain seems to be busy every day.

Comedian Steven Wright says, "Cross-country skiing is great if you live in a small country." I do love to cross country ski and snowshoe.

However since mid-December, my husband and I have been suffering from sore throats, head colds and yucky chests. Like everyone else in western Michigan, I'm sure. It is hard to go out and play in the snow when you are chugging cough syrup each night and slathering yourself up with that lovely aphrodisiac, Vicks VapoRub. Ummm, how sweet it is.

That great weather predictor, Mr. Groundhog, saw his shadow and according to him and the meteorologist, this stuff is here for at least four more weeks.

All this indoors time has inconveniently coincided with the TV writers strike. What's a person to do? Read? Talk to your family? Enjoy quiet time? Perhaps you may want to consider building an ark because when the snow melts we are going to be in for big flood problems.

My daughter was told today at a large store in Grand Rapids that they were out of snow shovels and road salt. They also said they weren't sure they could get anymore this year.

Things could be worse, though, folks. Delaware in the U.P. (Keweenaw Peninsula that sticks out into Lake Superior) has had over 210" of snow so far. That's over 16 ½ feet. Timberline, Oregon, has had 550" for the year and it is now piled to the third floors of buildings. Their ski lodges are complaining that folks can't get through all the snow to get to them. Even our capitol, Lansing, has had three times more snow than they normally get. Due to wind changes, the lake effect has moved inwards. Yippee.

Because of it being too cold, too icy or too snowy, school kids have had their fill of days off. Well, at least their parents have.

Churches have been cancelled more than once. People can stay home and make snow angels outside.

Would you like some snow trivia? Snow falls at 3 miles an hour.

What do snowmen eat for breakfast? Snowflakes.

Why does a man shovel snow? For the same reason he climbs a mountain, because it's there.

What do you get if you cross a snowman and a shark? Frostbite.

Mae West said, "I used to be snow white, but I drifted." Tallulah Bankhead said, "I'm as pure as the driven slush." And then there's the common parental cry, "Don't eat the yellow snow."

And I say – snow, snow go away, come again some other day - but not for a long, long time. We've had enough. We had a lovely white Christmas but we're lookin' at Easter in the not too far future. You can leave now, snow. We are sick of slip sliding away. We are sick of shovels and snowsuits and boots and hats and being chilled to the bone. We are sick of gloom and slush and hazardous roads. From now on the only kind of blizzard I want to enjoy is one with Reese's peanut butter pieces in it, a dollop of hot fudge atop it, in one of those blue and white Dairy Queen cups. Let it snow. Let it snow. Let it snow . . . no mo.

Splendor in the Snow

Our daughter gave us snowshoes for Xmas. When she mentioned she might give them to her sisters, I quickly said how much I would love them too, even though I had no idea what they really were.

It took us until now to get proper boots to use with them and today was the day we tried them out. We first walked across the lake. What an odd feeling. I wouldn't say it was a religious feeling but I truly was aware that I was walking on water. Never having done anything on frozen water before, that was quite a heady experience.

I am not a fisherman (ice or regular) nor a swimmer nor a boater. I do love to pontoon but my experience with that is to go out with dinner and something good to read and just float. From the middle of the lake everything looks different - The homes, the trees, the sky. I kept hearing birds chirping and loved the sound. Then I realized there were no birds. It was the cold snow squeaking as I walked.

We came upon a lone ice fisherman who had a larder of blue gills he had just caught. When one doesn't ice fish, it is hard to understand how that is such a popular hobby.

If I had to choose between putting a line down an icy hole to get a fish I would throw back or going to a movie or something – the movie or something would always win.

However, it was easy to see how much the man was enjoying ice fishing. I noticed his lightweight shanty and how it seemed so much more modern compared to the wooden ones I used to see on the lakes.

Later we walked from one end of the lake to the other. As we did, we saw him pulling his icehouse behind him, walking away. It was great fun to watch. It reminded me of a little kid – "if you don't play the way I want, I will take my house and go home". I had never seen anyone carry their "house" away before.

Bright sunshine. Lots of snow. Today was a perfect winter day, except for the very low temperature. Wherever I went, people said, "Isn't it a beautiful day?" We Michiganders are so happy when we see the sun. We realize that can be a rare treat here. We also assume that sunshine means warmth. It did not today.

I remember in Seattle I was told that the residents never use umbrellas. "Umbrellas," they said, "are for tourists. We natives can take it. We don't even blink at raindrops." That is how we in Michigan are with sun. We don't need much warmth at all to call it warm enough to "go with it". I always laugh when it gets up to 45 degrees and folks go without coats. I guess that is a positive way to live in this state, although some may call that a state of denial.

Cross Country Skiing, Sledding, Ice Skating, Ice Fishing, Snowmobiling, Downhill Skiing, Snowboarding, Snowshoeing – Michigan's winter wonderland of delights. There are enough choices for all of us to find one we like and enjoy it. I am looking forward to snowshoeing again this weekend. I just need to find boots for the dog.

The Stage of Life

At Your Age

So, I am playing Scrabble with my Scrabble Club and Miss Connie says, "I went to the Doctor recently and before he could say anything, I said, 'There are three words you cannot say during my visit - *At your age'*."

He just looked at her, likely thinking "at her age, they always get feisty".

She later told about going to another Doctor and saying, "Look, I've had this back pain longer than you are old." We all nodded, but of course, she was right.

Another member, Miss Mary, told how she had gone to Canada for eye surgery. It was all very organized, lines for this and that, but you never saw the Doctor until he was actually to do the eye surgery on you. When she got in there and saw him, she screamed with panic. He looked fifteen, okay, perhaps eighteen. "Do you know what you're doing?" she asked him. Shockingly, she said, he did seem to know what he was doing.

I remember having our furnace replaced a couple years back. One of the guys who used to goof around with my son when they were teenagers came to the door. I looked at him with wonder and asked, "What are you doing here?" I am sure I said it in a nice way.

He said, "I came to put your new furnace in." My mouth dropped. I was stunned. Surely this couldn't be true. I remembered the things these "kids" had done as they were growing up.

I asked him, "Do you know how to do that?" I am sure I said it in a nice way. He assured me he did and I let him into the furnace room with deep hesitation. This couldn't be. It really couldn't be. And, come to find out, he did a fantastic job and I would recommend him to anyone. Isn't life surprising sometimes?

How did people in authority, holding scalpels over us, putting our new furnaces together – all get to be so darn young? And when did the phrase, *at your age*, get to be so nasty, or irritating, at best? No matter if it's true.

There are good things about that phrase, though. At *our age* we no longer need to pretend we like to golf or that we will joyfully pick it up when we have time. The time has come and we choose instead to read a book, go for a walk, take a nap, whatever, just not golf. Does anyone want to buy a lovely set of ladies clubs? But then again, *at my age*, I can be fickle and I might just use them someday. But then again, maybe not. How much will ya give me?

At our age we don't have to go see the fireworks. We have seen them and they scare our dog, who is also *of that age*. Watching them on TV as the Boston Pops play is just delightful and, oh, so easy. And most of those Boston Poppers are *at our age* too.

Another thing I've noticed *at our age* - leftovers have become standard cuisine. My son and my niece, Alison, claim they don't eat leftovers. How interesting. *At our age* it is just the way it is. You cook one day and eat off it for days, quite happily so. We are so easy that way. If I served new food each night, my spouse might get dizzy from all the epicurean excitement, and, *at our age*, that is never a good thing.

One more thing I have observed, *at our age* we have seen a lot of repeats, not just on TV or in the movies, but in life. The more things change, the more they stay the same. We are quite smart *at our age*, smart and smug. You could even call us wise, or not, but you probably won't want to mess with us. You know how we can get *at our age*.

Older Adorable Angst

So … the other day I am speaking over in the Detroit area. In my talk, I used as an example for something - how I hate my hair. Trust me, the example fit.

After the program, a young twenty-ish woman came up to talk with me. "I just wanted to tell you how much I like your hair," she said. "I was sitting there thinking how nice it was to see an OLDER woman comfortable in her own skin, blah, blah, blah, blah, blah." She said some other nice things, but I never really got past the OLDER, OLDER, OLDER, OLDER. It was like flashing neon in my mind.

When I got home, I told my husband and he understood. I whined to him. "OLDER. Why can't I just be middle or medium? Why do I have to be OLDER?"

He truly empathized with me. He had been there.

One day a few months ago, he had called me. He was obviously distressed. He said it had begun a while ago. When he would go into restaurants the waitresses would all call him, "Honey" and then it moved on to "Sweetie". But then, one day, the big one. A young woman looked at him and said, "You're so ADORABLE."

He moaned. "ADORABLE. No one calls studs ADORABLE. They only call you ADORABLE if you are old, harmless and over the hill."

I assured him he was NOT over the hill. He was still on top of the hill. Perhaps hanging a bit over the edge of it.

His angst had begun a few years before. A little boy had run by his office doorway. The little guy then yelled, "Whose Grandpa is *that*?" Of course, this was before we were grandparents.

I remember when our first Grandson was a baby. I had him at the grocery store and someone said, "Oh, your grandchild?" I was rather hurt that they assumed I was the Grandma and didn't, even for a second, wonder if I was the baby's mother. I mean, don't they know that Joan Lunden had twins not long ago and she is near my age, somewhere near. Well, actually, a surrogate had them for her, but her Nanny takes care of them and she pays for it.

I related the incident with my Grandson to my daughter. "And she immediately thought I was the Grandmother," I moped. My daughter looked at me oddly. Actually her look said a lot. "Are ya kidding me?"

I guess I was lucky it was that daughter. One of the other ones would likely have just looked at me and said, "You're nuts."

I don't have a problem with aging. Well, that's not true. I really don't like it at all. I like maturing, gaining wisdom, being at this quieter stage of life. The aging part, I could do without. Why do we have to age just to become wise, more peaceful, etc., etc., etc.?

All this reminds me of my friend, Mary Ellen. A few years ago she went shopping with her only daughter. She wanted to buy a new sofa. She looked and looked. Finally her lovely chipper daughter said, "You need to really think this over because this is your last sofa." Mary Ellen straightened up and briskly retorted. "It is *not* my last sofa. I have a couple of sofas left in me."

I guess that sums it up. I may be OLDER. My husband may be ADORABLE. We may both be at the top of the hill, holding on by the skin of our chinny chin chins. But, if we are lucky, we may still have a couple of sofas left in us.

Addendum: I had just finished this and went to get my hair cut. My hairdresser had skin lotion for sale. I picked it up and was looking at it when she came up and said, "Oh, you don't want that. That's for *young* skin."

As if that wasn't enough, the next day my friend, Donnie called. Donnie and I both turned a big number this year, one with a big fat zero on the end. We often commiserate.

She called to say that yesterday she had the cable man come to do something with her computer. She mentioned he looked 18. As he was leaving she said to him, "I usually turn my computer off. Should I leave it on all the time?" To which he replied, "Most people leave them on all the time, but the *elderly* usually turn them off."

And it goes on and on and on. Gotta go now. Donnie and I are meeting to discuss how soon we need to slit our throats.

Age Is Just a Number

The esteemed George Burns once said, "Young. Old. Just words." That is true. But if they are just words, then why do birthdays with zeros in them feel so traumatic? Thirty, forty, fifty, sixty, seventy, eighty, ninety – just words. But when they happen to you, Oh, Boy!

Not long ago, my friend, Jody, turned 30. It was very hard for her. The day of her big day, I saw her and asked, "How are you doing with it?" "Oh," she sighed resignedly, "I decided to *just go with it!*" I loved that. And, in the grand scheme of life, what other real choice is there? We might as well just "go with it".

My friend, Jay, turned 80 a couple years back. I remember one day she said to me, "Moe, I am seventy-something on the outside, but inside I still feel like I'm 16."

I don't think the mind ever catches up with the body or the years. Diane Sawyer says, "Inside every older person is a younger person *really* surprised!"

When you are 39, turning 40 sounds unbelievable. When you leave your forties and enter 50, many go into shock. At that point we begin realizing our life is moving on, ready or not.

Les once said, "When I turned 50 I had to let go of a lot of things I thought I would always do. I had to accept the fact that many of them I would never get done." Reality bites.

Aging takes all of our "someday I'll…"s and shakes them up. Coming to terms with who we are, where we've been, what we've come through, what we've accomplished and where we're going, is sobering. These kinds of thoughts can jolt our boat, perhaps sink it.

I think traumatic thoughts of zero birthdays are universal. Show me a person who doesn't blink at turning "zero" birthdays and I'll bet they checked out mentally a long time ago. Even for the most positive thinker, the big "O's" can rattle their cage.

Eubie Blake said, "If I'd known I was going to live this long, I'd have taken better care of myself." I am guessing most of us can identify with him.

Age isn't a state of body. It's a state of mind. I know that is true, but I bet it was some young perky person who said it. It seems to me that after a certain age, if you don't wake up aching in every joint, you are probably dead. As I hobble around with arthritis, big scars on my knees, my chiropractor's phone number embedded in my brain, and Tylenol decorating most rooms in my house, age certainly feels like a state of body. And most days I feel like my state is succeeding from my union.

Talking today with my friend, who just turned seventy, I said "Seventy isn't old . . . if it is someone else." We are quick to tell others, "In this day and age, that is young."

Whatever age that is. Sixty is the new forty. Seventy is the new fifty - And on and on. It is so easy to talk like that to someone else. We aren't personally invested. And not only that, we believe it. Until it hits us right where it hurts, on our own birthday.

It does seem like people are younger at older ages than they used to be. This sounds like a Yogi Berra comment, but it really is true. People who are celebrating their golden wedding anniversary still look young. Folks in their eighties are as physically and mentally "with it" as folks much younger. My friend, Elmer, is nearing ninety and is sharp as a tack physically and mentally. Our aunt Julie just turned 85 and doesn't seem "old" in any way.

George Burns, when he was well into his nineties, commented, "You can't help getting older, but you don't have to get old." Ah, yes, life changes. We age. "Young. Old. Just words."

Too Old to Die Young

My husband has joked for a while that we are too old to retire early and too old to die young. I have to agree with him. But that isn't true for many of the celebrities that have colored our lives.

In middle school I loved listening to my record player and singing my heart out to Ritchie Valens and Buddy Holly. "Oh, Donna" and "Peggy Sue" lit up those years. Then there came the sad news of the plane crash that took their lives. Right around that time I remember when Patsy Cline was similarly killed. Many have tried, some have come close, but none have matched her unique voice - "Crazy", "I fall to Pieces".

The next big blow came while I was in high school. "President Kennedy has been shot."

The world was never the same. Martin Luther King, Jr. and Bobby Kennedy followed. A new violent wave hit America and turned our world upside down - So many promising lives taken by a bullet.

Marilyn Monroe began a long line of celebrities taken down with pills. The list goes on and on. Some took them on purpose. Some didn't. They still all went down.

As I was raising my kids there were more shocks. Elvis did what he thought he would do – died at age 42, just like his mother had. Ricky Nelson died in a plane. Roy Orbison died of a heart attack. They were the cream of the crop, the rock and roll crop. I still know almost every word to most of their songs and their music still lights up my life when I hear it, which is quite often as their CDs are frequently played at our house.

Not long after they died came the sad morning when I had to tell my teenage son that John Lennon had been murdered. My son was a huge fan. We were excited about and loving John's new comeback CD. Recently I visited New York City and saw where he was shot and the Central Park Strawberry Fields Memorial to him - "Imagine".

A few years later my son called to tell us that Princess Diana was killed in a car crash. No one could believe it and a light across the world was dimmed.

Only two years later came the news that John Kennedy Jr. was lost in a plane crash. As the world hoped he would be found alive, shock filled us when he wasn't - Camelot no more. The reality of his death is one I still find hard to believe.

And now Michael Jackson dies suddenly. I heard a friend say, "He was a weirdo." I guess I have to agree he wasn't "normal". However, none of us have had to walk in his shoes or be in the spotlight and pressure under which he lived since he was a very young child. I think he was one of the most gifted musically, yet sadly, a lost soul.

When Michael Jackson played at the Palace we took our family. All, except our youngest who was only five. She is still sad that she didn't get to go along. When Michael died our older kids immediately got out his songs and played them. Since his death we have gone back in time enjoying his unique beats and voice again. They lift our spirits and we are hard pressed not to sing along and move with his tunes. For sure he gave us many "thrillers" and he is "gone too soon". He was on the verge of a comeback and in my heart I feel it would have been some fantastic singing and moving. He had the gift. Whether the world would have accepted it is left to wonder.

In my life to date, I, like most of you, have lost many personal friends and family members. It seems to have really kicked in since I turned fifty. People who were special to me. Here. There. This one. That one. Some go quickly. Some don't. I now buy sympathy cards in bulk. I don't like that.

I keep thinking that my life is a great big garden of flowers and with each one that passes, a flower is taken. There are still many flowers left, but the garden is not as lush as it once was. So it is with the celebrities in our lives. They are a backdrop to our garden. They color it with songs, speeches and movies. The backdrop thins. The colors dim.

As Michael Jackson sang, "We are the world. We are the children. We are the ones who make a brighter day…" How does your garden grow?

Retirement Advice

People are giving me a lot of advice these days about how I should live with my husband's new retirement. "Oh, this will be the best time of your life." "You will both love it." "You will wonder where you ever found time to work." "It is going to be great."

Though they are loudly cheering me on, I remember that line about, "He protesteth a little too much." Sometimes I wonder if these friends "supporteth a little too encouragingly".

Every once in awhile, I hear a whole different tone. When my friend asked her sister how she liked her husband being home all the time, she replied in a horrible guttural tone, "He gets the mail." My friend gasped. "Oh, my, I'm so sorry." It seemed her sister had always gotten the mail and when her husband retired he just took this task over. The nerve of some guys!

A group of friends were giving me the retirement pep speech recently. Each saying nice sweet positive things about how great retirement would be. Suddenly the party took an ugly turn. Someone mentioned the grocery store. The pitch of the place went up several decibels. The rosy glow seemed to turn red and a bit ugly. Basically, the common advice was, "Don't ever go to buy groceries with your retired husband!" There were several sad tales to verify this claim. It seems one man wants to push the cart. Say it ain't so, Sam.

Another puts everything he sees in the cart. Oh, no, an indiscriminate buyer. One asks the price of every item. Another reads all the labels. Women, of course, have by now perfected the art of grocery shopping. We race thru the store at breakneck speed only getting what we need. Of course, we stop when it comes to self-check out. That is over the line and we happily stop to wait for a real person.

One man gets perturbed if his wife puts stuff in "his" cart. He also straightens the order of things she puts into said cart. She probably doesn't know how to put stuff in the cart in a proper way yet. She has only been grocery shopping for 45 years.

They also complained about how the men have to talk to everyone they see in the grocery store. And talk and talk and talk. Sigh.

So, after all the advice I have heard in the last few months, I am not sure what I should have my husband do in his new retirement. Isn't it my job to give him things to do? I'm not sure. However, I do have a few ideas of my own. I'm guessing he will love them. I wouldn't call it a honey-do list, just some great thoughts. Perhaps my ideas are a bit off the beaten path, but why follow the same old routines, right?

For starters, I think he should always unload the dishwasher and always fold and put away the laundry. That would be way cool . . . for me. And why not? He enjoys order and things in their place. Neither of those are values I participate in much. And just because he already does these things sometimes, doesn't mean he won't love, love, love doing them each day for the rest of his life. I mean how much more rewarding can life get? Why should I always get to do the peak chores?

I was also thinking he might enjoy having clean up detail on my car. It seems to always be a mess and I would love to have a personal car valet. Ahhh, just the thought of it makes me smile.

But the thing I am most excited about is this. My friend, Gayle, often shares things her husband has said to her. It always goes like this. "Babe…" "Babe…" "Babe…" I love that. My mate never calls me "Babe". I think he called me Baby once when I was whining about something but I don't count that. It had a different ring to it. I am pretty sure he always calls me the same boring thing, my name.

So I think he should consciously refer to me from this day forward as "Babe". I know it will be hard for him to learn such a new trick but think of the rewards. It will then come true, for me that is, what everyone has been saying about how I will just love his retirement. I can feel joy rising now as I think of that first endearment coming out of his newly retired mouth, "Hey, Babe, where's the remote?"

Thanks for the Memories

I don't do well with change. I want to do well with it, but the reality is that change is very difficult for me. I realized this when I began giving talks on change. As I analyzed why it is so hard for me, I became aware that it isn't the new thing coming that is so hard but more the ending of what is changing. I don't like endings very much. I hated leaving each home we ever lived in. I thought I might not live through our kids leaving for college. As I look back, I can see a long pattern of not liking big changes in my life.

So, when I have been anxious about my husband retiring, I think it is a lot more about saying good-bye to a life we have loved than it is about entering the new life that awaits us. Saying good-bye isn't fun. It is full of emotion and memories.

It is funny how when your spouse works someplace it becomes a part of you, even though you don't work there and it isn't really your life. And yet it is. It is definitely part of your life.

Sally, a dear friend, reminded me the other day that when she met me on the college campus, I was 24 years old and had pigtails. Ah, yes, and a baby and a toddler. And now I get the senior discounts. It has been a lifetime.

For most people, family is important. So it is with us and MCC has been a very dear extended family. Most of us grew up together through the last 38 years. We remember when each other were young, illnesses we have experienced, growth we have lived through. We watched each other educate and graduate. We have been joyful as people married, supported some through divorce, were happy as people remarried. We have mourned when people lost spouses or parents and been devastated when some lost children. These life experiences bond people together in a special way. We have made the journey together, good and bad, easy and hard, through laughter and tears.

Besides the great people who have also worked at this college and their families, we have had the wonderful opportunity to get to know people throughout the entire county. I doubt we would have gotten to know so many of these great people if it had not been for being a part of the college. Each town in this area holds people dear to our hearts and what a rich blessing this has been. So many good people and so many good times.

Our children are now grown but they each have vivid memories of romping at MCC. They played on the rocks outside the administration building. They played hide and seek in the library, halls and under my husband's desk. They remember each office he had and it is part of their childhood. When Don became a Ph.D. our daughter, Cara, was a pre-schooler. She told someone, "My Dad is a Doctor, but not the kind that can do you any good." After he had been President for a short while she asked me, "When do we get to move to the white house?" I think they call that 'unclear of the concept'.

Our dog, Clancy, loved the college so much that when he died we spread some of his ashes on the MCC grounds. We had to. It was his favorite place to visit. We knew he would want to be there.

Some of my greatest peaks were also there. Being a part of the first Women's Festivals remains at the top of things I am most proud of. Growing together bonds and enriches all of us. We don't have to get paid to feel part of a work setting.

So it is with a heart filled to the brim that I say thank you to each of you who has been a part of our lives at and through MCC. I have tried to think of something profound to close with but the thing that keeps playing in my head is Bob Hope singing, "Thanks for the memories." Our cup runneth over.

100 Years Young

Recently I had a very special treat. It was so special that morning I told my husband I felt like a kid on Christmas morning. I was so excited. My treat was I got to have lunch, one-on-one, with a dear lady, Charlotte Miel, who is 100 years young. How lucky was I!

We spent a leisurely afternoon together and it was a total delight to be with her. We had lunch at Clifford Lake. Both enjoyed a glass of wine, nice lunch and a big dessert. We had to celebrate her 100th birthday, after all. It was a great discussion and such a high for me to have the chance to spend time with this treasure.

It isn't just that she is 100 years young that makes her special, though that is special enough, to be sure. What makes her special is her quick mind, her wonderful sense of humor, her kindness, her sensitivity and her beauty.

My friend lives independently, drives to church and women's club. She does her own grocery shopping.

Of course, she is an avid exerciser. She walks outside most days unless bad weather keeps her in. I noticed how easily she scooted up and down the steps. I, on the other hand, still consider that to be something of a marvel, having had two total knee replacements. She didn't seem to have any mobility problems at all.

We discussed normal things: children, spouses, travels, friends, activities, life, aging. I asked her if she knew anyone else that was 100. "No," she replied. How odd that must seem.

Her attitude was extremely positive and her laugh came easily. I assume these are qualities that have added to her longevity.

We left the restaurant and she took me on a tour of her local town, showing me many things I had never seen. She then took me to see her local library where they greeted her as if she was the best thing they had seen in years. They shared with me how she is their number one patron, meaning she was the first one to get a library card there. It was obvious they think she is a treasure too.

Many books have been given in honor of her 100th birthday, as well as in memory of her dear husband who died a year ago at the fine age of 99. She wowed me by saying she is in the process of reading *all* of the books donated for them. She said, "If people were so kind to donate them, the least I can do is read each of them."

I hope I can be like that when I am 100 years old. What a role model she is for everyone.

After our wonderful visit simmered in my memory awhile, I realized I had some questions I hadn't asked her. I called her today.

Charlotte was born in 1907 and she told me that, at that time, the life expectancy for a woman was 49. Her parents died young, 56 and 65, so her longevity isn't hereditary.

She and her wonderful mate were married 71 years. She commented, "Oh, we had such a happy time together."

I asked her what advice she had for marriage. "Talk things over quietly and straighten things out without harsh words."

On parenting. "Know what your children are doing." Her children are now 63, 67 and 69. She has seven grandchildren and seven great grandchildren. "And they are as nice as they can be," she said. "They all call often, about once a week."

I asked her what it was like when women were allowed to vote. "My parents were quite active in public affairs and we just went out and voted."

She said she physically feels good. "It is just harder to sleep now and I don't have much of an appetite."

As I left her home the day of our lunch, she was about to prepare food for her family that was soon to gather at her home for Christmas. We made plans to meet for lunch again in the near future.

As I drove away I thought of Eubie Blake who said, "If I had known I was going to live this long, I'd have taken better care of myself."

And I wonder, if the rest of us get to live to be 100 years young, what do we need to do now to take better care of ourselves? It seems the simple things have served my friend well: love, kindness, laughter, positive attitude, staying active, exercise, reading, faith and family.

Note to self - KISS. Translation: Keep it simple, stupid.

Insights and Inspirations

A Zippity-doo-dah Lesson

Last weekend my grandson, who is three, was coming up to help us put in our pontoon boat. He was excited to see it come in on a truck and watch them put it into the lake.

The next day he was to go on an Easter egg hunt at John Ball Park and he was very excited about that too. Both events were cancelled due to freezing weather and snow.

I watched the little guy, who had been so very excited to do these two things, as he got the news that they wouldn't be happening. He looked sad, said, "Bummer." And then went on and had two great days, enjoying other things.

He was a great example of how to act when we are disappointed. Shake your head sadly. Say "Bummer" and go on and have a great day. Lessons from the very young.

I thought of how often we are all disappointed in life. Sometimes from life itself. Sometimes from other people. Sometimes from the weather and sometimes from our own sweet selves.

I realize that I often let my disappointment linger, sometimes turning into depression or crabbiness. Oh, how I hate to say that, or admit it, but I am quite sure my husband and family would readily agree with me.

What I have come to learn in my life is that sometimes I need to put on my attitude, just like my clothes, consciously. I believe that most days my attitude is on and positive.

But, every once in awhile, it is not, and that is when I have to kick myself in the ole attitude.

A few years ago, Michael, a friend in Chicago, called me from Loyola University, where he works. We had a nice chat and when it was time to go, he said, "Well, it was great talking with you, Maureen. Make a nice day."

I remember holding the phone in my hand, thinking, 'what are they teaching them at Loyola?' because that was weird. No one says, 'make a nice day'. What you say is, "Have a nice day". Everyone who says, "Have a nice day", really cares about you and your day. Right?

But, after thinking it over, I decided Mike was brilliant. As Robert Schuler says, "Your attitude is in your hands."

Attitude is one of the main things I believe in. It is one of the topics I first began speaking about. I have felt passionate about attitude for many, many years. And yet, when I heard Schuler's comment, I realized that I still was giving my attitude away.

I could be going along, having a zippity do dah day. And then someone would come along and light my fire. My day would go up in smoke. I would always feel powerless. It wasn't my fault. They did it to me.

Now I have learned that I either let someone ruin my attitude and day or I do not let them. I make the choice. It is in my hands. That has been very empowering.

I can't say that I never let others ruin my day anymore, but I can say that it rarely happens. This has really changed my life and the lives of those around me.

Life, the world, the weather, other people, can all disappoint or upset me. But what I choose to do with my feelings and attitude, are decisions I get to make and live with.

How great it is to watch a young little person, confronted with disappointments ruining his day, and then to see him make a choice to go on and have a conscious zippity do dah wonderful day. Perhaps we were all able to do that when we were three. Luckily, in case we have forgotten, it is still a power we hold within our reach.

Little Pebbles Turn into Big Irritations

My two titanium knees are having their second birthdays. They have allowed me to walk for exercise – something I hadn't been able to do for a very long time. It feels wonderful to have that freedom again, but as Rosanna Rosanna Danna, a.k.a. Gilda Radner, used to say, "If it's not one thing, it's another!" Now I am plagued by a bone spur on top of my foot. I had never even known you could get a spur on top of your foot. It makes my tennis shoe hurt and makes it very hard to walk for exercise. But, alas, I have solved the problem. I have found a nice pair of walking sandals. Other than making me look even more like a geek, they work fine and I am able to still enjoy my walks. That is, until I get a pebble in my shoe, which happens once or twice or sometimes more, each and every time I walk.

Here is how the scenario always goes. The pebble starts to irritate me. I know it is there. I ignore it. Maybe it will just go away, I think, even though it never has. It continues to bug me. Then it begins to hurt. Soon I can't really walk normally and I am not really enjoying my walk anymore. I am consumed by the nasty pebble in my shoe. I next try to reach under my big ole sock (which completes my geekiness look) and knock it out. This has only worked once, but I always give it the ole college try. Eventually, I have to stop walking completely. This means my walking partner has to stop too. I remove the entire shoe; take out the itsy bitsy pebble. It is always just a speck of a thing. I wonder how something so teeny can be so debilitating. How it can diminish my entire walking experience until I deal with it.

Each time this happens I think about how this is a metaphor of life. We have pebbles in our shoes emotionally, physically, spiritually. They rub us the wrong way. They irritate us. They diminish our experiences. They darken our lives. We try to ignore them. We try to take short cuts to deal with them. They still raise their ugly selves and demand our attention.

Sidney Simon said, "When we shove our feelings under the carpet, they make ripples for us to trip over." This is true whether it is emotional feelings or physical feelings. We can deny something is bothering us or that something is a problem for us, but our body never lies. The problem always shows up, whether we want to deal with it or not, whether we think it is a problem or not. It demands attention. And then we are left with our only recourse; to deal with it, remove it if we can, to try to make it all better.

The good news in this process is that our life journey can be enhanced, healed, eased.

Whether it is as simple as a pebble in our shoe when we are out for a walk, or whether it is more intense important items in our emotional, spiritual or physical agendas. Dealing with these problems can help us ease on down the road of our lives.

When my daughter, Donna, was little, something was going on and I said to her, "Donna, nobody said life would be easy!" I remember she stood at the top of the stairs; hand on hip and retorted, "Nobody said it wouldn't be either!" Removing our pebbles may not be easy, fun, or anything we want to deal with, but we are often called upon to do so. May we all have the courage to remove the pebbles from our shoes, whatever they may be and wherever that process takes us.

A Potpourri of Perspectives

One day I was speaking in Livonia. There was a nun also speaking. We sat together at the head table at lunch. She wore the old-fashioned nun outfit. It is technically called a habit, but I like to call it an outfit.

She told me that she had been at an elementary school that morning and a little guy had said to her, "Boy, Sister, I bet your Mom was surprised when she had a nun baby!"

I loved that. He was sitting there thinking – "You got a boy, you got a girl, oh, my God, you got a nun!" Such was his perspective.

We all have different perspectives on the world, on our life situations, on nearly everything.

A waitress brought a guy his steak. When she set it down, he said, "You've got your thumb on my steak."

She replied, "I had to. I didn't want it to fall on the floor again." They each had their different perspectives too.

When one of our daughters was in college, she called home and said she had something to tell us. She said we weren't going to like it and we would likely be really upset. I remember feeling like that old TV show, *Sanford and Son*. I kept thinking to myself, 'It's the big one.' Not even sure what that would be.

When she got home she broke it to us gently. "I got a tattoo."

I was so excited - I nearly jumped with glee. I thought perhaps we should all run out and get tattoos. In reality, I can see now that I was relieved. She had taken my perspective and gotten it in order.

Life is a challenge. It is often a rat race. We get stressed. We get overloaded. Our perspective takes hit after hit after hit.

And then along comes something to shake our cage, to rattle our world, to help us regain our perspective and remind us of what is really important.

This week a dear relative was diagnosed with cancer. This week a dear friend's sweet little child was diagnosed with cancer. A friend's husband was recently diagnosed with cancer. It seemed like each of these came out of nowhere. People are living their busy lives and then WHAM.

Perspective, it's the filter through which we look at our world. How are we doing with that? It isn't something that happens to us. It is usually an unconscious decision we make as we view our life and our world. Do we need to adjust our focus? Are we appreciating enough, loving enough, sharing enough, praying enough?

I love to take photos of nature. I see something that inspires me and I angle my camera. I adjust my focus to make it look the best it can. I need to remember to do the same with my perspective. Some days my perspective is grey and I feel like I am in a great big funk. Many times I can't even figure out why.

I need to remember to treat it like I do photography. On those days I need to angle my mind, adjust my mental focus and try to look at things the best way I can to make them look the best they can. This takes some work but it is worth it.

As the hilarious comedian, Flip Wilson, used to say, "What you see is what you get." Perspective. It is one of the few things we really get to control, no matter what life throws our way.

Coloring Outside the Lines

I was never good at coloring. I always found it hard to stay in the lines. Now, as I look at life, I think that might be a good way to live our lives, a bit out of the formal lines.

A couple years ago I had a "Cinco de Mayo party en Junio". Cinco de Mayo is a national holiday in Mexico, similar to our 4th of July, and they celebrate it on the 5th of May. I was too busy in May but wanted to do the party anyway, so I did it in June and called it Cinco de Mayo en Junio. Folks laughed at that but they came, celebrated and enjoyed. People don't really celebrate Cinco de Mayo in June, but why not? We colored out of the lines and it felt good.

Last week I experienced a couple out-of-the-lines events. They were a lot of fun and, oh, so good for the spirit.

First, was at my exercise class. On Wednesday, we had Christmas in July. As we began the class, someone said, "But it is June." We all had a good laugh over that as we realized, yes, it was June. But Christmas in

June just didn't sound as good as Christmas in July. And why do things always have to make sense?

As exercisers entered, a big wooden snowman greeted them while Jimmy Buffet was singing *Jingle Bells* and a lighted tin Christmas tree sat next to the sound system. Exercise was done to Christmas tunes and everyone sang loudly as we laughed and got fit. Cries of "Merry Christmas" were yelled to anyone who came near. Afterwards a snowman cake was shared by all. We don't usually eat cake after exercise but it was not only Christmas in July but also someone's birthday, very good reasons to eat cake.

What was amazing about the event was the excitement it generated among the participants. People came excited. They brought things to add to the silliness. Laughter abounded. Christmas in July (or June, whatever) is coloring out of the lines, but what fun.

The next coloring-out-of-the-lines event was a birthday party to celebrate my father in-law's 100th birthday. Several people said to me, "Wow, he's 100 years old?" To which I replied, "No, he died when he was 81, but he would have been 100 this week." Then they sort of looked at me oddly, which people often do.

This little birthday party involved about 120 people, mostly close kin. We camped and hung out for several days celebrating his 100th birthday and, of course, family. A big birthday cake decorated with a tractor and "happy birthday 100 years" on it was enjoyed along with enough food and beverage to feed an army.

A mass was celebrated outside with everyone singing and praying together. A tour of the family homestead and other family sites was taken. It involved 8 vans full of excited, emotional celebrants looking and exploring our past, enjoying and relishing our present and looking ahead to our future.

Family flew in from all over the country for this birthday bash. Cameras were clicking. It was not a formal event. It was not a normal birthday party. I'd have to say it was coloring-out-of-the-lines. It was wonderful and no one there will ever forget it.

As we look at our lives, they are usually very much routine. We do this. We do that. We do it this way. We do it that way. We do it the right way.

We go to bed at the same time. We get up at the same time. We eat at the same times. We have routines and stay on routines. We celebrate things when it is the right time. Life is too busy and full to mess with the order of things. Most of us just hold on tight and keep going with the normal flow of life assuming it is the right thing to do. We color in the lines.

But what if? What if everyone just colored outside of the lines once in awhile? What if we had picnics in the snow or had more birthday parties for loved ones who have died? What if we celebrated Valentine's Day in August or took a walk at midnight in the dark? I am guessing that once our minds are unleashed we can come up with all kinds of out-of-the-lines experiences. And, if we do, I am also guessing we will look back at all of them as wonderful, fun and uplifting. Perhaps we will realize we are all Picassos in our heart.

Comfort Zones

Jerry Seinfeld quips that the biggest fear people have is speaking in public. He goes on to say that at a funeral most people would rather be in the coffin than giving the eulogy.

We all have fears and comfort zones. As we age it is important to keep pushing those boundaries or they limit the quality of our lives. Every time we do something that is uncomfortable and accomplish it, our world becomes bigger. It never recedes. We can do more. We are more.

Once I had the honor to interview Mary Kay Ash, the cosmetics founder. I asked her how old she was. "I never tell people my age. It limits what they think I can do."

What a wise woman. What a true concept. Often we limit ourselves. Sometimes our peers do it to us.

Recently I asked some women if I could wear a current fashion or if they thought I was too old. Half said I could. Half said I shouldn't. The ones who thought I shouldn't were all my age. The younger ones all said, "Go for it."

George Bush did a parachute jump for his 75th birthday. "Old guys can still do stuff and they might as well go for it! It was one of the biggest thrills of my life." He felt so triumphant that on his 80th birthday he jumped again.

Dick tried skydiving a few years ago. His experience was a bit rough. He hit a wind gust and broke an ankle upon landing. Would he do it again? "It was a great experience and I have never regretted it. It was something I had always wanted to do."

Connie says, "I bought pottery for years from "real" artists". Encouraged by others, she recently began making pottery; doubtful she would every show it to anyone. To her surprise, she now does stunning pieces of pottery that she proudly gives.

Her husband, Gary, is legally blind. Armed with special lights, magnifiers and carving knives he has made lovely relief woodcarvings. Gary and Connie got out of their comfort zones. They could always do pottery and wood carving. They just hadn't tried yet.

Our cousin, Joan was dragged to a painting class knowing she wouldn't be able to do it. She now has a house full of marvelous paintings she has done. She could always paint. She just hadn't opened all of her gift of talents yet.

A few years ago I joined the community choir, a huge growth step for me. At the last concert I sang a short duet. When it came time, I was so afraid I thought I might throw up. But I gave it a shot because I feel it is important to keep pushing ourselves to do new things. I am sure to others it was no big deal, but to me, it was a huge deal and I felt so proud for taking the risk. Growth was the payoff.

Penny, Gisela, Harriette, Shirley and other local women have all walked 60 miles in the Susan J. Komen breast cancer walk. Did any of these women think they could do it in the beginning? No, but they trained, they finished and they had glorious growth experiences.

Beverly began scuba diving in her sixties. She and her husband then sold their homes, bought an RV and for seven years they have traveled as full-time RVers. Bev says, "Those who don't take risks limit their lives and live in fear. The choice seems easy. Jump into life with both feet. Life doesn't last nearly long enough. Make the most of it. Take risks. There's a lot of reward in doing the unexpected."

Katherine Hepburn said, "Everyone should do something that is very difficult for them and master it. It is so good for the soul."

Einstein said, "Most people only reach 10% of their potential." Ninety percent goes down the drain. What might you try that you haven't done yet? What talent, ability or interest is inside of you just waiting to be let out? Perhaps now is the time. Go for growth. Grow for you. You're worth it.

If I Had It To Do All Over Again

As life flies by, sometimes we need to sit back and take stock. How am I doing? What have I done? What do I need to change? How have I grown? These questions inspired me to write a poem, inspired by an anonymous poem I read years ago.

If I had my life to live over again, I would quit trying to be perfect.

I would believe in myself more and realize I am loveable and capable. I would be a good friend to me.

119

I would realize that if I take better care of myself, I have more to give to others.

I would put more quiet time into my days.

I would write more and express myself honestly, sometimes in a private journal for my eyes only.

I would find someone to talk with about my problems and not keep them bottled up inside.

I would forgive myself when needed and forgive others more often and quicker. You see, I have found that when I don't forgive, I am the one who suffers the most and the longest.

I would pray more and ask God for more direction in my life and then remember to listen to his answers. I would thank God more.

I would dare to dream more and remember my dreams instead of forgetting them as I age.

I've been one of those people who lived my life afraid of not being accepted. If I had it to do all over again, I would lower my guard and be less fearful of being hurt. I would realize that people are the flowers of life and I would pick more of them. I would make friends, not just with people like me, but with all kinds of people - people with different interests, opinions, lifestyles and ages.

I would hug and kiss more and pat more people on the back.

I would try to be less critical and not hurt others. I would compliment more, be more honest, show more emotion, cry and smile more. I would certainly lighten up and not take myself so seriously.

I would laugh more often. Sometimes I would be the only one laughing and that would be okay.

I would look into others eyes as they spoke and try to tune out all the distractions and to really hear what they were saying.

I wouldn't assume as much. I always thought I knew what other people were thinking and feeling or that they knew my thoughts and feelings and how much I cared. I now see it doesn't work like that. I must share my thoughts and feelings and hear their thoughts and feelings also. The things I never said are out there waiting some place with the things I never did.

I would sit back less and enjoy life more.

I would go for more walks and participate actively, joyfully and gratefully in living.

I would sing often and loudly and care less if I'm off key or don't know the words.

I would write more letters and make more phone calls – especially to those I love.

I would hold my children more, talk and listen to them more, read to them often. I would play with them more and clean my house and watch T.V. less.

I would be more romantic to my mate. I would write more love notes for no reason. I would say, "I love you" more and look into my mates eyes when he talked. I would hold and hug more.

If I had my life to live over, I would live it one day at a time and try to enjoy each day, each person and each challenge. If I had it to do all over again… but you see, I don't.

Neither do you. Now is the hour for each of us to care more and to celebrate ourselves, life, love and people more - For they are all precious gifts. We don't have forever, but we have today. Let us not waste a moment.

The Angrier You Get

So Richard moves his place of business to a new spot in town. He has a party to celebrate. His friend, Mel, sends him flowers. At the party, Mel looks for his flowers. When he finds them and reads the card, it says, "Rest in peace."

Mel is furious; leaves the party and returns to the florist. He screams and swears at the florist and demands new flowers and his money back. The entire time he is ranting, the florist laughs. "What are you laughing at"?

"Sir, just think, today someone got buried and over their casket was a big bouquet which said, 'Enjoy your new location.' "

I love that story. I also think it shows how some people get angry as their first response and others see the humor in life. These are both choices.

Anger is a normal emotion that we need to be aware of in our lives. We feel it. We need to acknowledge it, deal with it and move through it. Anger is a healthy place for us to visit. However, it is not a good place for us to hang out.

Anger begets anger. The angrier you get, the angrier you get, the angrier you get. If you add a D to the front of the word, you get danger. Something to think about.

Woody Allen, in his humorous way, said, "One of my problems is that I internalize everything. I can't express anger; I grow a tumor instead."

In a new health study I read, "Anger is more of a health threat than being overweight, smoking, drinking, etc". Wow. Who knew!

How do we deal with anger? Phyllis Diller suggests, "Never go to bed mad. Stay up and fight." Of course, it's better to use healthy tactics. Exercise it out. Write it out. Talk it out with safe positive people. Sometimes these things require counselors. It is worth it. Sometimes good friends will do the trick. We can use all kinds of responses that are positive. But beware of using addictions or other negative behaviors that may hurt you or others, and beware of rage.

An old famous philosopher whom I can't remember said, "We only get angry for one reason. They didn't do it our way." Whew. I have tried and tried and I can't think of a time this wasn't true.

They didn't do it the way I thought they should. They didn't say it the way I thought they should. They didn't handle it the way I thought they should. And on and on.

Not long ago I read a sign outside a church. It said, "When they anger you, they control you." I nearly jammed my brakes as I read that. What?

I thought about it. I don't mind if they anger me. I may not like it, but I can deal with it. But, whoa Bessie, I sure as heck don't want them to control me.

That thought has really helped me let go of anger. When I am in the midst of it, I remember that I don't want them to control me and it really does help to let it go.

George Jean Nathan said, "No man can think clearly when his fists are clenched."

It is easy for people to get into thoughts of "he made me mad", "she made me mad", "they made me mad". In reality, they can't make us do anything. They may lead us into anger but we allow it. We make the choice. We give them our power.

Simple explanations and solutions. Hard to practice. But then, nobody said life would be easy!

Being "Skeerd"

My grandson, Louie, has a new phrase, "I'm skeerd". Translated it means, "I'm scared." Usually he isn't really afraid. He just likes saying it.

Recently I was scared and it wasn't pretty. It made me think a lot about what fear does to us and the paralyzing consuming power it can have over us.

I had the veins in my legs stripped last week. I have had several major surgeries and compared to most of them, this was nothing to worry about - A piece of cake. No problem, the Doc said. Why then did I go into a giant state of anxiety?

I could track down why I felt afraid. Part of my fear was based on things people had said to me. They had definitely "skeerd" me. But even though I understood it, and even though I tried to be rational, I was still left with the anxiousness.

I was honest with my Doctor and told him I was afraid. I felt silly doing so but thought I needed to just get it out there. He calmly smiled and said, "Sometimes people are. It will be okay." That helped . . . a little. However, the fear critter still had a big hold on me.

A friend told me that if you have faith in God, you can't have fear. I believed her. And yet the fear held on, even though I do have faith in God.

Eleanor Roosevelt is famous for the quote, "You must do the thing you think you cannot do." I have always loved that quote and have had it on my desk for many years. However, she said more with it. "You gain strength, courage and confidence by every experience in which you really stop to look fear in the face. You are able to say to yourself, 'I've lived through this. I can take the next thing that comes along.' You must do the thing you cannot do." That is some wise advice, Eleanor.

People tell you to follow your gut, to listen to your voice within and it will tell you what to do. Unfortunately, my gut told me, "I am skeerd too". And the voice inside me just confirmed it. I was clearly no help for myself. I wondered if I shouldn't have the surgery because I was having all these misgivings.

I am sharing this because I think most of us have these kind of feelings crop up. I have had major surgeries done and did them without fear. Why then, did this small thing throw me for such a loop? I wonder if sometimes we are psyched for the biggies in life. We gear up. We give 'em our best shot. We are tough. We are brave. We are fearless.

But then along comes something smaller, something much easier, something not to worry about. And it tips us off our boat of control. Our heart beats faster. Anxiety swirls thru our mind, body and emotions. We fear the unknown. We wonder what happened to our ole brave self. Where did we go? Who is this "skeerdy" cat?

Recently my husband and I were flying and went thru a bunch of turbulence. I panicked and almost wrung his hand in half as I prayed a gaggle of Hail Mary's. He was nice to me but it was clear he did not have the fear I did. He calmly read his book. However, he could relate because he has had MRIs that have put him through this wringer of anxiety. Most of us have something like this that can grab us. One thing may not bother us at all, but another will give us the old what for.

There is a motivational line that says 'Fear is False Evidence Appearing Real'. That is true. But when I was afraid, it didn't help.

What do we do with fear? Prayer, of course, is one route. There are also the two fear busters – knowledge and action. The more we learn about things, the why, the how, the what, the less we fear. The more we begin to do things we fear, even when it is in baby steps, the less we fear. Prayer, Knowledge, Action - Some pretty good tools. Combine that with some good people to talk with and you've got a plan.

As I look back at my recent fear fest over my vein surgery, I can see it was all in vain. (Can you believe I wrote that before I saw the pun?) It all went perfectly, easily and quickly. The most traumatic and most negative part was the fear I put myself through.

In one of my favorite John Denver songs, he sings, "Somedays are diamonds, somedays are stones. Sometimes the hard times won't leave me alone."

I think fear fits in there. I think it is hard and heavy and can sink us like a stone. But if we can hold on, even though we are shaking in our boots, we can get beyond it. Perhaps not because we are brave and courageous but just because we held on, eyes closed tight, breath held in. And then we look back, the fear is subsided and life goes on. Until the next time.

Simplifying Life

"Simplify, Simplify." These are famous words of Thoreau and good ones to think about. There are three major ways we can simplify our lives and see a profound difference.

Number One: Simplify our possessions. Gulp. Does that involve cleaning and sorting? Yes, it does and in a major way.

Go through every room, every closet, every cupboard, drawer, shelf, box, pile. Get rid of everything you don't need or treasure. You can give it away, toss it or sell it.

When my first child left for college, I did this procedure. I went through my entire home, including my garage and storage areas. Since then I try to do it annually and after the first time, it has never been that big of a job. I am always surprised to see that each year I have stuff to toss, sell or give away.

What a wonderful feeling it is to have our possessions pared down to what we need, use and want. Another glorious benefit is knowing where everything is.

Number Two: Simplify your organizations. Whew. What does that mean? It means looking at all the groups and organizations you belong to. Which ones do you really find valuable? Ideally we need to both give the group something and get back something.

Have you ever wondered, 'how'd I get roped into this'? Perhaps someone else thought it would be a good idea. Perhaps you found it hard to say no. Perhaps you loved being in this once but now you would rather have free time or belong to another group. We only get so many hours. Why waste them doing other people's priorities? Ask yourself, do I really want to belong to this? Am I adding to this group? What am I getting from it? Then hone your organizations to what you really want to be part of.

Number Three: Simplify the people in your life. That sounds harsh. How can that be good? Sometimes there are people in our lives that have become toxic to us. They fill our lives with negativity. Perhaps we want to help them, but in reality, we can't as they don't want to be helped or have to help themselves first. Sometimes it is better for them to have us stop helping. These people might include our parents, grown children or friends. This simplification is not easy but the end result may be good for everyone.

Years ago I tried to help a woman who was depressed. After seven years I realized it was never going to happen. She had to want to help herself. I let her go with love. I still care about her and wish her well. I'm in contact with her but I don't hang out with her. I can't afford the negative energy.

There are so many people in our lives. Sometimes it is helpful to just look at the ones we spend most of our time with and evaluate if it is working for us and for them. If not, perhaps we need to simplify.

What we find when we do these things is that we have a lot of space in our homes, our schedules and our relationships. We can then fill these with other things we want to do or other people we want to spend time with.

Before we can grow, we need to make space within ourselves and our lives.

We have several months left of this year. If we start now to simplify our possessions, our organizations and the people in our lives, we can be enjoying the benefits of this simplification by the start of the New Year. Simplify, Simplify. If you don't like the results, you can always go back to a life of clutter, overload, too much to do and negative people. But, then again, perhaps Thoreau had it right after all.

Goal Setting and Gerald Ford

Am I the only one who feels like we just celebrated the New Years for 2000? Time is truly flying – and at sonic speed.

I love a new year! In fact, I love a new month, a new week. I get excited at the beginning of each month, each week – planning what to do, what to accomplish. I even get excited as the weeks and months end, always trying to cram a few more things into my "done" list.

I sit here anticipating the New Year - Another glorious empty calendar to fill. One year, 12 months, 52 weeks, 365 days, 8760 hours, 525,600 minutes.

I am an avid goal setter. Each January I plan goals in several categories: health, career, emotional, spiritual, educational, financial, recreational, home, relationships, projects, etc.

I try to look at them throughout the year and use them as a guideline for what I need to do. They are my maps. They give direction. They remind me what is important.

I have learned that if we don't set our own priorities, someone else will gladly fill our days with theirs.

I never get all my goals done. I may not even get most of them done in any given year. But I make progress and I am happy for that. I don't feel bad that I don't accomplish everything in a year. My eyes have always been bigger than my calendar. I have accepted it. So much to do…So little time.

I am encouraged by the quote, "No matter what your past has been, your future is spotless." This gives me hope that perhaps this is the year I will get all of my goals accomplished.

In 1971 when Gerald Ford gave his speech at the dedication of his Presidential Museum, he said the following:

> When I was captain of the football team at South High, I thought it was the greatest event of my life. But then I went to U of M and I thought that was the greatest event of my life. Then I married Betty and I thought that was it. Then I went to Yale and got a law degree and I thought that was it. Then I had my children and I thought that was it. I became a U S Congressman, I thought that was it. Then I became Vice-President and I thought that was it. But then I became President of the United States of America and I knew, surely, this was *the* greatest event of my life. But, what you people in west Michigan have taught me, is that *the greatest event of my life is the future.*

I am a professional speaker and since 1971 I have often used these comments by President Ford in closing my talks. His message is profound. Sometimes we don't dream big enough. We think this is as good as it can be, and lo and behold, something even better is waiting around the corner of our lives. The future.

So now we begin a new year. Right now it is a clean slate, waiting for us to direct it. It is calling for us to make choices: yes to some, no to others. We won't get to control all of it but we will get to control much of it.

It is time to get started. We have already lost one week, 7 days, 168 hours and 10,080 minutes. Time to begin. Time to *"get er done!"*

As my 3-year-old grandson, Danny, likes to say, "Ready, Set, Go!"

The Wisdom of a Child

This afternoon I visited with my friend, Emma Jane, who is 9 years old. We had a good time talking and laughing and I tried to absorb her wisdom.

Emma has just gone through a huge battle with cancer and guess who won – Miss Emma Jane. Gilda Radner said, "Cancer cells hate laughter and jokes and songs and dancing. They want to leave when too much of that is going on. They love gloom and depression and sadness and fear, but joy makes them want to move out."

If that is true, and I think it is, it is no wonder they moved out of Emma Jane who is now cancer free. Emma is full of joy, spunk, giggles, funny comments and big smiles. She is a great jokester and loves to pull pranks. One of her nurses at Children's Hospital in Denver knew Emma was a Bronco fan so she covered Emma's hospital room with Green Bay Packers signs while Emma slept. When Emma woke, she ripped the signs into tiny pieces and put them in an envelope addressed to the nurse. As Emma shared with me things that had helped her through her long ordeal, at the top of the list was fun time with the nurses.

I asked Emma if she got afraid. "Yes." Emma refers to this as being "worried-ish." She said she was helped a lot by reading books about cancer. She also said her family and friends were great support. She loved getting letters and cards in the mail and we talked about how we need to remember to do that for other people when they need to be cheered.

Emma was shocked by the gift of a laptop computer. Money was raised to buy it for her from people all over the country. Her Brownie leader organized the project. Her family added Skype, a Web-based videophone service, which allowed Emma to talk with and see her class, friends and family.

This contact was incredible and even allowed Emma to do spelling tests and still be a part of her school. "Hi peeps!" Emma would say cheerily as her face would pop up on the computer screen. Her classmates would scream, "Hello Emma!"

Emma asked her Mom only once, "Why did I have to be the one to get cancer?" While her Mom was trying to answer this in the best way possible, Emma quickly moved on to another topic. She is all about living in the moment and full of life and a positive attitude.

I asked Emma what she had learned through all this. "I learned lots of stuff about blood and platelets. I'm a lot smarter about hospitals and nurses and doctors. I now know that finger pokes are way better than IVs."

Her advice to the world is simple, yet hard to do. "Stay strong. There's no quitting. You have to just get through it and then it will be okay."

Emma gave me a trick she used and one we could all use in many challenging situations. "Count to four. Breathe in on one, out on two, in on three, out on four and do what you have to do."

In her long and ferocious battle with Ewing's sarcoma, a rare childhood bone cancer, Emma went through five surgeries, 25 radiation treatments, 14 week long chemo treatments, several blood and platelet transfusions, and untold difficulties. She did it all without complaints.

She had to relearn how to walk, how to get out of bed and how to dress herself. She lost her hair but assured me, "Oh, that's not one of the hardest parts at all. At one point my friend and I pulled it out with our fingers and acted silly doing it." Her comments reminded me of something I recently heard Michael J. Fox say. "Vanity is the first thing to go."

She did tell me, though, that she hated it when people call her a boy.

The hardest part she said was when they found out she had cancer and her parents cried. "I hated to see my parents cry." That is a pretty love filled example no matter what direction you look at it from.

Next Emma will undergo another huge surgery to repair her spine that has been damaged by her cancer and the treatment for it. The surgery could take up to two days and will have a long recovery. Perhaps you will want to pray for this little sassy, adorable, bright curly haired girl.

"The hardest part will be the going to sleep part. I don't like that part." Emma said, but added she gets comfort from a prayer she and her Mom have redone. "Now I lay me down to sleep. I pray the Lord my soul to keep. God stays with me through the night and wakes me with the morning light" And with that, Miss Emma Jane smiled and asked me about my dog.

Tick. Tock. Tick. Tock.

Wherever I go the last couple of weeks, mothers are out and about. They are meeting each other for coffee or lunch, kicking up their heels, smiling, and catching up. It seems the kids are nestled all snug in their classrooms and schools. Ahhh.

On a further note, the snowbirds are gearing up to get outta Dodge, leaving us all in their dust and in the looming cold snowy season, which is sure to come, no matter how lovely it is right now.

Apples are popping up all over. Pumpkins are almost ripe. Leaves are beginning to turn brilliant and fall is in the air, even if just a hint. And, if that isn't enough to jar us with reality, and if memory serves me, the holiday rush is just around the bend. Sigh.

So here we are. Time to regroup for this year. Remember when it began and we were filled with high hopes of all we would do? Well, how's that workin' for ya?

Have you completed what you wanted to do, are you struggling with it, making progress, forgotten about it, or perhaps, blown it off? What were you caring about in the beginning of the year? What did you think you would do, improve, work on?

The good news is there is still a good block of time that we can refocus and get 'er done.

When New Years Eve comes and the New Year dawns, we can feel proud that we actually accomplished something we really wanted to do, even though it wasn't easy. Even though we had other things we really preferred to do. Yes, accomplishment and satisfaction are lovely gifts to give ourselves. They are also wonderful gifts of example to give our children.

As we ponder where we are in this realm, do we have health goals we need to aim for? Are there people we wanted to see? Places we wanted to go? Projects we wanted to finish or just begin? Was there something spiritual we were in need of? Financial? Educational? Did we want to try a new hobby?

One family I know is refocusing on their health. They each have things they want to improve on and have recently discussed them as a group. They range from exercising more to flossing their teeth, whatever each feels is important to them. They are going to meet through the rest of this year and stay focused on their goals, encouraging each other as they go. They also tossed in some money and the ones who do the best, come New Years Eve, will divide up the pot. A bit more incentive, eh?

What I like the best about their plan is it's individuality. It isn't about losing the most weight. It is about whatever health issues they feel they need to attend to and making those a part of their lives.

So, as we ease on into fall and begin the wrap up of this year, we still have time to refocus. We can still do what we wanted to do and here are some steps to guide us.

Think it over and decide what you want to work on. Write it out in specific detail. Be realistic. Consider the time you have and what it will take to do it. Break it into steps, baby steps, even. Make a plan.

Everything begins with a single step. What makes dreams reality is continuing to take those steps, one after the other.

And, then, of course, we need to add that magical ingredient that makes all things happen – action. It may not even be hard to do. It is a necessity, however, to accomplishment.

Perhaps it is a good time to take a quiet walk alone and think about these things. Where are you now? Are you happy with everything in your life or are there some things you want to adjust, focus on, or improve? How do you want to want to look back on this year?

We only walk this road once. The clock of our life is ticking.

Tick. Tock. Tick. Tock.

A Plethora of Advice

Here we are again. Another year of commencement addresses full of inspiration, words to live by and advice. Do we need to be a graduate to find meaning in them?

Tim Russert, the renowned news commentator who died suddenly of a heart attack, said, "After sitting through years of commencement speakers and giving many of them myself, I have to confess that I can't recall a single word or phrase." Can you? Do you remember any of the inspiring words you've heard or even who the speakers were?

Barbara Bush spoke at my daughter, Colleen's, graduation. I remember a couple of gems that she delivered and have tried to live by them. One was, "Here is the secret to parenting. When your child wants to lick the beaters, be sure to turn off the motor." She changed my life. I haven't stuck a beater in my kid's hands while the motor was running since. Oh, and in closing she said, "Try and do a little good every day." That's been a little harder to live by.

Tom Brokaw spoke at the College of William and Mary. From the air you could see the words, "Hire me", taped on a graduate's mortarboard. He advised, "We may not have given you a perfect world but we have given you dynamic opportunities for leaving a lasting legacy as a generation that was fearless and imaginative, tireless and selfless in pursuit of solutions to these monumental problems." True that.

Desmond Tutu spoke at the University of North Carolina Chapel Hill. "Go on dreaming. Go on being the idealistic people you are."

At Notre Dame President Barack Obama said, "Have confidence in the values with which you've been raised and educated. Be unafraid to speak your mind when those values are at stake. Hold firm to your faith and allow it to guide you on your journey."

My favorite advice from the ones I heard this year was from First Lady Michelle Obama who spoke at the University of California. "Remember that you are blessed and remember that in exchange for these blessings you must give something back. You must reach back and pull someone up."

Following her lead, Holocaust survivor Eli Weisel spoke at Bucknell University. "There must be at least one person on this planet who needs you, one person you can help. Don't turn away. Help."

In a special tribute to honor Tim Russert on the anniversary of his death, NBC showed him doing clips of many of his commencement addresses. His cheery smile delivered, "People with backgrounds like yours and mine can and will make a difference." He also shared, "Have a wonderful, meaningful and decent life. Work hard. Laugh often. Keep your honor. God Bless." Listening to one who died so suddenly, his words seemed to have special wisdom.

A commencement speaker at a local academy said, "Have fun. Give it your best shot. Keep improving."

My niece, Michelle, teaches at a high school and was the commencement speaker. She gave lessons she has learned in the last ten years since she graduated from high school. "You need determination, perseverance and a sense of humor. Be open to new experiences and remember that you can change. Do things that make you happy, love others and choose your attitude. Remember to be grateful and to tell people you appreciate them."

So, here is a plethora of ideas for young people to live by. But wait. What about the rest of us? Perhaps it takes a person who has lived a solid journey of life to absorb them and really take them in and turn them into reality. Perhaps it takes people who have loved and lost; gotten and ended jobs; married, divorced, parented; lived single; become a grandparent; volunteered; walked to a different drummer; taken the road less traveled; followed the crowd; won and lost; given and taken; prayed, pleaded and waited for answers; learned and grown; been hurt and recovered. Yes, most of us have taken these turns in the roads of our lives. But it is never too late to stop, pause and reflect. In doing so, we can find meaningful advice in each of the speakers mentioned above. In doing so, we can fine-tune our lives and directions. We can grow. And therein lies our choice because change is constant. Growth is optional.

What's Important?

Seemed like a pretty good Christmas holiday this year. Roads were good enough to drive on most occasions, though not all, and we still had a beautiful snowy white Christmas. Now, onto the New Year!

As the year ended, most every TV show, newspaper and magazine spouted lists of top ten things for the past year. Some lists were of good things, some bad. It got me thinking of my own top ten lists.

When I think of the top ten good things of last year, I keep thinking of the same thing for number one. Having my grandsons greet me by running to me, jumping into my arms, burying their little sweet heads into my neck and yelling, "Nina". No matter how hard I try to think of other best things in my life last year, this memory keeps filling up my mind.

The only other thing I thought of was laughing so hard at my nephew, Patrick, that I thought I might stop breathing. To laugh really, really hard is a special event, for sure.

I don't want to bore you with my top ten great things of the past year. What I want to do is nudge you to think about your own top ten best things of last year. What were they?

Might you make your own list?

The Daily News listed local top ten stories, most of them tragic. The same kind of stories filled the Grand Rapids Press and the local TV stations - Murder, embezzlement, tragedy and sorrow. We can each come up with our top ten list of bad things about the year.

Friends and relatives died. People we care about got cancer, had heart attacks, lost jobs and homes. There are certainly negative things that happened in each of our lives but let's not focus on those.

My friend, Dotti, said a wise thing recently. We were at lunch with Carol. Her husband, Jim died a year ago, a superb human being.

As we sat and talked about how hard it is to lose a spouse, Dotti said she had not only lost a husband, but she had also lost a baby and a grown adult son. I responded to her, "I can't imagine how horrible that must be."

She said, "It is horrible, really horrible, but you get through it. Life goes on and you survive. I remember waking up one morning and thinking I could lay here and cry all day or I could get up and do something good in the world. I decided to get up and do something good and I have been trying to do that every day since."

What profound advice from a wise woman. Best not to focus on the negatives of the past.

If we take some time to ponder the top ten good things of our past year, it helps us realize what is important to us. For most of us, I am guessing it comes down to many of the same things. Family. Friends. Pets. Good work. Good books. The crispness of a winter walk. The hot sun warming us on a summer day. The experience of laughing really hard. Listening and talking to someone we care about. Doing nice things for others. Refining ourselves into better human beings. Prayer. Song. Good food. Good chocolate and a nice glass of wine.

I could go on and on. It reminds me of *The Wizard of Oz* movie. At the end of the film Dorothy says, "If I ever go looking for my heart's desire again – I won't look any further than my own backyard."

Hopefully, for most of us, the top ten things we enjoyed last year are right around us, waiting to be enjoyed again in the New Year. Happy New Year! May your cup runneth over with good things.

Tears and Commencements

What is it about graduates in gowns and mortarboards with tassels that get us? What is it about that often-heard tune, "Pomp and Circumstance", that gets us? Put the two together and they really get us.

Recently I was at our local community college graduation ceremonies. I had tears in my eyes as the graduates marched in. I talked to several other people who experienced the same heartfelt emotion. Many of us didn't know the graduates, yet we still felt this surge of deep feelings. I am betting there were people all over the county and country feeling the same thing as they recently watched graduates marching.

I remember being a high school graduate. As I sat at my commencement I was thinking 'my life as I knew it was over and in front of me was a big black hole of uncertainty. What would I do? Where would I go? What would my future hold?'

I am guessing a lot of graduates felt the same exact way this year. The more things change, the more they stay the same.

When I graduated from high school, I was expected to leave home. Going on to school was not an option. I moved to Grand Rapids and got a job.

I was later encouraged by my future mother-in-law to check out financial aid. I set up a meeting, and when I left that meeting, I was enrolled as a student at Grand Rapids Community College. I also had educational grants, student loans and a work study job. I was on my way to higher education, a dream I never thought I'd get a shot at.

I think graduates who have college as an option may take it for granted. But as I recently stood watching the many Community College graduates marching in to graduate, I knew many of them had experiences similar to mine. No options for further education. And then along came help in the name of student loans, grants and work study jobs. Call it luck. Call it blessings. But never call it *for granted*. For those of us who never thought we'd get a shot at higher education, it is sincerely sweet.

I was in my mid thirties when I graduated from Michigan State University. The four year education had taken me 17 years. When I sat at my commencement, my children in the audience, I remember thinking. 'No one graduating today is as excited as I am. None of these other graduates can possibly be feeling the joy and pride I feel at this moment.'

Perhaps they did feel just as proud, but I couldn't imagine that.

So, why do I get teary at commencements? I am pretty sure it is because they held such emotion for me personally. Fear. Sorrow. Joy. Excitement. Pride. Too many emotions to list. I don't think I am the lone ranger here. I think there are many people who feel like I do at commencements. We each have our own life journeys and they color how we look at graduates and graduations. For many graduates it is what they expected they would get to do, just another stop sign in their highway of life. But for others, like me, it is lit like neon. It is glorious. We can't believe we made it. We never ever thought we'd get the shot. Higher education for many is not a given. It is a gift. It is a supreme struggle. It takes everything we've got.

As the Montcalm Community College graduation was ending, the President asked the graduates, "How many of you are the first in your family to graduate from college? How many of you are parents? Grandparents? Dislocated workers?" To each of these questions, many graduates stood, beaming and hooting.

But at those times, happy and proud as they are, we still look ahead at the rest of our life's journeys and wonder how we will maneuver. As we contemplate, it is good to remember Winston Churchill, "This is not the end. It is not even the beginning of the end. It is only the end of the beginning."

He Who Laughs...Lasts

Questions Nobody Asks Me

So there is this guy I know. He just went to have a professional photograph taken. The young female photographer asked him, "Are you a runner?" I am sure he immediately perked and puffed up and replied, "Yes, I am. How did you know?"

To which she replied, "You have such a hard body." When he told me this, I burst out laughing and said, "Well, you can bet those are words no one has ever said to me."

Thinking on this, there are other things no one has ever said to me. For example, no one has ever said to me, "Are you able to gain weight?" Nor has anyone ever cautioned me, "You have got to quit exercising so much." Nope. No one. Not ever.

No one has ever said to me, "I wish you could come out of your shell." No one has ever asked me, "What is it like to be so shy?"

When asking me what I do for a living, no one ever, not even once, asked me, "Are you a model?" "Are you a doctor?" "I bet you're an engineer."

No one has ever suggested, "You must be a nurse." There are clearly people who have the gift to be nurses and those who don't. I must have been on the wrong end of the line when they handed out that gift.

No one ever looks at me anymore and asks, "How young are you?" Nope. That one blew right on by me. The other day a man delivered a freezer to my door. He looked at me and said, "How many grandchildren do you have?" What a jerk. By the way, I have two.

Never has anyone said to me, "I bet you were your high school valedictorian." And, of course, I wasn't. How do they know? Going along with this thought, I have never been asked, "Are you a member of MENSA?" Although, if it has something to do with menopause, I could qualify. Talk about a club you don't wanna be a member of. But then no one asked me if I wanted to join that either. It just reared its ugly head one day and I had to join.

There are other questions I have been asked but can only respond with gales of laughter. For instance, "Do you knit or crochet?" Mary tried to teach me once. She ended up in tears. And I'm not joking. She sadly told me it would be a group I would never be a member of. No hope for me. I have had to buy sweaters and mittens my whole life, making them was never an option.

"Do you like to fish?" Another question that I can only laugh at. They clearly don't know me. However, I did fish once with my Dad and Uncle in Lake Ontario. I caught, all by myself, a big ole salmon. It was something like 32" and 26 pounds. I was bruised for quite awhile after reeling that baby in. I love that I did it but I never wanted to do it again. My grocer carries lovely salmon, don't you know.

I have never had anyone ask me what it is like to be so neat and tidy. I have had people say, "How can you work in all this clutter?" They apparently don't know how it works. It works because I know where everything is. Translated that means I know which pile it is in. Usually. Most of the time. But then, sometimes, I don't. I hate it when they're right.

I guess the other thing I hate is how they never ask me for any I.D. when I ask for the senior discount at places. They just look at me and never doubt. No questions asked.

Humor – The Sunshine of the Soul

Another one bites the dust. Comedians, that is. First Harvey Korman and now George Carlin. Bummer.

We saw George Carlin once. He was wet-your-pants-funny. I often think of his routine on how we all have so much stuff as I live in my world of stuff. I have remembered his list of seven words you can't say on TV for many years. I suppose that is not something to be proud of. I now hear five of them routinely on regular prime time TV. Who'd a thought?

Harvey Korman was wholesome and wonderful. His best thing was trying not to laugh at Tim Conway. Deeply etched in our minds is that hysterical skit where Korman is the patient and Tim is the dentist and keeps injecting his own body parts with Novacaine. It is one of the funniest things I have ever seen.

And then there's Carol Burnett. My favorite was her as Tim Conway's secretary, Mrs. Hahwhiggins. I also loved Carol as Scarlet O'Hara wearing the drapes.

There are so many wonderful comedians. Some I don't even remember their names. One guy did a routine on Letterman years ago. He said, "Your sister is a dirty rotten scumbag. I don't mean that in a bad way." I always loved that. He actually added a couple nouns I can't use in this column but I think the funniest part was "I don't mean that in a bad way".

I record David Letterman each night. I don't care about his interviews or skits but I love his dumb lines and silly on the spot humor. Last week he said, "It is so hot in New York that on the way home my GPS said, 'Hey, wanna stop for a beer'".

Physical humor is one of my very favorites. Lucille Ball and Ellen are masters and prove that humor is not just witty words.

David Sedaris is a wonderful NPR kind of comedian. His books are delightful to listen to. If you aren't familiar with him, check out his books and have a good laugh.

Some people just don't laugh enough. One woman had surgery and the Doc said when he opened her up, a "ha" came out.

Humor is the sunshine of the soul and the main ingredient of mentally healthy people. If you aren't laughing enough, you might wonder what is going on in your world. You should probably call your fun friends and get laughing.

Humor gives a gazillion benefits for our health, mental well-being, communication skills, sales skills, parenting skills, and on and on.

I often ask audiences to think of someone they love or loved working with. Then I ask them to raise their hand if that person had a sense of humor. They all raise their hands.

For my husband and me, laughter abounds on both sides of our families. When his brother died, our nephew did the eulogy. It felt like a comedy routine, except for all the crying that went along with our laughter.

As we look at our grandsons, one of the joys is their already budding sense of humor. It is one of the greatest gifts we can give our children and ourselves.

Life is tough. Humor is what God gave us to help us get through the hard times. It doesn't make it all better but it is like a spoonful of sugar making the medicine go down.

A Buddhist told me, "We believe what we practice, we get better at."

I think my dear friend, Nelda Cushman, did it best. Just a couple days before she died, I went for a ride with her. We stopped so I could go to the bathroom. As I was walking in, she yelled out the car window, "Hurry up, I'm dying out here."

Nelda practiced humor her whole life, no matter what went on. It carried her all the way until she was knock, knock, knockin' on heaven's door. We better all get practicing.

Crackpots and Crockpots

My friend in San Diego has a neighbor boy who is 8. They banter back and forth and tease each other. Recently the boy wrote him a note.

"Dear Craig, You are stoopid. Love Billy"

Lynne Dalrymple of Belding told me recently that one of her favorite funny lines was from Homer. Homer Simpson, that is. "Everyone's stupid except me." And don't say you haven't ever thought that.

Having written some heavy things lately, I thought it was time for a little silliness. For those of us who have to live through this cold winter, they say laughter is an instant vacation. They didn't say it would be warm, however.

I always save fun things I read and want to share a few with you today. Perhaps they'll take the chill off.

Henny Youngman once said, "When I read about all the evils that alcohol and heavy drinking can do to a person, I made a decision, to quit reading."

I have a daily calendar that you tear off each day. Here are a couple of my favorite fun quotes from it.

"Even if you don't believe a word of the Bible, you've got to respect the person who typed all that." Lotus Weinstock.

"I hate to spread rumors – but what else can one do with them?" Amanda Lear.

I find both to be true.

Recently I was in a bathroom stall at Van Andel Arena in Grand Rapids. There was advertising on the inside of the door. It was an ad for a crock-pot. I thought of the old real estate rule, location, location, location, and wondered who made this weird ad placement decision. What an odd meeting that must have been! "Hey, I've got a great idea on how to sell more crock pots." I bet a crack pot had that idea.

I am currently listening to a book on CD by the witty crime writer, Janet Evanovich. They recently asked her on NPR how she went from writing romance novels to mysteries and she said, "I hit menopause and began to have more thoughts of murder than romance."

Humor seems to be everywhere if we slow down and enjoy it. Shopping for Valentine cards I saw one that read, "I love you more today than yesterday. Yesterday you really got on my nerves." Ah ha - An honest card.

Today is four years since I had my knees replaced. I celebrated by going to the orthopedic surgeon for a check up. They gave me about 10 sheets of forms to fill out. I refused and gave them back to her saying, "Nothing's changed." She did not like that. It reminded me that I recently read this, "If L.L. Bean can remember what color sweater you ordered for Christmas last year, why should you have to fill out a new medical history every time you go to the doctor?" Amen, brother.

Another question to ponder is why are there cars named after cougars, jaguars and mustangs. But never, not even once, has a car company named one after a dog. Perhaps that is what really began taking down the car companies. Would it be so bad to have a nice car named the lab or a cute sports car named the poodle? How about the terrier? Maybe even something sleek and low called the dachshund. Come on; get outta the box, you car engineers.

I watched part of a PBS special on humor tonight. It reminded me of one of my favorite lines by Gracie Allen. "They laughed at Joan of Arc, but she went right ahead and built it."

Okay, all of this has been trite but true. Maybe you got one laugh out of it. Maya Angelou says, "When I laugh I know I've done something wonderful for my body and my spirit."

Keep laughin' folks and remember you don't stop laughing because you grow old; you grow old because you stop laughing.

Goofin' Goofballs

My friend, Carol, went to the post office and mailed a large package. She then went about her day with a sense of accomplishment.

The next day her husband brought their mail in. "There's a big box for you," he said.

"Really," she said. "I wonder what that could be."

You guesseder Chester! She had sent the package to herself. It went to Lansing overnight and returned back in time for the mail carrier to pop it in her truck and bring it right to Carol's front door, all for $12.47. Double the cost now as she returns to the post office to re-mail it to its true recipient.

Carol has a terrific sense of fun and told this as a great story on herself. We all laughed and we all identified.

After Carol shared this with me, I had to go to the post office. When I got there I gave Pearl, our wonderful frontline postal clerk/friend, a scolding. "Pearl, what are you doing? You aren't supposed to let us mail packages to ourselves. You need to protect us from ourselves. You need to have a list of local goofballs, like Carol and myself, who can't be trusted to mail things to whom they should go to. Clearly we need supervision." Pearl just laughed. Goofballs, indeed. She obviously knows who we are even though she hasn't supervised our behaviors yet.

We all do dumb things like this. Don't we? I certainly have a wealth of them in my closet of memories. Though I try hard to forget them.

I have a wonderful recipe for Apricot Slush*, with lemonade, OJ, Apricot Brandy, etc. You freeze it for a refreshing summer delight.

I also have a wonderful recipe for asparagus soup* which you make with chicken broth. I recently was making a huge batch of asparagus soup and used my homemade frozen broth. As I diluted it into the soup, I noticed what a lovely shade of amber it was. Rather unusual for chicken broth. How nice, I thought.

When the soup was done and about to be given away in portions, I gave it a taste test. My, how sweet it was. Rather odd, actually. You guesseder Chester! I had used my frozen apricot slush instead of the chicken broth.

I fed it to my husband that night, watching him closely. Not much of a reaction. "How's the soup?"

"A little different, but really good."

Well, chefs cook with wine all the time, so I am going to pretend I was just being creative and not a lame brain.

When my poor children were young I got them up one morning and made them the most beautiful pancakes for breakfast. Truly a picture, they were. Butter. Syrup. Lighter than usual, very lovely.

The little jerks wouldn't eat 'em. They complained about the taste and got very obstinate. Of course, I told them to "Eat up. It's not every day I get up to make you such a delightful breakfast." They gagged a bit and finally went off to school.

Later I realized it wasn't pancake batter I had used but left over onion ring batter. Uuuuuuuw. I just prayed Social Services wouldn't find out. Poor little children, scarred for life. They talk about it still. Goofball. Lame brain. Bad Mom.

My friend, who prefers to remain anonymous, is extremely bright. However, he also has had these kinds of experiences. He took his cat to the vet because it had a lump. A tumor, he worried. The vet came in and said, "O.K. Show it to me. Yeah, that's a nipple."

My friend replied, "But, it's a boy cat."

"Yes," the vet said, "So are you."

"Oh…"

"That will be $127.00."

When talking to my husband, he says he thinks the more creative people are, the more they do these kinds of things. He is trying to make me feel better.

The good news about all of these kinds of behaviors is they are universal. Aren't they? Please say they are.

Just think how boring life would be without incidents like these to laugh about. And laugh about them we do. Who knew that when God gave us a sense of humor? He meant it for us to laugh at ourselves first. What else can we do?

*See chapter 15 for recipe.

Things Aren't Always What They Seem

Has everyone had the experience where you see someone you know; you wave like crazy; they get close to you and give you a puzzled look; you realize you have never seen them before? Sometimes I look at them like, 'WHAT???' Sometimes I pretend I never waved. Sometimes I am even honest and confess, "Sorry, I thought you were someone else". This confession comes with a feeling of major stupidity. Please tell me I am not the only one who has done this.

Things aren't always what they seem. Sometimes we think one thing and it turns out to be not what we thought at all.

An old family story is about my father in law, a hardy eater and a hard working farmer. His dear wife always made oatmeal for breakfast. One day she was not able to make breakfast. Perhaps she was giving birth to one of their eleven children or something. So he made his own breakfast and went off to work in the fields. At noon he didn't eat lunch and said he was still full from breakfast. At supper he said he didn't want to eat and said he was still really full from breakfast. She asked what he had had for breakfast. As the story goes, he said, "I just had some oatmeal." When pressed further, it came out that he had very well "just had oatmeal". However, he hadn't cooked it. He had poured a big dish full of the old fashioned oats, covered it with milk and sugar and chowed down. There were no quick oats at the time. There was just the kind you cook on the stove. His big bowl had cooked and expanded in his belly all darn day. Yep, he sure wasn't hungry for a long while. That oatmeal just wasn't what it seemed.

Recently a fun friend told me a great story. It seems her legs had itched all day and she kept complaining to her husband about it. Hour after hour felt like itch after itch. Just before bed he came to her rescue. He told her to lie down on the bed and he would put some cream on her legs to soothe them. She is a good trusting soul and did as he suggested. As he was applying the cream she began to complain. "This feels gritty. It isn't even soaking in."

In a calm voice he kept telling her to "Just relax. Quit complaining." I wouldn't be surprised if he added, "Trust me." But she didn't really tell me that one.

At this point, I am on the verge of being like Mrs. Lockhorn in the cartoons who was on the phone once and said, "I have to hang up now. I've already told you more than I know."

Back to my friend - She tried to relax but it didn't seem to work and she just couldn't quit complaining. She grumbled, "It almost feels like it's turning into a cast."

Apparently he left the room and after awhile she couldn't stand it anymore. She got up and rinsed the cream off her legs and went back to bed. The next morning at breakfast he said, "I have a confession. I thought I was putting cream on your legs but when I looked at the tube this morning, it was minty Crest toothpaste. *Sorry.*"

They are, as I said, a fun couple and so they had some good laughs over this. So did I when she told me. As she was telling the story, toothpaste was the last thing I had expected. Crest. No way. Things just aren't always what they seem.

Oh, I shouldn't tell you their names. So I won't. However, for the extremely astute, their name rhymes with shagahorn. If you need a further clue, they live on a local lake. If you need one teensy weensy more clue, they usually go to mass on Saturday night and sit in the front row. On the left of the center aisle. Oh, and they go away for the winter . . . to Arizona. But I will not tell you their name. No way, Jose! You can't make me. Uh-uh.

This way you might think it is someone else, but remember, things aren't always what they seem.

Kids Say and Do the Darndest Things

So, my oldest grandson is about to turn five. He goes to Young Fives. What is that, you ask? Is it preschool? Well, here is a great way to explain the difference between Young Fives and Kindergarten.

Last week his teacher was doing a pizza project with the kindergarteners. She asked them to give ideas for great pizza toppings. They said,

"Cheese	Sausage	Olives	
Pepperoni	Onions	Ham	
Pineapple	Mushrooms	Green Peppers."	That sounds normal.

She asked the same thing of the Young Fives. They answered,

"Cheese	Pepperoni	Pineapple
Pears	Mashed Potatoes	Mushrooms
Candy	Carrots and . . .	Sprinkles."

And that's the difference between Young Fives and Kindergarteners, in case you've been wondering.

Not long ago our wonderful priest was doing a first confession with a second grader who was getting prepared for her first communion. When the child finished her confession, Father raised his hand to give absolution. "Faster than you could imagine," Father said, "the child jumped off her chair, leapt up and gave me a high five." Now, how cute is that?

My daughter, Donna teaches. She was doing a lesson on the difference between *want* and *need*. Most of them seemed to be getting the concept but one boy was really misbehaving. After this went on for a while, she felt she had no recourse but to cancel his recess. He threw his head on his desk and began to wail about how he wanted recess. Boo hoo. Another student looked at him and said, "You may *want* recess, but you don't *need* recess." That one had clearly gotten the lesson.

Recently another of her students wrote her a note, "I'm going to be bizzy this weekend."

Ok, it's wrong, but it sure is cute.

A month ago, our two-year-old grandson was walking around our living room. I was sitting in front of the toy box, blocking his way to it. I said, "Louie, do you want to get in the toy box?"

"Sure", he replied with a lot of gusto. I opened the toy box lid. When I turned back, he had crawled *into* the toy box. It wasn't what I had in mind, but he sure was excited about his interpretation of "get in the toy box".

A young boy heard his state representative speak. Later he told his teacher about it and described her and her work. "She goes to the capitol and works very hard there. She's a public serpent." This, of course, does not reflect on the state rep but on the listening ability of the student. However, I'm guessing a lot of folks would agree with this description if it were about other politicians.

It is now deer season. Oh, happy day. We went to Grand Rapids over the weekend and the roads and places seemed eerily empty. Hunters all a hunting, I guess. On Sunday even mass was quite empty. Hunting again? Some area schools close for hunting. All this reminds me of a child who was asked to say what the four seasons were.

The child answered, "Well, you know, they change. Let's see. There is deer, pheasant, rabbit, and I can't remember the fourth." Sigh.

Delicate Questions vs. the Truth

We are really just a bunch of liars. Aren't we? I mean think of the many times someone says something to us and we reply with what we *should* say and not what we really are thinking. Oh, and don't tell me you never do that.

Sitting at brunch with my family, we got laughing over this idea. It began with something simple. I had just been doing quite a bit of entertaining and had noticed something I have noticed many times before.

Whenever you ask someone if they take cream or sugar in their coffee, they always say, "No, just a little milk." Or, "No, just a little sugar." No one ever just owns up to it and says, "Yes, I want it all." They always give you the "No" first. I think they are all in "cream and sugar denial".

We began laughing and coming up with more. What about the call in the middle of the night… "Did I wake you up?" My husband could have been sleeping soundly for eight hours and he would say, "No." I am usually lying next to him thinking, 'You not only woke him up, you woke me up and this better be really, really important.'

There are other questions that are delicate to answer. "Can you tell I lost three pounds?" You know you better say yes.

"Would you like to see all my vacation pictures?" That is often followed by, "This is my third cousin on my mother's side." Or, "Isn't this a beautiful tree?"

How about, "Want to see this book of photos of my grandkids." Now that I have two absolutely adorable grandkids, though, that one seems more legit. If you want to see pictures of my grandkids, call me a.s.a.p. Just kidding.

Have you had, "Can I bring my pet snake?" Or even, "Can I bring my cat?" Or sometimes this is a hard one, "Can I bring all my kids?"

One I have had problems with a couple of times is, "Can I bring my new wife?" I remember saying no a couple of times and that didn't go over very well. In fact, they never returned. But the first wife did and that was okay with me. Sometimes loyalty takes precedence, right ladies?

My friend, Linda, came up with this one. What about, "Isn't that a cute baby?" Hmmmm. But, of course. Somehow when you say, "That sure is a baby," it loses something.

As we got going on this, someone said, what about, "Is my breath ok?" Whew, yeah, sure! Just don't mind me as I back away quickly, eh.

I remember going to someone's house and as we entered they had an easel set up. I began praying, "Please let it be Pictionary." Of course, it wasn't. We got a nice long look at how to build an Amway pyramid. Mental note: Next time they call, I am busy, I know I am/will be/must be.

There was a couple more. "Want to see the wedding albums from all my marriages?"

"Want to help me..." You don't know what is coming and you think, 'Heck, no.'

"Are you busy Saturday?" You desperately wonder what is coming and fear fills you up. And then the other shoe drops. "Want to help me move?" Or, "Can you come help me cut a tree down?" Or, "Wanna help us move the piano upstairs?"

Once my mate heard a recipe on NPR for the Thanksgiving treat, horseradish Jell-O salad. He went to the store, got all the ingredients and made it for us. I remember his, "How'd you like it?" We had to tell him the truth. We couldn't have that kinda thing again. We gave him an E for effort though – and for creativity too. I am afraid we burst his bubble, though. He hasn't cooked since.

That is the trouble with questions like all of these. When asked, the person who has to answer is treading a very, very fine line. We can pay for our answer for an extremely long time.

How about the classic, "Honey, does this make my butt look big?"

Putting the Fun in Funerals

Funerals are sad events and rightly so. We leave behind someone we have loved and enjoyed. Their memory remains in our hearts. Hopefully, those memories are good. Even more hopefully, they make us laugh when we remember the loved one.

I have been to some funerals where we cried and laughed in equal measure. Those are the best, I think. Humor heals, don't you know. It heals us emotionally and when someone we care about dies, we need that.

When Dick Burk, a local accountant, died, his friend spoke at his service. I still laugh when I think of it. He said, and may I paraphrase, please. "Dick was never a great dresser. He wore things that didn't always match. Once he bought a leather plaid tie in Spain. He wore it with everything, whether it went or not. Quite awhile later I asked him, 'Are you still wearing that tie from Spain?'

"He replied, 'Nah, it got so much gravy on it, I had to fry it up and eat it." Now that's funny.

When Don, a local Ferrier, died, they asked folks in the audience to share memories. Many did. So, I couldn't resist. I shared how we had taken La Maze classes together. It was at a point where the women were on the floor relaxing and the men were supposed to tell us to relax different parts of our body. He said to his wonderful wife, "Relax your left hind leg." Oh, my.

When my brother in law died, his son did one of the eulogies. We were concerned he might not be able to get through it. He began, "It is such a shame my Dad isn't here. Nobody liked to tell you how great he was like he did." That broke the ice and it went on from there - A grand mixture of laughter and tears. Gerry would have been so proud.

We all hope to leave a legacy of something, a memory folks may remember about us and our lives. Humor is a great one to leave. A lady in Flint came up to me after a talk. She said, "You are right about humor being important. My dad died six months ago and my ten year old son recently came up to me and said, 'Know what I miss the most about Grandpa? His laugh.'" What a legacy.

When people die, it is a great tribute to write the survivors a note and tell some of your fun memories of the deceased. It brings brightness into their sadness. It stays in their memories. What a gift.

I had the great honor of doing the eulogy at Nelda Cushman's funeral. She was one of the funniest people God ever did make. Tom said to me afterwards, "I didn't know a person could laugh and cry so hard at the same time." And we surely did. Nelda had a gazillion stories to be told about her and they all left us filled with joy and sorrow at her loss. I still miss her tremendously and she resides in a special fun part of my heart.

Last week I heard another funny funeral story. Perhaps the funniest I have ever heard. We missed the funeral and could only go to the wake. How sorry I am I missed this.

Apparently at one point in the service, they got the grandkids up to share their fondest memories of Grandpa. One said, "My grandpa was the only man I ever knew who could snore and fart at the same time." Now that's a true legacy.

The Magic in a Smile

As we were leaving church Sunday, it was cold and damp. I heard my name, turned, and saw Kathy, a friend and local realtor. She had a huge smile, came over and chatted. When we parted it was noticeably warmer and I commented to my husband on the power of a smile.

Smiling is simple. It takes less muscles than frowning. It is free. But sometimes we forget, or are too tired or too busy or just plain out of the habit.

Do we know how our face looks? Everyone around us does. What a sobering thought.

A couple years ago I was at the post office and ran into a man I knew. I asked how he was. He replied, "Great, just great." I said, "Really?" and he returned, "Yeah, everything is just great!" All I could think was 'he oughta tell his face'. His face showed no hint of joy or smile or great.

Before I get too critical, let me share that not long ago I was at daily mass. As it ended, Father was walking down the aisle and gave me a big smile. I smiled back. As I did so, I felt my face crack and knew that it had not done that action yet that day. It was about 1:00 p.m. Granted, I had been home in my office all morning, alone. Actually, I was with my dog, and gifted though he is, he *never* smiles. Neither had I.

Many years ago, I remember going to church and not being happy with a sermon. Afterwards, my husband went to the store. A friend from church asked him if I was sick. When he got home and told me, I was stunned. I kept saying, "I am not sick. What would make him think I'm sick..." My daughter, Cara, replied, "He probably saw your face during the sermon." The truth hurts. For some reason I was sure I had hidden my inner feelings. Not so much. Our face is our billboard to the world - For better or for worse.

Smiling is contagious. It is hard to give one and not get one back. It is hard to get one and not give one back. They make us feel better.

Smiling is great for customer service. I know as I go in to Walgreens, I am always greeted by more than one smile. It gives me a good feeling to enter their store. Many establishments and churches have folks to smile at us and usher us in and out. This is a golden touch. This is good for us, as well as for them.

Studies prove that a smile comes through the phone. It is easy to know if the person answering is smiling when they hear it is us – or not.

A smile lifts us. I have been so sad, heart aching over something, and someone will give me a big smile. Many times I don't even know this person. I am always struck by how that lifts me. It is almost magic.

In his book, *Still Me*, Christopher Reeves, a.k.a. Superman, told of the horse accident, which left him paralyzed. He was telling his 4-year-old son, Will, that he would never run with him again. Or lift him up, or play ball with him, or…In the midst of this, Will interrupted with, "But you can still smile." Christopher goes on with, "that was when I decided that maybe my life still had value, because until then, I had been thinking of ending it all." What a powerful lesson for all of us. Yes, we can still smile.

Smiling is a gift we can give the world. It makes the world a better place. It makes us better people. It is usually the folks who never smile who are the least fun to be around, the least open, the least warm.

So as Nat King Cole commanded in his classic song, "Smile".

Chuckles with Children

Art Linkletter was right, "Kids do say the darndest things."

Yesterday I was in the coffee shop and a mom was sharing that her 4 year old was really attached to the neighbor lady who had been ill. The little girl wondered why the neighbor was ill and the mom explained that she had a cyst on her ovary. The little girl seriously thought this over.

That night she was talking with her dad and was telling him how sick the neighbor was. She told her dad, "and she has a system on her Oreo."

A few years ago I was walking thru Woodland Mall at Christmas. A little girl was getting off of Santa's knee after having her photo taken with him. Her mom reminded her, "What do you say to the nice Santa?" The little girl turned back to Santa and said, "Oh, I forgot. Charge it."

One day a couple summers ago, our friend was chatting with her young son. He had burped and wanted to know more about what that was. She explained it was gas and that you cover your mouth and say, "Excuse me." He was content with her explanation and ran out to play. Awhile later he ran back in and said, "Hey, Mom, I just burped out my butt."

Children are one of our best resources for humor. They keep us young just by being around them. They delight us in many ways. They bring lightness and brightness to our worlds. What a treasure.

A couple years ago I went to church in Florida. It seemed like everyone there had white hair. No children. No crying or talking during mass. Kinda boring and way too quiet and proper. I prefer kids in church. I love it when a kid blurts out near the end of Mass, like one did at St. Charles once, "Is he done yet? He should be." Luckily, he was.

One of our favorite stories is from the old Art Linkletter show. Art asked this little boy if he wanted to say something to someone out in TV land. The little guy said, "Yes." He then stuck up his middle finger to the TV camera and said, "Here's to you, Herbie, and I really mean it." Poor Art. He didn't have that 3-second delay button that is so routine now.

Kids are known for honest opinions. Beware what you ask them.

Recently a little guy was asked if he wanted to share something with his brother. He replied, "No thank you." His mom said, "We're selfish, but polite."

We have a ratty old book in our home that is filled with funny things the kids said as they grew up. It is absolutely hysterical and guaranteed to make us all laugh until tears run down our faces. I am sure it would not be all that funny to someone else. But to our family, it is the very best of humor and fun. It would be what I would grab if our home were on fire.

Yes, kids do say the darndest things and for that we thank God. They lighten our loads and our hearts. All we have to do is take the time to listen . . . and laugh.

Silliness is a Friend

Sunday the doorbell rang. I opened it to find my friend, Bev, dressed as "The Queen". This may not sound weird, but Bev lives in Arizona and I live in Michigan. She came here for work, but also as a surprise to watch the Academy Awards with me. She was dressed as the Queen in homage to the movie being up for best picture.

As I looked at her in her royal costume, I was speechless. She looked so silly in her crown, headscarf, et al. Silly and wonderful! What a gift of joy she brought with her silliness.

Silliness is highly underrated. It is one of the main things we can do to ward off burnout. It is a huge deterrent to stress. It seems when we can allow ourselves to be silly and to enjoy silliness, really enjoy it - we are healthier and happier.

Kermit, a pastor, once said, "A perfect life is a blend of nonsense and purpose." What insight.

In this day and age we are filled with purpose. Educators are serious about educating. Business is serious about business. Health care is serious about health care, and on and on. As a society, we are on missions to do things of purpose. This is good, but it can and does lead to lots of stress. When we have serious stress, we suffer. Work suffers. Families suffer. Marriages suffer. Health suffers.

Isn't it wonderful, then, to find out that something as silly as silliness can be a balm and even a preventative measure?

What do we do to be silly? Won't we seem foolish? Won't we look ridiculous? Do we care?

Silliness comes in all shapes, sizes and perspectives. What is silly and fun for one may be downright ridiculous and dumb for another. Personally, I love physical humor. I think it is silly and delightful. I am talking about the old kind reminiscent of Lucille Ball, Carol Burnett, Tim Conway, Harvey Korman, and more recently, Ellen or Kramer on the *Seinfeld* reruns. Their silly humor makes me laugh out loud, feeling better along the way.

I heard a speaker say one of her favorite silly things to do was to wear a red, round, Styrofoam nose when she drove on the highway. She said she loved it when a couple would drive by and only the man would see her. He would tell his wife, and before the wife could look, she would take the nose off. I loved her ingenuity and silliness.

When our kids were younger, one of them had a neon skeleton mask that got left at our house. My husband and I have had lots of silly fun with it. One of us would sneakily put the mask on after we were in bed. When the other would glance our way, there would be the skeleton face all lit up in the dark. It may not sound fun but every single time it would make us laugh with surprise and silliness. Then the other would hide it and, months later, when it was least expected, there would be the face again. Always bringing delightful silliness.

None of these things may seem funny or silly to you. They don't have to. The point is that they were silly enjoyment for those doing them. That is the trick. To participate in and enjoy silliness. And to give ourselves permission to do so, balancing our purpose along the way.

My three-year-old grandson, Danny, often says, "Try it. You'll like it." That is how I see silliness. Whether you dress up and surprise your friend as the queen, wear a red nose on the highway or a neon skeleton mask to bed - Come up with your own silly idea, make silliness your friend. Besides being fun, this could reduce your stress, improve your health and keep burnout at a distance. You and those around you will benefit. Try it. You'll like it.

For the Health of it

Giving Blood – A Good Idea For Others

She looks at my chart. "Your birth date? Address?"

I reply and then ask, "Does it say chicken in there, because it should. I am really afraid. I hate this. Am I the only one?"

"No," she replies. "Most people hate it and they all tell us so. Men are the worst. Men faint much more often than women."

I know that should make me feel better. It doesn't.

She then comes at me with the needle.

"Wait." I stop her. "I forgot to tell you they always use a butterfly needle because they can never find my veins." She looks at me, quite kindly, actually, as she gets the butterfly needle. She has more patience than I think I would have with me.

She pokes me. The worst is over. I survive. Go figure.

A man in the waiting room tries to commiserate with me. "I can help anyone who is all bloody, but all I need to do is watch them draw my own blood and I nearly drop over."

I ask my friend, Marty, how she feels about blood tests. "I've never had a problem. I have good veins, but I'd rather have a baby than have my finger pricked."

What is it about having your blood taken that is so unnerving to most of us? The nurse tells me it is something from our childhood. I doubt that. I never had my blood drawn when I was a child nor was I ever poked with needles. I think I am just a big chicken for no reason. I don't know about all the rest of the fearful folks.

"What made you go into this field," I ask the woman with the needle in my arm?

"I had to give blood so much as a child and I thought I could do it better than they did. I had 18 surgeries by the time I was 28. That was a lot of needle pricks." I am with her on that one.

When I return the next day to pick up my blood test results, I ask the other phlebotomist some similar questions. She tells me she gives blood every 56 days, which is as often as a person can. She adds, "Every 2 seconds, someone in the U.S. needs blood. About 60% of the people are eligible to give blood but only 5% actually do. You know it's the greatest gift you can give, and it's the only gift that truly comes from the heart."

Of course, I have never even considered giving blood. It takes all I've got to get my own blood tested. In fact, when I hear the Red Cross on the answering machine, I tell my husband, "It's for you."

I ask her how long it takes to draw my blood for a standard blood test. "About 3-5 seconds," she says. Gosh, I thought it was at least 30 minutes.

My daughter, son and husband all give blood on a regular basis. I admire them. Not enough to join in, however, at least not yet.

I discuss it with my friend, Julie. She tells me her sad tale having to do with needles and blood tests. Then she adds that donating blood is on her bucket list. She obviously wants to conquer her fear.

For those of you who don't know what a bucket list is, it comes from the movie of the same name, starring Jack Nicholson and Morgan Freeman. The bucket list is a list of things you want to do before you kick the bucket, so to speak.

My blood-giving daughter sends me some statistics. One out of every 10 people admitted in the hospital needs blood. Blood can't be manufactured. It has to come from a donor.

When you give blood, they only take one pint. This regenerates in your body within 24-48 hours. Giving blood causes no adverse affects to your body but there are positive affects.

Giving blood is not dangerous. Everything is done in an extremely sterile way so you remain safe and sanitary.

I am now thinking that this is a good idea for other people to do. Personally, I am still not sold that it is a good idea for me to do.

But then the phlebotomist throws out one more statistic, which reels me in. I am not saying it will, but it could, perhaps. "You lose one pound when you donate blood."

Creative Dieting

You are probably not going to believe this, but I swear, it is true. Recently I was in a restaurant bathroom in Grand Haven. Two teenage girls were also there and one said to the other, "I'm on a great diet. You eat 12 cookies a day and nothing else. You can eat them whenever you want." I was not only stunned by what they said but by the seriousness with which they discussed it. Were they kidding? I think not.

There has been so much said about dieting. My favorite diet book is by Kaye Ballard, "How I lost 10 pounds in 53 years." I never read it but I just love the title and think she must be my kind of person.

The other day I saw a sign in a restaurant, "It took a lot of willpower but I finally gave up dieting." Now that is something I can relate to.

I also relate to the one, "Inside me lives a skinny woman crying to get out. But I can usually shut her up with chocolate." I could have written that one. Oh, wait, I just did.

The cardiologist's diet is, "If it tastes good, spit it out."

David Letterman often shares his successful diet. "You can eat anything you want that you find in your pocket." Ewwwwwww.

Sensibly I heard said, "People are so worried what they eat between Christmas and the New Year, but they should really be worried about what they eat between the New Year and Christmas." Whatever.

I heard someone say, "Why doesn't Sara Lee have to say, 'See your doctor before you eat this cheesecake." Hmmmm.

There are all kinds of healthy foods on the market now. Some of them are even good. When I think back on the kind of "diet" foods available when I moved here and first joined Weight Watchers, whew, things have sure improved big time. I expect to get an award some day for having joined Weight Watchers more than anyone else in the history of the company. I even got to goal once, for a couple of days. Like my youth, it was short-lived, even shorter.

The soup aisles are stocked with lots of healthy soups. If you add enough salt to them, they are palatable.

I have read that treats like movie popcorn and fettuccine alfredo should have warnings that say, "If you eat this you will die." I could let go of the popcorn but I do love a hit of alfredo once in awhile. Life has to have a little yumminess, don't you think?

As life has gone on, I have known several people that I admired because they always ate healthy and exercised faithfully. They were folks to emulate. Unfortunately, most of them died young. Dang. That just ain't right. So it leaves me with a dilemma. What to do? What to eat? What to shun on my plate?

I think a lot of how we do with all this is our heredity. I exercise as I do. I eat as I do. And when I see my relatives, gosh darn it if we don't all look the same. Our bodies are little replicas of each other. For good and for bad.

A few years ago, my cousin, Sandy, and I went on a Richard Simmons cruise for a week. It was a blast. We exercised with Richard morning and night. We went to classes with him each day. I have pictures if you ever want to see us in our glory. We loved it. I always found it interesting that all women I told about this thought it sounded like fun and all men just turned pale.

While on this adventure, I heard my cousin say to a lady, "I've always had a problem with food. I even ask for seconds at communion."

I guess we each have to make our own way on this stuff. Most folks struggle getting the right food in and exercising the right amount. We battle. We give in. We get inspired. We fall off the wagon. But one diet I always have managed to stay true to is from Miss Piggy. "Never eat more than you can lift."

Getting to Know Kidney Dialysis

I have never been to a kidney dialysis center before. They run 48 patients at a time. Each patient goes 2 ½ to 5 hours at a time, 2 – 3 days a week. The center runs machines from 5:30 a.m. until 11:30 p.m., Monday through Saturday. I am at one of 12 centers here in Rochester, New York, where I was born and where much of my family lives. New centers are soon to open and are already booked with patients.

I am here with my dear Uncle Bill. On the way he says, "I don't know why you want to go sit in there all afternoon when you could be out enjoying this 70 degree sunny day."

"Because I love you," I reply.

I came here to see him. He's the closest thing I've had to a father. Most people take having a father for granted, but some of us never got that normalcy.

The staff here is pleasant. The sun is shining in the huge windows. Patients are all hooked to their machines in big rooms facing the nurse's station. They each get a TV to watch but none seem to watch it. One lady is on her cell phone. One man drums his fingers. The time passes slowly. Several are missing limbs. The patients are all races, ages and both men and women. Some look healthy. Some don't.

My wonderful aunt, a nurse and quite an angel in life, buzzes around chatting to all the patients. One man hands her a bone he brought for her dog. They all know her name. "Hi, Mary," they say as they perk up when they see her.

Today she leaves shortly and I stay. I am gladly giving her a much needed, but not necessarily wanted, break. She is happy to tend to my uncle 24/7. They are and have been deeply in love for 62 years.

Besides being a beacon of love, they are also a beacon of faith. They don't just go to church and pray. They reach out to all they see, in any way they can. They are to many people, as they have always been to me, a lifeline.

We need beacons like them. I am reminded of that old song, "You light up my life", and the older one, "This little light of mine. I'm gonna let it shine." And they do, no matter what.

My aunt and uncle spend 15 hours a week here. It is like a part time job, this holding on to health and life. There are no weeks off or vacations from this schedule. This show must go on.

Some here are not as lucky as my family. They are here alone each time. They live alone and come alone by bus. When we leave, a few others are leaving too. Some of them put on their limbs to go home. As we walk and wheel out, the next group is walking and wheeling in.

One man has been coming for 16 years. He is only 57 and has already had two kidney transplants. Everyone has a story.

We all know people getting dialysis, chemo, radiation or some other treatment. The easy life doesn't necessarily go on forever.

My uncle has had to give up a huge list of things as many others have. It is not a given, that we get to have and do what we want forever. I am reminded to be extra grateful that I can use salt, eat all my vegetables, have a glass of wine, and even drink as much water as I want. He can only have a few ounces of liquid a day. It hits me in the face that these things I take for granted are not rights. They are blessings.

It is also a blessing to quietly sit here for four hours next to my uncle as he goes in and out of sleep, and the fluids go in and out of his body, and the love flows in and out of our hearts. And I thank God for this man and this moment. I am blessed.

High Anxiety – A Trip to the Dentist

"Lie back. Relax."

I think to myself, 'fat chance'.

A TV hangs above me. Music blares in my ears. He suggested something soothing. "Forget that," I said. "I want rock and roll and make it loud, please." But it is still not enough. I can still hear them. And see them.

There are two of them. All I see are their eyes. They are wearing masks. But then so am I. Mine is different than theirs. Mine is connected to a gas hose. I am whiffing nitrous gas in deep breaths. They tell me to just breathe normally. Easy for them to say. I want to feel it as fast as I can. Some call this laughing gas, but I'm not laughing.

He gives me four shots to numb my mouth. Isn't that enough for a small army? It may be, but it is not enough for me cause I still feel 'em. He says, "I just can't get you numb enough." Words you really do not want to hear. I suggest he just hit me with a hammer. It can't get much worse.

I ask for a pad of paper and a pen, thinking I may take notes for a column. The only word I write is damn. He agrees.

I have always hated to come here. They are very nice to me. I really like them. They are excellent at what they do. That still isn't enough. I don't want to be here. They know it. He says, "You have to quit fighting me." And then that big word again. The one that really has no place here. "Relax."

My whole life I have had soft teeth. Another way to put it is I have had bad teeth. My husband has good teeth. As a former dentist once told me, "It is such a shame your children all got your teeth." I agree. So do my children. My husband is ready to retire. He is not even retiring young. He has still never had a cavity. Is that even normal?

I am now getting five cavities filled in a torture chamber, although a very lovely one. I don't think it is right for a woman to sign up for social security and have to go get five cavities filled within a few weeks of each other. That just can't be in the natural order of things! I wonder how this happened. Somehow something has messed with my mouth and not in a good way. I don't think it has anything to do with the fact that I crave chocolate about once a day. It must be the environment.

I lay there tense, trying to ignore them. They are using nasty tools: drills, buffers, picks, and a whole motley mess of stuff that I don't want in my mouth. My tongue has swollen to the size of Philadelphia. My lips feel like Goldie Hawn in that movie where she had them all Botoxed up. I know Botoxed isn't a word but you get my drift. But with all this swelling and puffing, I can still feel the bzzzzzzzzzzzzz. I swear they are using something that could rip up cement.

The song playing now is "I wanna go home." Boy, do I.

After awhile they ignore me. They might as well. There is no way I can chat with my mouth loaded. They are discussing what they had for Easter dinner. They think that ham is so blasé. He had lamb chops with mustard sauce and they were divine. I couldn't hear what she had. The torture chamber was just too loud at that point.

They told me it would only take an hour. They were wrong. They meant it would only take an hour for a normal person. Apparently they forgot to read my chart, the part where it says in big red letters: she is a great big chicken – cluck, cluck.

Finally it is over. Everyone is glad - Especially the people in the waiting room for the last half hour. The doc jokes how I really made him earn his money today. I give him my sincere apologies. I really am sorry. It ain't easy being a big chicken – cluck, cluck. I wish I was brave. I wish I didn't mind going to the dentist. I like him. He even gives me a big hug as I leave. I think he wants me to come back. I can't imagine why. I think if I was him, I would refer me to another doc a.s.a.p. Any excuse would do. Who needs a patient like me?

It is now hours since the big ordeal. My mouth has resumed its normal feel. Philadelphia has left my tongue. Goldie has left my lips. I think I need a little chocolate.

Epilogue: The next day the kind doc called to see how I was after my trauma. I told him fine and that I was sure I'd forget the whole thing in about ten to twenty years. The mailman then brought the lamb chop recipe*. I love my dentist, I thought. But I sure don't want to go see him for a while.

*See chapter 15 for the recipes.

The One Word That Changes Everything

"I have one word that will get all your audience's perspective in order, no matter who they are."

I just looked at her in disbelief. What could she possibly be going to say? How could she say just one word that would get everyone in line? But she did. She looked at me and said simply, "Cancer."

I still get chills when I tell that story. I have used it for many, many years in my talks. It always has a dramatic but important effect. I clearly remember the woman in her late 30s that shared it with me.

She went on, "Six months ago, I was busy and crazy like everyone else. I went to the Dr. and he said I had cancer. Immediately my life cleared up. I quit thinking about and doing what wasn't important. I began focusing on what was important and letting the rest go."

What wise advice. We can learn from her, no matter what the state of our health or our age.

Last week I spoke to about 250 female cancer survivors. It was a daylong event with incredible programs, demonstrations and information.

I have spoken to cancer survivor groups many times and always feel they have a special aura about them. They have been to the edge, looked over and learned. They are wise. They have their perspective in order. I think cancer is a life enhancer. It makes people think about their life and priorities. So many others just exist in life, letting days go by one after the other without ever thinking consciously about what they want.

To prepare my program, I asked a couple of friends who are cancer survivors what they thought was the best advice they could give.

Mike, my dear brother in law, has just finished a phenomenal battle and ended his chemo. He had clear thoughts on this. "Do what you can do something about. I couldn't do anything about the chemo or the effects of it. I could continue exercising and working. I only missed one day. I kept thinking, I have to be an example to my kids and show them how this is done."

Linda said she visualized the cancer cells being gobbled up. She advised that people live as healthy as they can in their lives and that they not look back when their treatments are over but only look ahead. She suggested it is important to reach out to others who are beginning this journey.

Several said exercise was critical to physical and mental well-being.

Jodie said, "An attitude of gratitude is my mantra. I went through some very difficult things – divorce, alcoholism and then cancer. I realized that each struggle gave me strength and qualities I needed to face the next one. They have been gifts. Also, I live by the philosophy, when you feel like you can't make it, fake it till you can. And it works."

I shared the above thoughts along with my personal message of the importance of laughter, smiling, positive thinking, setting goals, etc... With my friend's contributions, I was able to give the audience a worthwhile valuable message. Life is precious. It is short. There is no time to lose.

There are 3 kinds of people in life: those who resent what happens in life; those who consent to what happens in life and those who invent life. Inventing our life is clearly the way to go. We only get one shot - might as well make it count. After all, the message is for each of us whether we have cancer or not. We're all terminal.

The Miracles of Homer

Many of us have had dinner at Maxfields. It is a popular spot to enjoy a great meal. We don't think anything of driving there. We make plans to go eat and think about what we'll do when we get home.

Such was the scenario when Dr. Homer and his wife, Judy, set out for dinner five years ago. On the drive there, they hit a patch of ice and rolled their van. Dinner plans stopped and so did life, as they knew it.

Recently, Homer gave a talk. I was one of the fortunate to hear his story.

Homer and I have been friends since we moved here. Our boys were good friends. I always thought of Homer as a nice man, very friendly and positive, but I had no idea how positive.

I've never understood when people talk about spinal stuff – C5, C7, etc. Homer was the same way.

His neck was broken high, C5. Below the level of one's injury, they are paralyzed. His was an incomplete injury. Translated that means he had a chance of some movement.

Homer believes in miracles. Miracle 1: he is able to move one toe a bit. Potential.

Miracle 2: he can use his hands. Each night, to prevent his hands from curling, he wore a splint on every finger. He worked a ball. He now can steer to drive, brush his teeth, and eat with utensils – important tasks, for sure.

Miracle 3: his wife was uninjured. Judy, his wife of 43 years, gave up her teaching career and became Nurse Judy. Some days, he says, she is Dr. Judy. Their children visited from across the country every other weekend. Their son has now moved near them. "I am only as good as my caregivers," Homer said.

Many patients at Mary Free Bed Hospital are men between 17 and 30. Men take more risks – bow hunters falling out of trees, snowmobile accidents.

"There's a lot of money tied up in me. It is better to be injured in a car. Michigan's no fault insurance is a wonderful thing. Their goal is to try to get your life back to what it was."

He was in Mary Free Bed for four months at $4000 a day. While there he saw a wealthy businessman getting help with his walker. "Mary Free Bed is needed by all people."

Homer reminds people that one little misstep can change your life forever. One patient was paralyzed as he went through the traffic light because someone ran the light.

He praises physical therapy. "Physical therapy is like a job or marriage. The more you put into it, the more you get out of it. No pain, no gain."

He encourages people to enjoy their lives. "Do it now – plan for tomorrow, but live for today. People say, 'when I retire...' Don't wait." He was retired in one second.

He gave up a lot. "I cross country skied on new skis the morning of the accident. I used to walk the trail nearly every day. I often biked for miles on the trail. I loved to bow hunt. Now I terrorize my neighborhood by riding my electric scooter around. I love the freedom and independence."

He works on the computer and often visits people in the hospital or nursing homes. He drives himself to Rotary Club in his wheel chair in an adapted vehicle. He hits a key and the door opens and a ramp comes down.

He thinks of recovery as a job and works at it each day. He walks 300 feet with his walker for bone density and therapy. He keeps laughing and says it helps.

He looks at the positive side, "I could have been killed or been on a ventilator."

I asked him, "Did you *ever* get down or depressed?"

"No," he replied, "not ever." I'd say that was Miracle # 4: his incredible positive attitude.

Spirituality and Philosophy

Angels and the Voice Within

I believe in angels. I don't think they have wings and big white dresses. I don't know about the halos. It's a nice idea but I can't quite imagine them in reality. I can't decide if they would be shiny, glittery or all perky. At this point, I really don't need to know the specifics about how the angels look. I just believe in them.

Once I had a reading by a phenomenally psychic woman. One of the things she told me was that I had an angel on each side of me, guiding me, and that they were my Grandmothers who had died. This did not surprise me. I had always felt their strong presence and I really liked the visual she suggested. It was comforting to me. It still is.

Many of you don't believe in psychics and many of you don't believe in angels. That's okay. What I wanted to share was an experience I had the other day. There are a variety of ways to explain it. Here's how it played out.

I have a wonderful friend. She is a busy young beautiful Mom and career woman. She works out of town. She juggles it all. She always has a smile, always looks beautiful. She has a ready laugh and sparkly eyes. She has two children, a wonderful husband and a lovely home. One of her little children has had cancer. She is now doing great and is a happy pretty little girl, bubbling with life.

My friend has breast cancer and has just begun radiation. She has been heavily on my mind for about two weeks. About ten days ago I thought it would be wonderful for a group of us to send her some flowers. I never got around to doing anymore than thinking about it. It remained just an idea. Ideas usually take more than thinking, even when they are good ones. They usually demand action to become reality.

This idea continued in my mind, though. I look back now and wonder if my angels were whispering in my ears. The whispers became persistent and I wrote it on my to-do list.
"Buy flowers for my friend."

My to-do lists are quite large. I never get them all done so I end up moving things to the next day's list. This goes on and on. I really need longer days or perhaps just more energy in the days I have.

The other night I was still doing errands late in the afternoon. It was getting dark. I thought I would perhaps buy the flowers and then I thought I really should do something else on my list. But I just pulled into the florist and came out with a lovely bouquet. I was happy I was actually getting this done. It felt good. I planned to deliver them on my way home after just a few more errands.

And I did. It was a simple thing, really. It only took a few minutes. But what a reception!

I didn't think my friend would be home, but she was. Her young perky children were bouncing around. Her handsome husband was making dinner. She came to the door and gave me the hugest hug, crying as she did. She cried so hard her body shook. She said how much she needed this and that it had been a really, really bad day. She kept hugging me with more smiles and tears. It was a very special moment and more than I imagined. It was two women lifting each other up with love, late on a cold nasty day.

I left and drove away but could hardly see. Tears of gratitude ran down my face and I thanked God that I had listened to the voice within that had pushed me to do this. I gave my friend a gift but she gave me one too.

I drove home thinking how often I miss those nudges to do things. My angels talk and sometimes I am too busy to listen. My life is too noisy to hear them. Perhaps it's not my angels. Perhaps it's God speaking to me, the Holy Spirit or maybe my sub-conscious. Whatever the voice within is, it gives great ideas and good guidance. I need to listen more.

But listening is not enough. I also need to follow them.

Our lives are busy, especially at this time of year. But if we are open to these kinds of things, our lives can be so full. Yes, I believe in angels. I believe they lead me to do some good things that I might not think of on my own and I am really grateful that once in awhile I put their nudges into action. And those nudges become blessings in my life and sometimes in the lives of others.

Do You Have Enough?

Christmas is over. Did you get enough? Do you have enough?

Two things recently came across my life that brought that thought to mind.

One, I read that Kurt Vonnegut and Joseph Heller, both infamous writers, were at a party given by a billionaire. Kurt said to Joe, "How does it make you feel to know that our host only yesterday may have made more money than your novel, *Catch-22* has earned in its entire history?"

Joe replied, "I've got something he can never have. Enough."

What a powerful exchange!

In these hard times, many cut back their Christmas giving. Yet they had enough.

In a national scandal Bernie Madoff made off with billions of other peoples dollars. Many have been left wondering, "Do I still have enough?" Enough is a word that suddenly is describing dilemmas of people at every financial level.

What do we really need? What is enough?

People make money and buy things. They make more money and buy more things. George Carlin used to refer to it as our "stuff". And then people have to buy bigger houses to hold all their stuff. We end up with stuff we don't want. We have to give it away or sell it. We have way more than we need. We have way more than enough.

The second thing that happened recently was this. My grandson, Louie, just turned three. He wanted a trumpet. His mom found one and he opened it first at the party. He clenched it to his chest and said dramatically, "I wanted it." Then he blew and blew and blew and enjoyed it. After awhile his mom asked if he would like to open some of his other presents. He looked at her, smiled, and in a precious sweet voice said, "No, thank you." He had enough.

On a personal level, if I am honest, I have lost many things: my looks; my figure; at times my sense of smell; on hard days my mobility; some times I am sure I have lost my mind or at least part of it. But as I examine the state I'm in, and I don't mean Michigan, I realize that even on bad days, I have enough. Life is a funny thing. As it diminishes it also gets richer in many ways. I am wiser than I used to be. I am more tolerant. I am content. I realize how fragile health and life are and to have them today is abundantly enough.

If we take this to a broader level, John Bogle said, "Our world has quite enough guns, political platitudes, arrogance, disingenuousness, self-interest, snobbishness, superficiality, war, and the certainty that God is on one side or the other. But it never has enough conscience, nor enough tolerance, idealism, justice, compassion, wisdom, humility, self-sacrifice for the greater good, integrity, courtesy, poetry, laughter, and generosity of substance and spirit."

He goes on to say, "The great game of life is not about money; it is about doing your best to build the world anew. And that's enough . . . at least for today."

Ah, food for thought as we ponder the end of this year and anticipate the new one. What has made our level of enough in our personal lives? Do we have enough? Do we give enough?

Do we love enough? Do we laugh enough? Do we pray enough? Do we really live enough?

We have just enough time to examine our lives before our new year begins - Just enough time, but not enough to waste.

The Grand Miracle of Forgiveness

It is said that we teach most what we need to learn. I needed to learn to forgive.

I went to a class and the instructor asked who had a resentment they would share. My hand was up quickly and I was chosen. I told about someone who had hurt one of my children seven years before. The class loved it. They identified.

I was quite proud of myself until the instructor asked, "Why haven't you forgiven her?"
I was speechless. What a dumb question. When I finally thought of an answer, I said, "Because if I forgive her, she'll get away with it." I could see everyone agreed.

The instructor just got worse and said, "She got away with it seven years ago. You've been keeping that alive all by yourself." She told me how my resentments affected everything I did, said and thought. I immediately decided to resent the instructor too.

Her words gnawed at me. I knew she was right. I should let the resentment go, but I had no idea how to do it.

I am Catholic. I am educated. I have gone to counseling. One would think I would have learned to forgive somewhere along this road. But no one ever told me how. They just said, "Do it."

I went back to the instructor and said, "I have decided I want to forgive her, but I don't know how. *What do I do with all these feelings?*"

What a wise woman she was. She prayed with me and then taught me three steps to forgiveness. I have used them many times. I found I had a long list of resentments I needed to let go, some since childhood, some more recent.

The three steps the instructor taught me have changed my life.

Step One: The Act / Decision.

We decide intellectually that we want to forgive them. It is a decision we make to ourselves and our God. It doesn't feel good yet. We are still in pain. Lao Tzu said, "The journey of 1000 miles begins with a single step."

Step Two: The Process.

We need to feel/process all our feelings in this situation. We have to feel the hurt, anger, grief, betrayal, resentment, hate, or whatever emotions we have. We may need to write about them, to talk about them, to do whatever we can to work through them in positive ways. Once a counselor told me to walk and consciously think of my anger. It was a much more aggressive walk and a positive release.

When you see a man on the top of a mountain, you can bet he didn't fall there. Feeling our feelings takes time and can be very painful. In the film, *The Prince of Tides*, Barbara Streisand says, "Tears won't bring him back, but they might bring you back."

Sidney Simon says in his book, *Forgiveness*, "When we shove our feelings under the carpet, they just make ripples that we will trip on." Feeling our feelings is tough work but it liberates us. Hopefully, our pain will ebb.

I have physical scars where I have been cut. They used to hurt and be tender. Now they have healed over. I still see them. I know they are there and where they came from, but the sting is gone. So it is with our emotional scars. They heal over. They just become part of who we are and our life journey.

Step Three: The State of Forgiveness.

I believe that forgiveness is a God thing. I believe that if we do the first two steps, God will do his magic and bless us with the state of forgiveness. Often when we least expect it. Sometimes when we think it is impossible.

Inner peace is created by changing ourselves, not the person who hurt us. When we forgive we look at them through new eyes. We see them, we remember, but it doesn't hurt us anymore. We may even wish them well and go on our way.

We are imperfect people and we live in an imperfect world. Pain is inevitable. Suffering is optional. Forgiveness is one of the hardest things we will ever be asked to do. Is it worth it? You bet. Because we are worth it.

Marie Balter was locked in an insane asylum for years. She wasn't insane. Marlo Thomas portrayed her in a TV movie. When she was released she said, "I would not have grown one bit, if I had not learned to forgive."

Though forgiveness is a personal journey and a gift we give ourselves, the benefits radiate to our families, our friends and our world. I love the short prayer, "Lord, give me the guidance to know when to hold on, when to let go and the grace to make the right decision with dignity." When we are able to do this, a grand miracle is performed.

Forgiveness is a choice. We can choose to harbor hurt and resentment or we can choose to heal and give ourselves the peace we deserve. Don Juan, in *Journey to Xtlan*, said, "We either make ourselves miserable or we make ourselves strong. The amount of work is the same."

Hurts come in all shapes and sizes. They come in different ways. Sometimes folks mean to hurt us. Sometimes they don't even know they have.

What do we need to forgive? Not irritations. What we need to forgive are deep personal hurts. We need to forgive actions, what people have done, not who they are and what they are like.

When I began my journey of forgiveness, I really didn't want to forgive. I just wanted the pain to end. I wanted to feel healed. But to do so, I had to let it go and quit licking my wounds. Sometimes, I think it is harder to give it up than to go through what happened in the first place.

One woman shared that her counselor asked her, "How long do you want to bleed over this?" Is holding on worth the price we are paying? Would we rather be right than happy?

There are some people who are very difficult to forgive. Perhaps they're still mean and nasty. They're never sorry. We want them to beg for forgiveness. They don't. We want them to pay, to hurt as we have. They don't. Some of them even die and leave us with the whole burden.

A wonderful thing to learn is that we don't need their repentance to forgive. It is really not about them. It is about us, our healing, and our future.

Often we want two things. We want to keep our anger and we want to have peace. We can't have it both ways. The word forgive means to give up.

There are some important things that forgiveness is and is not. Forgiveness is not forgetting. We don't get amnesia when we forgive. Often we need to remember so we can protect ourselves.

Forgiveness is not trusting. We don't have to become a fool to forgive. Some people should never be trusted. Others we may be able to trust again. Each situation is unique.

Forgiveness is not understanding it all. I want to understand everything, to talk it through. That is usually a fantasy. We need to accept confusion as we forgive.

Forgiveness is not tolerating, excusing, or condoning. When we forgive we are not saying it was OK, nor are we saying we will allow it to happen again. Our forgiveness does not let them off the hook. They remain responsible for what they did.

Forgiveness can't be forced or phony. We can't forgive because it's our duty or someone told us to do it.

Getting even doesn't work. It's a game no one wins. When we forgive, we quit playing the game. We walk away. We leave the score unbalanced. We surrender . . . our resentment. We win . . . peace, joy and healing.

Forgiveness can't wait for the circumstances to be right. They may never be.

We need to limit our expectations of forgiveness. We must accept imperfect forgiving. Perfection locks us up. We may not get a rosy ending. We may never be best friends again. We may not kiss and make up. We may not like them again. We may have to let them go out of our life. We can still get peace.

There is no one way to forgive. We can forgive in many ways: face-to-face, by letter; by actions, silently within ourselves. Every situation calls for a different approach.

Portia Nelson wrote an autobiography in five very short chapters.

"Chapter 1:   I walk down the street.
There is a deep hole in the sidewalk. I fall in. I am lost.
I am helpless. It isn't my fault.
It takes forever to find a way out.

Chapter 2:   I walk down the same street.
There is a deep hole in the sidewalk.
I pretend I don't see it. I fall in again.
I can't believe I am in the same place again, but it isn't my fault.
It still takes a long time to get out.

Chapter 3:   I walk down the same street.
There is a deep hole in the sidewalk. I see it there.
I still fall in. It's a habit.
My eyes are open. I know where I am. It is my fault.
I get out immediately.

Chapter 4:   I walk down the same street.
There is a deep hole in the sidewalk.
I walk around it.

Chapter 5:   I walk down another street."

Most of us have hurts and resentments we need to heal. We have the power to choose healing or harboring. Lao Tse said, "If you do not change directions, you may end up where you are heading." Is that where you want to be?

A Time of Renewal

My grandson, Louie, is just three. One thing he sometimes does is when you hold his hand to walk with him; his legs go up and down and up and down. There's lots of motion but it's not necessarily forward. It's like he hasn't quite grasped the concept of "onward . . . Christian soldier".

I think that resembles my current faith journey. I'm moving up and down. I have lots of activity. I am not sure I have "onward" motion.

There have been times in my life when I felt my spiritual side was in high gear. There have been other times when my high gear was taken over by other important things. It seems almost everything we do is important, right?

As Lent is upon us, I feel like my sweet Louis. I have movement but I'm not sure I've got growth and I'm thinking growth is the purpose of Lent. Oh, my.

There is an old poem I love by an unknown author.

I got up early one morning and rushed right into the day.
I had so much to accomplish that I didn't take time to pray.
Problems just tumbled about me and heavier came each task.
"Why doesn't God help me?" I wondered.
He answered, "You didn't ask!"

I wanted to see joy and beauty but the day toiled on gray and bleak.
I wondered why God didn't show me. He said, "But you didn't seek!"

I tried to come into God's presence. I used all my keys at the lock.
God gently and lovingly chided, "My child, you didn't knock!"

I woke up early this morning and paused before entering the day.
I had so much to accomplish, I had to take time to pray.

I asked a couple pastors I admire how they would size up Lent in a couple sentences.

Pastor Jones said, "Lent is a time for Christians to take an introspective look at their relationship with Christ. It is also a time to embrace the world in its brokenness and do good by reaching out with compassion and love."

Father Phil said, "Lent is relational. When you fall in love with someone, you spend more time with them and other things fall aside. Likewise during Lent, we encourage people to spend more time with God and let other things fall aside."

I tried to ask a couple other pastors but never connected with them. Do I get points for trying? I hope so. I think I need all the points I can get.

From my perspective, Lent offers each of us a personal spiritual refresher time. Our churches can be vehicles for this but we each make our own journey.

We can do it in a variety of ways: services, speakers, music, events, prayer, reflection, forgiveness, reading, listening to our God. I think that is often referred to as silence. We get to choose how and what we will do.

That reminds me of the guy who said he gave up chocolate for Lent . . . after 10 p.m.

And the guy who just emailed me that he is again giving up smoking for lent. And I know he has never smoked. I won't say your name, J.B.

A former Lutheran Bishop said, "Lent is a chance to step back from our hum-drum thoughts, to go deeper into the spiritual God places in our lives. It is a time to reflect, give up and give in to God's actions. It is a time to forgive and allow God to renew us and make us whole."

I have friends who are atheists. I have friends who are agnostics. I respect their beliefs, but personally, my faith has lifted me throughout my life whenever I really needed to be lifted. It began as a child. It continues today. I don't know how I would have gotten through my life without God actively in it, nor through this week, nor today.

Lent offers us a special time to focus on our own spiritual state. Whether you decide to give up stuff, go do stuff or think and read about stuff, may it be a rich time of renewal for you.

Father Cummings, chaplain on the battlefields of Bataan in World War II, coined the famous phrase; "There are no atheists in foxholes". Why? Because they "gots" to believe to get through it. With the state of our country and world today, I think most of us "gots" to believe to make it through too.

A Doctor held a stethoscope to a small boy's chest. "Can you hear that? What do you think that is?"

The little boy looked at him and said, "I bet it's Jesus knockin' "

So I leave you with this. Knock. Knock. Who's there? Lent is our time to look within and see who's knockin'.

Facing Death With Courage

This fall I lost 3 very dear friends. I still find it hard to believe they are gone. Each held a special place in my life journey. We raised children. We read books. We took sewing and Spanish classes. We talked. We laughed. We cried. We aged. What they left me were rich memories and lessons on how to live and how to die.

Nelda went to the doctor because she was tired and was given two weeks to live. She was in a room with two friends. After the doctor left they were silent, and then Nelda said, "Well, I guess it's adios amigos!" Ever the witty woman, she kept her keen sense of humor till the very end.

Nancy was ill for a while. They diagnosed her with one thing but when she didn't respond to the medication, they re-diagnosed her with ALS. She died about a month after. Daily she was stripped of her ability to do things we take for granted. In the midst of this, she kept her dignity and caring nature.

She could only visit for a few minutes but would want to know how we liked the book that book club was currently reading. She proudly showed pictures of her grandchildren and told me what nice people they were. She told me "there is nothing to do but accept it".

Marge was ill with emphysema for a long time. She told me she wished she could talk to young people about smoking. She wanted to tell them and show them the consequences. We visited often. Once I snuck my dog into the hospital in Grand Rapids to see her. She loved it.

All three of these women were bright and gifted. Nancy was a brilliant artist. Marge was a gifted nurse. Nelda was a wonderful florist. But they were so much more. They were mothers first and foremost. They were proud grandmothers. They loved their lives. They were strong, brave, independent, interesting, gracious, and fun. They each faced death with courage, faith and resolve.

I am just one of many people who loved these women. I am just one of many who are left with the great loss of them. I feel blessed to have gotten to spend time with each of them as they neared the end. We shared tears, memories, faith and laughs. I got to hug them, tell them I loved them. I don't know if it made them feel better but it made me feel better.

Recently I saw Joe Namath on 60 Minutes. He said, "Life hurts a lot of times." And so it does. It hurts a lot of times when I think of the loss of these dear friends, and of other dear friends who have died recently.

When they say, "Rest in Peace" I think it has a double meaning. I think it also means, "Rest in Piece" – a piece of our heart, a piece of our memory. I never want to lose the precious wonderful pieces of each of these women. I am sure they will be a part of my life forever. What lessons on life they have taught. What lessons on dying they have shown. I am more because they were my friends. I know many of us will rest in peace with them, with pieces of them in our hearts.

Love, Lent and Action

We have all heard of or experienced Fat Tuesday or Mardi Gras. It seems that in our area, paczkis, the Polish filled donut has become a "must have" for many people on the night before Ash Wednesday. My friend, Julie, said she sent her husband to get some paczkis around 7 p.m. on Fat Tuesday. They told him they were cleaned out but that they had 7000 in the store that morning. It's hard to imagine the munching mania that hit our area that day. People must have been flying in the door thinking, "I've gotta have a paczki right now. Make that a dozen, no, two."

This sweet mania precedes the forty days of Lent, a time of soul searching, repentance, reflection and taking stock. It is to remind us of Jesus withdrawing into the wilderness for forty days. Most Christian churches follow the practice of Lent and there are many ways to go about it.

One Lent, years ago, I came upon some ideas in Reader's Digest. I followed the suggestions and have thought about it every year since. Seeing we are still in the beginning stages of Lent, I decided some of you might enjoy the ideas. Here's the gist of them:

First week – The Hand of Love
Write a letter a day to a friend or relative, someone near or faraway. Tell them how much you appreciate them. This doesn't have to be lengthy. If you can write it on nice paper and send it, they can relish it for the gift it is. Email doesn't have near the impact as a letter in one's mailbox.

I remember I wrote to my elementary principal who had been a positive influence in my life. He wrote right back and it was wonderful to have that reconnection.

I also wrote our jeweler and our pharmacist. I was so grateful for the kind help they always gave us. I don't know if they remember that but I do because the process felt so good.

Second week – The Voice of Love
Phone two or three people each day for a short chat. Perhaps just to say hello, thank you, I'm sorry or I'm thinking of you. Call people you have meant to phone but never seem to get around to doing it.

I am not a phone person and this is a hard one for me. However, when I actually get the call made, it feels great to hear the other person's voice and have a heartwarming visit.

Third week The Deed of Love
Take something you have made or bought to two or three friends who mean a lot to you, but for whom you rarely express it. Take perhaps a baked good, flowers, or a small item that says, "I care about you."

Fourth week – The Heart of Love
Make a list of at least ten people for whom you will pray daily. Include friends and some you don't particularly like. Consider forgiving some who have wronged you. Perhaps you need to forgive yourself for something.

Fifth week – The Mind of Love
Look inward. Pray for yourself and work on your spiritual side. Meditate.

Sixth week – The Victory of Love
Get outdoors and breathe in spring. Get together with friends. Be joyful. Treasure faith, hope and love in your life. Celebrate.

There are lots of ways to go about Lent. Attending church services, reading spiritual things, giving up things, doing positive things.

Lent is sort of like a spiritual time out. We slow down our busy lives to think about how we are doing and where we can improve in our spiritual life. Lent can ground us and help us remember what is important to us.

I guess I'll close with one of my favorite prayers. "Oh, Lord, help me to be the person my dog thinks I am." Clearly I have work to do on this.

Family Feelings

Lookin' Like Kin

I am in a mad stage of cleaning everything in our house. It seems soon my husband is going to be in the house 24-7. I think this will feel better if I have everything in order. I am grasping at straws, I know.

So we came upon our passports and found they expired a couple weeks ago. Dang. How did that happen? This following a conversation about as soon as he retires we will drive to New York to see my family. We always drive through Canada. So now, Houston, we have a problem.

Off we go to Walgreen's to get new passport photos. They take twenty minutes so we run do an errand and when we return my husband goes in to get them. As he comes out, I ask, "How's mine?" He gives it to me.

I gasp. "It's of my mother!"

He laughs. "Isn't that amazing? We come in and get our pictures taken and when we get them, they have taken one of your mother and one of my father." We have a good, yet sober laugh. Sigh. Bigger sigh. When did this happen? I saw his coming. I never saw mine.

Years ago my grandma died. I remember going to her funeral. I looked at her. Yep, she was dead. But, a few years later, I got up one morning, walked into the bathroom and looked in the mirror and there she was. Grandma had risen.

When I met my husband he looked like himself. He also looked just like his brother, Bill. So much so that more than once after we were married, I went up to Bill and hugged him, thinking it was my husband. Bill was always nice about it, but it was still a bit unnerving - Kin that looked so much alike.

Somewhere along the line, my mate began looking like his Dad. Isn't life funny that way? Can you relate?

And it isn't just looks that liken us to our kin either. My poor daughter! She comes to visit and very often people say, "Oh, I heard you laugh and thought it was your Mom." Or they say, "You must be Maureen Burn's daughter. You look just like her." I'm afraid that's not really a compliment either.

I remember when I was a young teen, my cousin and I discussed how much we hated our feet and how we wanted to go on a diet to lose weight in our feet. I have my Mom's feet. She had her Dad's feet. My son has my feet. His son has his feet. We all have the same feet. I hate mine. They have big fat toes. My girls were blessed. They got their Dad's feet.

A couple years ago I got a call from a new sister. She had just found out that my father was also her father. This was a big surprise to both of us. He had just died but there was no doubt about our kinship. We have the same voice. How odd. I thought I was talking to myself. Then I met her and saw my nose, my eyes and a lot of my personality. We could not deny each other. Kin.

Sidebar. It is amazing to me how many people I know who have found new siblings in their adult years. It seems there were a lot of kids being born after the big war and their parentage didn't come to light until years later.

As we look at our families, it is interesting to note how our bodies, looks and personality traits resemble each other. Looking at a photo of a family in the newspaper this week, I couldn't help but notice how they looked alike in so many ways. At a funeral last week, our friend's children got up to speak. We didn't know their children and it was so neat to see one look like their Mom, one like their Dad, one spoke with her Mom's voice, one was built like his Dad, one was a combination of both his parent's faces.

Perhaps now is a good time to look at yourself, your mate and your family. Think about all the resemblances. Let them know whom they take after and how. If we don't keep our history alive, who will? Maybe it is just faces, feet, laughs, looks, or other traits, but they are ours. And therefore, they are special. Someone else is a lot like parts of you. Kin. Kinda cool.

Lessons Left for the Living

There's a tear in your eye, and I'm wondering why, for it never should be there at all. For your smile is a part of the love in your heart . . .

What's on my mind today is a heavy heart.

As many of you know, my husband's brother, Gerry, died this past week. He was my brother in law, but after 42 years, laws don't count and he was like a brother.

Gerry was an unbelievable role model for those who knew him and he leaves lessons for us all to learn from and live by.

When Gerry was about 30 he was diagnosed with Parkinson's disease. He proceeded to live the next 32 years of his life in a body that continued to betray him.

Gerry came from an Irish family of eleven children. When he told us of his diagnosis, he said, in his typical positive demeanor, "I'm glad that if one of us had to get this, that I'm the one, because I know I can handle it." *Lesson One: Believe in yourself.*

He also said at that time, "Everyone gets dealt their card in life. At least I know what mine is and I can deal with it." *Lesson two: Be positive.*

As Parkinson's robbed Gerry of mobility, facial expression, even speech, he continued to lift others with his indelible sense of humor. He might not say anything all night and then knock folks over with one comment, which would be right on and so very witty. *Lesson three: Keep laughing.*

Last week when we all gathered at his side, everyone knew it was the end. Most of us had prayed for years that God would take him and end his suffering. But, there, when we knew God was answering our prayers, his wife and I laughed amidst our tears and said, "But, God, we didn't really mean it." How true. We wanted his suffering to end. No one wanted him to go.

Gerry went to Catholic School and College and was raised in a faith filled family. He married a woman of strong faith. That faith was the glue that held them together through this long ordeal. I really don't know how people get through things like this without it. Lesson four: Keep the faith.

The experiences I am sharing are not ours alone. So many of you have experienced deaths, losses, severe illnesses with those you loved. We need only turn on the TV or open the newspaper for a daily dose of tragic tales, deaths and woes. They are abundant, universal, and often random.

Life isn't fair. We can't have it both ways. We can't erase life situations that we don't like. Many of us have wondered why Gerry had to suffer so hard and so long while other folks are living healthy lives as they do awful things. I suppose if we ran the world we might do it differently. But we don't.

We usually don't get choices about if these things will happen or not. Our choices are often limited to the very lessons Gerry taught us. Believe in yourself. Be positive. Keep laughing. Keep the faith.

Gerry was sent off like the treasure he was. Surrounded by a room full of people who loved him deeply. Irish music playing quietly in the background. Prayers wishing him God's Speed. It likely doesn't get any better than that.

Moments after he passed, our daughter, Donna, said, "Well, Grandpa is already introducing Gerry around heaven." What a healing visual. And even though we don't know for sure, we choose to believe, and it heals our hurting hearts.

When Irish eyes are smiling, sure, 'tis like the morn in spring.
In the lilt of Irish laughter You can hear the angels sing.

I think I can hear them. I really do.

A Wonderful Brother and Milk

I went to see a movie the other day, *Milk*, starring Sean Penn. For those of you who may not know what the film is about, it's about Harvey Milk, not homogenized or pasteurized. Harvey was the first openly gay man to hold a high public office in America.

Many of you will remember 1977 when Harvey Milk was assassinated in his office by a fellow worker. It was a turning point for gay rights throughout the country.

Anita Bryant, formerly Miss Oklahoma, led the opposition with a conservative righteous perspective. One of her quotes was, "If homosexuality were normal, God would have created Adam and Bruce."

Wherever you are in this realm, one cannot see *Milk* without thinking about how far we have come in 30 years. Today it is hard to find a TV show without a main gay character. Gay organizations are in high schools and colleges, even in small town America. Barney Frank is gay and a widely respected U.S. Congressman who chairs the Financial Services Committee. Ellen DeGeneres is a beloved talk show host who recently married her girlfriend. I could go on and on. It's a different world.

Today in the "list of things not to be proud of" Michigan ranks as one of the highest in America in hate crimes. Many are gender based. Recently in Wayland, a teen was beaten by peers because of her sexuality. History repeats itself even when it knows better.

Milk left me a puddle of sobs. It brought up pain I thought I had long gotten over. Isn't that the way we are? As my friend, Linda, recently said, "Grief files itself away but it is never gone. It pops out when least expected."

Ten years after Harvey Milk was assassinated, my brother committed suicide. He was gay and there seemed to be no place for him in the world. This led to depression, which led to a bottle of pills, which led to his death.

John was bright, handsome, fun and kind. I was twelve years older and loved caring for and playing with him. He was a joyful child, always quite effeminate. When he was little, he liked to play dress up. This caused him to be mocked and taunted by others. He was called, "girl", "pansy", and other words I don't want to repeat.

As John grew up and came out, I remember the sadness I felt for him. It wasn't for his sexuality. I never thought it was a choice. One would only have had to know him as a toddler to know it wasn't a choice he made. He was who he was, just as I am who I am and you are who you are. My sorrow was for how hard his life would be. Times were different then. Things were closeted, denied. Tolerance was not common. People hate what they don't feel comfortable with or understand.

I have debated long and hard over whether or not I should write about this. It is easier not to. Why do it? Why open up? Why expose things others may judge harshly?

But I feel I must. I can't get the movie or the history off my mind. My heart is sad as I remember it all. And I feel I owe it to my wonderful brother.

Oprah always asks interviewees what they know for sure. I know some things for sure.

I know my brother was one of the kindest men I have known. I know he was a really good person. I know he was treated horribly in his life and was the victim of more than one hate crime. I remember him coming out of work in Grand Rapids and his new car had been turned upside down and the windows had been beaten out by haters, just because he was different.

I know I couldn't do enough to help him.

As I think of all this, the song "Somewhere" keeps playing in my mind.

"There's a place for us, somewhere a place for us.
  There's a time for us, someday a time for us,

Time together…Time to care, someday, somewhere . . .
We'll find a new way of living.
We'll find a way of forgiving, somewhere . . ."

This is a new time. It is a time to care. It is a time of a new way of living.
It is a time of forgiving.

What else I know for sure is that I wish my brother had been born now
instead of then.

He never had a shot. He deserved one. He was a beautiful child of God.

Giving Birth for the Second Time

I just gave birth to my son for the second time. The first time I hurt
with physical pain I had never known before. I remember lying on the
delivery table, alone with the pain and the son churning inside me.

I remember the cold steel of the room and the solitary noise of the clock.
I counted the pains and thought of all the women I knew who had lived
through this childbirth thing. This realization gave me hope that I, too,
would make it.

A while later, my son was born. My husband and I were ecstatic.

Joy filled moments that last a lifetime. Phone calls to relatives. Weeks of
new found bliss - An adorable baby.

Jumped high. Crawled on his belly. Emptied cupboards. Threw food all
over and wiped the rest in his head. Early teeth. Early words. Early joy.
The only son with which we were to be blessed.

Years rushed by. Three beautiful daughters entered our life. Individual
careers and educations blossomed and bore fruit. Busy schedules. Fun
times. The family kept going and growing.

As babes grew to toddlers to school age to teens, joys expanded and frustrations grew. Dangers seemed greater as peers replaced some of our parental influence. School, friends and activities consumed our kids as we tried to prepare them to one day face life on their own.

The mother turned 40. The boy turned 18. He was ready to go. She knew this was true.

Echoes in my mind of the many parents who told us along the way, "Enjoy those kids. They grow up way too fast!" I knew this was fact and I enjoyed the kids with gusto. But now I wondered. Can one ever really prepare for your children leaving, for their entering the real world on their own and for them walking away and not looking back?

As parents we give. We give life. We give help. We give rides, advice, discipline, money. We give love.

And then one day we give birth for the second time.

We unload the car, the suitcases, the boxes. We help them make their bed and get settled. We hang around for a few "parent" moments and then we leave.

Again I give him birth. Birth to a new life, a new start – his college and adulthood. They are no longer on the horizon. They are here. Today. This hour. This moment.

The pain is different than the first birth. Before it was physical and with an end in sight. This pain is in my heart. It makes me sob and shake and hurt deep inside. Once again I look at other parents who have made it through this, but I'm not sure how they did it. I'm not sure when and if one ever feels better. This is my first time.

With those we love we become vulnerable, with our children the most. We don't hold back. We love them with inseparable bonds that deepen through years and years of caring. We are left so open, so raw.

Final hugs, I love yous. We leave. We drive home enveloped in our loss, our pain, our sorrow.

We head home knowing home has changed. The home that held three girls and a boy is now a home of three girls. It looks different ahead.

I think of how I gave birth to this boy, but he gave birth to me as well. He gave birth to my motherhood. Before him I was a young woman. I worried - Was I ready for motherhood? Would I know what to do? Now I am seasoned, a veteran.

As we drive home our eyes and thoughts flood with tears and memories of this son we've left behind. All the times. All the years.

I wonder how I'll be tomorrow. Life goes on, I know, but I can't imagine how.

Epilogue. Looking back at this time, my life was full of anxiety over my nest emptying. What would our family be like when it was not what it was? Would it survive in tact and remain close? Now I know the answers. The kids all left and entered adulthood. We all survived and grew up together. Our family remains in tact and close, just different.

Last Child Leaving

Here's to all you Moms and Dads who just took your little ones' hand to the first day of Kindergarten and let go. I remember those days well. They were scary, painful, sad, and full of change and newness for my little one and me. But today I'm in a different place.

Here's to all you Moms and Dads who drove your bigger ones to college, unloaded the van, helped them get settled and then left them and drove home. The actual leaving is hard, an emotional letting go. The drive home is worse – silence, tears, reminiscences. The return home is worse yet. Empty drawers. Empty walls. Empty rooms. Technicolor memories. Panoramic loss.

There's a good side to this, I'm sure. More time for me. More time for us. Less rush. Less mess. Less laundry. Less cooking. But less life.

I feel part of me has been used up, the mothering part. This used to be my playground. Now it is empty.

"I'm going. You did a good job. Thank you very much. I don't need you anymore. I'm on my own now. Bye."

My mothering part is in shock today. It may have been my best part. It does not know what to do with this new extended role. It doesn't like change. It liked active mothering.

I tell myself today's a new beginning, a new time of life. I must get myself together: career goals, personal goals, things to do in the house, friends to see, places to go. Life goes on. But it goes on differently and it will never be the same.

Today I can't get into my new life. I need time to mourn, to lick my wounds, to wallow in my memories, to focus on my loss, the joys and regrets.

Was I a good enough mother? Probably not. Did I teach them all I should have? Probably not. Did I tell them how much I love them? Probably not; it's an impossible task, after all. They can never really know the depth. If they're lucky, they will one day when they experience parenthood themselves.

My life has been rich these 18 years. Rich with that cheerful face so full of life and all its experiences. Rich with busyness. Rich with kid events. Rich with juggling. Rich with chats. Rich with joy.

How do some parents handle children leaving home with such ease? I wish I knew. I feel like I've been cut to the bone. Gaping wounds. Grief bubbling through everything I try to do.

I'm happy for my child. I really am. My feelings are purely personal. They are purely selfish. I cry for me. I dance for them. It is what I want for them. I am just sad I have to pay the high price of letting go in order to let them have it.

Epilogue: I still feel tremendous emotion as I reread this. Endings are hard for me, whenever and however they come. I have found I treasure the entire extended journey of parenthood and the close wonderful relationships we still have with our children. It is a joy I could not have imagined when I wrote this. The family as we knew it changed. It became bigger and is now full of our children's adult lives and the lives of their children. My oldest grandson just went to pre-kindergarten for the first time today. The parenting cycle continues. Hold on tight. Let go.

Time Flies from Tot to Thirty

My baby turns 30 today. Whew, where did the time go? I remember that hot summer well. I was big as a house and overdue.

A friend's mother said, "You don't even begin to feel old until your baby turns fifty." She was in her eighties at the time and a bundle of energy. She had just given a talk on writing your memoirs. Her baby, who is now in her eighties, seems to be taking her energetic advice, living life to the fullest, squeezing out every last drop.

In one of my favorite old movies, *Ferris Bueller's Day Off*, Ferris says, "Life moves pretty fast. If you don't stop and look around once in a while, you could miss it." I say amen to that.

We are a rushing bunch, we Americans. We have information, communication, and entertainment surrounding us at the drop of a hat.

My grandsons left here last night. As they drove away in their fancy new car I heard them asking to see a DVD. That would be from their car seats. I am still using my VCR at home and audiotapes in my car. Oh, I can use DVD's but I am not totally comfortable with them yet.

When recently visiting my now 30-year-old daughter, I would no sooner eek out a question about anything and she would have looked up the answer on her Blackberry. I was in awe. I still want to look up things in books. Recently I was wishing I could buy a new set of Childcraft books for my grandkids. I'm sure they'd love them. For those of you who don't know, those were World Book encyclopedias for little ones.

I just finished three days of "Nina Camp". Translated that means "Grandma Camp" but for some odd reason my grandboys call me Nina. No one knows why, but I like it. When they arrived, I said, "There's no TV at Nina Camp". The four year old just looked at me eerily.

My friend, Barb, is an absolutely wonderful preschool teacher. She has recently been studying the idea of what happened to play. It seems our youngsters have lost the creativity of play and of being able to amuse themselves with nothing. It was something many of us had mastered, especially those of us who grew up on the isolated farms of America.

Today with safety concerns, rushing, technology, enormous opportunities and day care as a necessity, children are taking a whole new road to play. I am not saying it is bad, but it is different. Adults are faced with similar dilemmas.

Our days are full to the brim. Lives are whizzing by. Babies come and turn into 30 year old adults in such a short span of time. We look back with wonder. John Jensen said, "The trouble with life in the fast lane is that you get to the other end in an awful hurry."
Who wouldn't agree with him?

I remember when my friend, Nancy Fox, died. I don't know why but it really struck me then that there was no u-haul following her hearse. I had heard that phrase before but at that moment the reality hit me. It stung again as other friends passed. All their stuff, all their busyness, their calendars, their concerns – left behind. And in some cases, no one even wanted some of the things they had cared for so deeply. Hmmmmm.

Robert Byrne said, "The purpose of life is a life of purpose." Sometimes we need to stop, take a breather and think about our purpose. Who am I? Where am I going so fast and why? What difference will my life make? Am I happy with all of these answers? If not, what do I need to adjust on my life journey? Pretty serious thoughts for a hot summer day, but those are the kind of thoughts I am having on this hot day as my baby girl is turning thirty.

We need to be careful of this life we have been given. Jean-Paul Sartre summed it up with, "Everything has been figured out except how to live."

On Holidays Throughout the Year

A Pause for Love

The Beatles sang, "All you need is love." Such is the tone of Valentine's Day.

Love is a broad term. There are oh, so many ways.

We have the romantic kind. Hollywood would have us think that is about sex. It isn't really. It is about hearing the one you love tell a story for the 499th time and still laughing because you think they are still funny. It is about physically caring for them when they have lost all of who they were when you first fell in love with them. It is about laughing together, crying together, fighting together and talking together. It is about just being near each other and having that be enough.

Real romantic love also has the element of forgiveness, the starkness of reality, the job of tolerance. When you consider all the parts to romantic love, it is a wonder we ever stay romantically in love. It is quite a task. It is also one of God's greatest blessings.

We love our children. They light up our lives. They give us purpose. They drive us crazy. They worry us. They make our cup runneth over with joy. At times they even empty that cup. I have always loved the quote from Lillian Carter. She was Mama to President Jimmy Carter, the evangelist Ruth Carter and the beer drinking Billy. She is quoted as saying, "Sometimes when I look at my children, I wish I'd remained a virgin." I am sure she was joking. Perhaps not. It is still a great line.

We love our extended family. There is a special bond with kin. It feels like an old shoe. When I am with my aunts and uncles, cousins, in-laws – it feels so good for my spirit, so nurturing. We may not always agree but we always love each other. We will always be there for each other. We are extended family and what that means is extended love.

We love our friends. Friends are the family we make for ourselves. When it comes to friends, I feel like I won the lottery. Friends walk the road of life with you. It is sometimes a smooth walk, sometimes bumpy, sometimes icy, sometimes foggy. But they are always there to hold your hand, push you along and give you just what you need. Yes, it was a pretty cool day when God came up with the idea of friends.

So it turns out that Valentine's Day isn't about chocolate. It isn't about flowers. It isn't about cards. It is just a reminder in our busy lives to pause for a minute for love. It is truly the pause that refreshes.

On Being Irish

Whether you are Irish for a day or a lifetime, St. Patrick's Day is a joyful time.

Checking with the local McDonald's, it seems a lot of you were Irish as you enjoyed Shamrock Shakes. Three thousand were sold in our county this season. For some, having a Shamrock Shake is as Irish as they get. That's okay. Although the shakes aren't authentically Irish, they are green and tasty. My niece, Nikki, has them done half and half with chocolate. Besides being yummy, this proves the Irish are creative.

Sometimes I think others shake their head in wonder over all the Irish fuss. We used to host a big St. Patrick's party with friends. The first year, I remember a guest asking, "Who's St. Patrick and what do you do on St. Patrick's Day?"

That is a good question.

St. Patrick is the patron saint of Ireland.

Mostly folks celebrate by eating corned beef and cabbage, drinking green beer and other libations, enjoying talk and laughter with friends, and listening to Irish music. I have a delicious corned beef and cabbage recipe* I found last year. It will make you wish St. Patrick's Day came more often. Tim, a high school teacher finds this day very dear to his heart. He spent time during college in Ireland. Tim showed his class a video of beautiful Ireland, played Irish music and gave an Irish quiz.

Maureen, a Professor at Grand Valley State University, enjoyed the day with her family at a program of Irish music, dance and stories. She said she "was very touched by the stories of how hard life was for the Irish coming to America".

My husband is a purebred Irishman, 100% authentic. His 4 great grandparents came over "on the boat" and ended up in Hubbardston, Michigan. Some of them settled for a time in Rochester, New York. My ancestors were there also. After some research, he has found they were all members of the same church at the same time. Two generations later we met at a party in Grand Rapids. The luck of the Irish.

This St. Pat's we went to Shiels Tavern in Hubbardston to watch the Irish Dancers perform. What a treat they were! Ages six to eighteen all dancing together. Wonderful dancers, wonderful girls and a wonderful coach. We also visited a lovely gift store, The Celtic Path. We rifled there for a long time and came home with some Irish clothes and other special items from the homeland.

At Shiels there were grown men dressed from head to toe as leprechauns. Most folks were wearing green and Irish "stuff". One lady sat down with her green beer and turned her shirt on. It lit up with green lights. I'm not sure if she was lit but her shirt sure was.

What is St. Patrick's Day all about? I think it is about pride in Irish heritage. It is said that what doesn't kill you, makes you stronger. The Irish have survived famine, horrible ocean crossings, war, poverty and discrimination. In spite of these things and in spite of sad tales like *Angela's Ashes*, they are a happy lot. They know what perseverance, faith, family and fun are all about. Their music and humor have brightened the world and continue to do so. Because the Irish are known for their wit, I am going to share an Irish joke.

Mr. Finnegan walked into a bar and ordered martini after martini. Each time he removed the olive from the glass and put it into a jar. When the jar was full and the martinis all drunk, he went to leave. "Ah, sir, would you mind tellin' me what you're doin'?" asked another customer. "Nothin'", said Finnegan, "my wife just sent me out for a jar of olives."

St. Patrick's Day is over. Irish shenanigans and silliness must now be put away. It's time to get back to normal life and Lent. Ah, but it 'twas fun while it lasted.

*Recipe in chapter 15.

Irish Luck

Top of the mornin' to ya, or almost. Ah, yes the luck of the Irish 'tis a well-known thing. Are you lucky? What is luck?

I looked it up and it is defined as fortunate, charmed, blessed and success due to chance. Those all sound right. I know lucky in love. I know lucky in Vegas. I have heard of luck meets a lady.

Rodney Dangerfield must not have been Irish. He said, "My luck is so bad that if I bought a cemetery, people would stop dying."

I am especially fond of the line; luck is when opportunity meets preparation. You betcha.

I have a lucky Irish daughter. She wins stuff all the time and always has. It is quite uncanny to know someone who is so lucky. What an unusual phenomenon and one I do not share with her. Lucky her.

Jean Cocteau said, "We must believe in luck for how else can we explain the success of those we don't like?" I have heard that used. Some people like to diminish others with this kind of rationale.

St. Patrick's Day is more than luck, however. It is about shamrocks, parades, laughter, and of course, food and drink. Green beer is a St. Patrick's staple. As I am not a beer drinker, it doesn't matter to me if it is amber or green. I still don't like it. However, there are other delectable Irish delights to treat yourself to this week. You don't have to be Irish to enjoy.

A couple years ago I found a recipe for Corned Beef and Cabbage* that is yummeee. It is also easy. Corned beef is on sale right now and the veggies are cheap. You'll feel lucky.

Cooking cabbage, though, reminds me of a sentence I read in a novel. "The house always had a strange smell, as though she had found some vegetable to boil that no one else knew about." How colorful is that? It takes you right there. Rest assured, though, that the recipe above will smell mighty fine.

For dessert you might want to make Irish Whiskey Bread Pudding*. The first time I made it my husband wasn't around. I called his brother and asked him, "Is Irish Whiskey like regular whiskey? Do I really need to use it?"

"Oh," he replied. "Irish Whiskey is unique. You definitely need to use it. It's smoother and much better, totally different."

I'm not much of a whiskey drinker either but I went right out and bought me a bottle. I never did get around to sippin' it but I sure do get raves on the bread pudding.
I'm bettin' if you sip as you cook, you may end up feelin' mighty lucky.

To end your meal or just to celebrate, you may want to make a lovely cuppa Irish Coffee. Alex Levine said, "Only Irish Coffee provides in a single glass all four essential food groups: alcohol, caffeine, sugar and fat." He must be right because it sure tastes good, better than good even.

In a mug put 2 t. sugar mixed with 2 T. Irish Whiskey. Add hot coffee and top with whipped cream. Relax and enjoy and I'll bet your Irish eyes will be smiling. If you drink a few of these your Irish eyes will likely cross and then close. Beware.

Oh, and don't forget to squeeze in a Shamrock Shake sometime this week to make the holiday complete. And if you are really, really lucky, all this merriment won't stick to your hips. Happy St. Patrick's Day.

*Recipes are in chapter 15.

Church, Chocolate and Easter

One of my daughters went to Mass in another state on Easter Sunday. The Priest was giving a children's sermon. He asked, "Who can tell me what Easter is about?

A little girl enthusiastically raised her hand. "It's about that Jesus guy. They put him on a cross and put him in a cave; and if he comes out and sees his shadow, we get candy."

How did Groucho Marx say it? "Close, but no cigar."

I listened to an audio book by David Sedaris, an NPR humorist and author. He was telling of being in a French class in France. It was full of people from different countries, cultures and religions. The teacher had them explain how Easter was celebrated in their country and faith.

He told about Jesus, the Passion and Resurrection. He did this in very broken French, which he then translated back into very broken English on the audio book. When he finished his description of American Christian Easter, he then took a big sigh and continued. "And then there's this big bunny…"

The combination of Jesus and the Easter Bunny - What a puzzling duo! However, it makes for quite a special holiday, something for everyone to partake of. Even my Grandson, Louie, who is just one and barely walking, can enjoy Easter. He likes bunnies and candy. Jesus and religion are still a bit out of his realm of understanding.

In the last few days I have been to Meijers, Walgreen's and Hallmark. They were filled to the brim with Easter candy, cards, decorations, artificial eggs, baskets, and on and on.

As one drives around town, there are trees laden with colored eggs. Blow up bunnies adorn yards.

The Grand Rapids Press had a photo of a six foot, anatomically correct, chocolate sculpture of Jesus, standing with arms outstretched and called,

"My Sweet Lord". It took 200 pounds of milk chocolate to make. This was done by Cosimo Cavallaro, described as a quirky food artist. The New York art gallery said the fact that it was to be unveiled during Holy Week was just a coincidence. Not surprisingly, many were in an uproar.

The Easter Bunny and Jesus. Lamb and ham. Candy, colored eggs and baskets.

All living together in our world. One wonders, how did this all begin?

In pre-Christian times, the rabbit served as a symbol of new life during the spring season. The bunny was first used as a symbol of Easter in 16th century Germany. The first edible Easter bunnies were made of pastry and sugar and produced in Germany in the early 1800's. The Easter bunny was introduced to American folklore by the German settlers, who arrived in the Pennsylvania Dutch area during the 1700's. The children believed that if they behaved, a nest of colored eggs would be their reward. They built nests in their hats and bonnets. In later years, elaborate Easter baskets replaced their hats.

Last Sunday we participated in a community service in a parking lot. Pastors represented the Methodist, Congregationalist and Catholic churches. Each prayed and shared a couple thoughts. Then we all sang and processed back to our individual churches for our Palm Sunday services.

It was a great example of what my Aunt Mary told me years ago. There are many roads to the same place.

Easter is a time for Christians to celebrate. It is a time for little children to enjoy the bunnies, eggs, baskets and candy. It is a time for families to come together, enjoy a spring feast, and share what is important to them. For many that will be based on their individual faiths.

In the words of Mother Theresa, "If we truly want peace in the world, let us begin by loving one another in our own families. It we want to spread joy, we need for every family to have joy."

Reaching Out on Mother's Day

Mother's Day. Hallmark cards. Oh, happy day - But not for everyone.

As I was thinking about Mother's Day coming up, I thought of all the people for whom it is not a joyous day. As a friend told me today, "I just try to get through it. I can't wait 'til it's over."

Many have lost their mothers. Perhaps they died recently, perhaps years ago. It still leaves a big hole in their lives that Mother's Day brings up.

For others, they don't get along with their mothers. Some mothers no longer speak to their children. Some mothers are disappointed with their children and vice versa. Communication is scant, stilted, and almost non-existent. I read a quote by Thomas Berger, "Reinhart was never his mother's favorite – and he was an only child." Though humorous, for many this is true.

I have had several women tell me that when their mothers died, it gave them peace. The fighting and bickering were over; the criticisms stopped. The very difficult relationship had come to an end. Not every mother-child relationship is roses. Apparently, no one promised that everyone gets a rose garden.

Sometimes illness affects mother-child relationships: Alzheimer's, cancer, pain and suffering. All of these difficult conditions can affect one's happy mother's day.

Then there are all of the women hoping and trying to have children. Perhaps they haven't been able to conceive; perhaps they haven't found a partner yet. For many, mother's day is a big fat reminder that they don't have what they really, really want.

Many mothers I know have had children die. No matter how this happens, a mother is left with a tremendous void that Mother's Day brings to the forefront.

There are some mothers who should never have had children. They have done a poor job of mothering. They were never up to the task. These children grow up with a lot to deal with. Mother's Day reminds them that others did a lot better in the mother lottery.

Last week my daughter and I were shopping in Holland. A lady in her sixties owned the store and her mother, in her eighties, worked along side her. They were clearly having a nice time together. We commented on how nice that was. "Well, my mother and I get along fine," she said, "but I don't get along with my daughter. I love her, but I don't like her." What do you say to that? But I think, for many, that is reality. On the right hand, things are great. On the left, not so good.

Life is a mixture. Good. Bad. Easy. Hard. Hallmark. Painful.

Why am I writing this? Perhaps it will make each of us think of all the people we know who may be having a hard time this Mother's Day. It could be for any of the reasons I mentioned above or something else. Perhaps each of us could do something nice for one of those people. Spread a little love. Write a note. Give a call. Visit. Flowers. Hugs. Love.

And if we each reach out a bit, if we each spread a little caring to someone who is hurting, then we can go to bed Sunday night and feel, yes, it was a Happy Mother's Day.

A Myriad of Mothers

After the 2004 tsunami, there was a wonderful picture book, Owen and Mzee. A baby hippo was stranded alone and a 130-year-old giant tortoise mothered him from then on.

Mothers come in all ages, sizes, colors, and species. All forms of motherhood are special.

Last night I watched a beautiful elderly mother having dinner with her adult son. They came into the restaurant holding hands. Both were all dressed up. They seemed to have a lovely time together and share a deep bond.

Mother's Day is tomorrow. Mothers everywhere will be celebrated.

The expectant mother - I remember finding out I was expecting my first child and wondering, "Can I do this? Am I ready? Will I know how?" And then it happens and God gives you what you need.

New moms. I have a dear friend who is just expecting her 2nd baby. Her first is a toddler. She is glowing . . . and tired. The glowing may fade. The tired may go on for a long, long time.

I have a friend, Gayle, who has 10 children. She is always glowing. As I meet her children, it is not surprising that they are just like her – radiant. She home schools all of them. She is a grandma of a toddler. In her spare time she is in a book group, choir, etc. I think she got a double dose of energy.

I am not sure how I ever had the energy to raise four children. As the kids grew up and left the nest, so did my energy. It never really returned, however the kids did, and I am grateful for that.

There are old mothers. Cliff's mother is 106. Not long ago she quit work. She is amazing and still keeping busy. In the future, there are going to be a lot more mothers like her – living productive lives well into triple digits. I am guessing I won't have the energy for that.

There are very young mothers. I was at a play recently, chatting with a stranger. She was a beautiful black woman and I guessed we were similar ages. She said she was waiting for her mother who was in the restroom. I asked how old her mother was and she replied that she was . . . I tried not to act shocked... 4 years older than me. I quickly calculated and asked her how old her mother was when she had her. "Fifteen", she replied. She told me they were more like girlfriends than mother and daughter.

Single mothers. We all know mothers raising children alone. This is an enormous responsibility and often very difficult. There may be a special goal post in heaven for them.

Adoptive mothers. As I watch my friends who have adopted children, I am aware that mothering is not about blood. It is about love.

Birth mothers. Friends who have had a child and given it up for adoption have done so for the true betterment of the child. This is a selfless action.

Stepmothers. A special role and challenge. Often a positive gift for both the step mom and the child.

Foster mothers. What a gift they give to the children in their care, mothering them and letting them go with love.

Grandmothers. Great Grandmothers. Great-Great Grandmothers. Grandmothering might just be the coolest of all - The joy without the responsibility.

Godmothers. This can be a dear relationship and opportunity. It is always an honor.

Mother-in-Laws. I hate how mother-in-laws get the short end of the stick. I am a mother-in-law. I try hard to be a good one. I cringe when I hear the world referring to mother-in-laws in negative ways. Wouldn't it be nice if mother-in-laws were as highly regarded as other mothers? When it is, it is a beautiful thing.

Mothers who have died. I have several people I care about who have recently lost their mothers. It doesn't seem to matter if they are young or old themselves. When their mother dies a piece of them does too. I ache for my friends as they experience their first mother's day without their mother. I hope they are blessed in special ways and memories to help them through it.

Tomorrow there will be a lot of cards and gifts given in honor of mother's day. None of them will be as valuable as the gift each mother was given when they were given the opportunity to be a mother, no matter what form of mothering that was. As Whitney Houston once sang, it is "the greatest love of all".

What Happened to Thanksgiving?

Early November 1, I was sitting at a restaurant reading and doing paperwork. I was quiet, alone, enjoying my solitude. All of a sudden my brain stiffened, is that Christmas music I hear? No, it couldn't be. I listened intently. It was Christmas music. Well, perhaps it was just one winter song, surely a lone lyric. But, much to my surprise, and the woman across from me, whom I immediately asked, "Is that Christmas music?" And to which she confirmed in stunned dismay, "I think it is!" Even though we didn't know each other, we were joined in instant shock and irritation. I mean, just a few hours ago I was trick-or-treating with my adorable grandson. My pumpkins are still out. Do we have to be bombarded with Christmas carols ALREADY? And bombarded we were for the next long hour while "Let it snow" was followed by "I'll be home for Christmas" and "Chestnuts roasting on an open fire" and a gazillion (or so it seemed in my irritated state of mind) more holiday tunes.

Later that day I went to several stores to buy Thanksgiving computer paper. I am greeted by, "Lady, we don't have anything for Thanksgiving. We go right from Halloween to Christmas." Their looks add, "Are ya nuts?"

Afterwards, I was at a mall and there in full color display was Christmas. A huge tree was decorated in the center, Christmas in full regalia and alert. Everywhere I looked, the same message. Buy, buy, buy, Christmas, Christmas, Christmas, rush, rush, rush. At least that is the pressure I felt as I continued my errands.

What happened to Thanksgiving? It appears to be so far in the back seat of commercialism, I'm not sure it is even in the car anymore. It has been just plain run over.

This all reminds me of a few years ago when I tried to buy a bathing suit in early August. They looked at me like I was alien. Over and over I was told, "Lady, you can't buy a bathing suit in August. If you want a bathing suit, and definitely if you want any selection of choices, you need to buy in January. By August we are into fall and winter clothes." And that reminded me of when I tried to buy snow boots in January. I was told I needed to buy those in September. I have lived in Michigan most of my life and as crazy as Michigan weather is, and it is really, really crazy, you know it is. But I have never seen snow in September (Oct. 1, yes!). Nor have I ever gone swimming outside in Michigan in January.

I really don't think I am a Christmas grouch. I have always Christmas shopped throughout the year and been proud of it, especially in mid-December when I have half my stash bought already. But I have also enjoyed having Christmas begin the day after Thanksgiving. I have loved the progression of school starting, Halloween, Thanksgiving and then Christmas. It is the way it is supposed to be. But it is truly no longer the way it is.

Personally, I cannot sustain the peak of Christmas/Holiday joy and excitement for 8 weeks. I need to ease on down this road, not have it shoved down my throat so quickly.

However, this commercial mania is contagious. I am growing less and less thankful by the minute. The whole thing reminds me of a horse race where the horses have blinders on and run fast without being distracted by where they are. In my mind, where we are - is the first of November. Where we are is over three weeks from Thanksgiving. Where we are is ordering turkeys, considering pies, enjoying the fall color still in bloom. Where we are - is anticipating Thanksgiving, knowing full well that Christmas is right around the corner, but, thankfully, still in the back seat of our minds. This whole thing reminds me of a favorite quote by Lily Tomlin, "The trouble with being in the rat race is that even if you win, you're still a rat!"

Thanksgiving Thoughts

As it is Thanksgiving weekend, I thought I'd take you on a quick trip down memory lane - A very quick trip. Do you remember when being called a turkey was "in"? You big turkey! I even had a sign up in my garage that said, "No turkeys allowed". It was a big circle with a turkey in it and a diagonal line across it. I gotta admit. I still feel like a big turkey on many days. You too?

Another Thanksgiving thought. Isn't it funny how we all like what we like at Thanksgiving dinner . . . and don't mess with it? We have always laughed about the stuffing at our family gatherings. My mom made stuffing kinda dry, just right, actually. My mother-in-law made it kinda soggy. I liked hers but I never loved it. Her kids, however, loved it. I think it boils down to whatever you grew up with is the right way. My family now eats stuffing kinda dry, because to me, that is the right way.

For years we had Thanksgiving with my husband's brother's family. She didn't like my green bean casserole as I use frozen beans. She had to bring her own, made with fresh beans and with a real no-no, cheese in it. She was the only one who ate it, but no one cared. It is the way it is. We each want it our way. I eat jellied cranberries. Absolutely no one else at our table would touch them. It is correct, in my mind, as it is what my mother always served. My family mostly hates black olives. But one daughter and I love them. I buy 2 cans for us to eat as we fix dinner. We actually buy them for the dinner but they always get eaten before hand. One year they did make it to the table but no one touched them. No one wants them at dinner, just before dinner. It is the way it is.

There is an old story. Great Grandma always cut the end off the ham before she cooked it. Grandma always cut the end off the ham before she cooked it. Mother always cut the end off the ham before she cooked it. And I have always cut the end off the ham before I cooked it. It is the way it is. It is right. But one day, I asked Great Grandma why she cut the end off the ham before she cooked it. "Because I didn't have a big enough pan," she replied.

We each have our own *usual* for Thanksgiving dinner. We like what we grew up on because it reminds us of our past. In reality, there is no right or wrong. It is just what we like. And that's okay and reason enough to do it *our way*.

Gratefulness and Great Fullness

"If you're happy and you know it, clap your hands." It is that time of year, time for us to clap our hands together and be grateful. And to do that, we get a national holiday, an enormous turkey dinner, family good times, football galore, and gratefulness to go along with our great fullness, which comes immediately after the meal.

A favorite author of mine, Anne Lamott, says her main prayers are, "Help me, help me, help me" and "Thank you, thank you, thank you."

Thanksgiving is truly more than turkey and more than football. It is about giving thanks.

Fitness Magazine came up with 3 things folks can do to alleviate their stress. One was to enjoy nature, another was to have fun, and the last was to have an attitude of gratitude.

I think a good exercise is to write a paragraph of things for which you are grateful. I like to do this without qualifying that these things are the ones I should be the most grateful for. I just write them without putting my pen down, whatever comes into my mind. This is a wonderful daily routine.

There are so many things we are and have that we take for granted. A few years ago I had a nasty fall and was taken away by ambulance. I ended up okay but had lost my sense of smell. Not so bad. A sense of smell is nice but who really needs it? And then they told me to get fire alarms in my car and other things I hadn't considered. I also discovered smell is a very large part of taste. So, most of my sense of taste was gone too. I remember people said, "Oh, how great. I wouldn't eat then!" But that way of thinking didn't work for me. I always thought, if I can't taste that first brownie, perhaps I'll taste the second or third. After three years a kinesiologist brought my sense of smell back. I was very grateful, even though for my entire life before this, I had never thought of my sense of smell, let alone been grateful for it. Granted, this all may seem minor, but it opened up my mind to all I have and had that I had never really been grateful for. When you think of it, most of what we have is a gift and there aren't many of our gifts that we are responsible for.

In a recent article, Michael J. Fox, who has suffered Parkinson's disease for years, said, "I am so blessed." In the same line of thinking, my dear friend, Nelda Cushman, told me as she was dying, "Moe, how could I be more blessed?" These attitudes of gratitude are unreal. I am in awe of people like this - Normal people with abnormal gratitude. I am thankful for their inspiring examples.

When my husband and I dated, Ed Ames had a hit song, "My cup runneth over with love." If we take time to think about it, most of us do love so many people and so many things. Yes, it is true that hard times have hit our area, but most of our cups are still half full and in many ways, they runneth over.

So, if you're grateful and you know it, clap your hands…together and give thanks. This is the time. This is the holiday. "Thank you. Thank you. Thank you."

Christmas Decorations –
The Beat Up and the Beautiful

Decorating for the holidays, what a joy it is! Or at least it's a joy when it is all done and we sit back and immerse ourselves in our homes and our family's Christmas decor.

Each year, since we have been married, I try to get one nice decoration for the holidays.

Each year something gets tossed because it has become worn, faded, etc. Basically, it has done "its thing".

Once in awhile, someone will come over and give a negative comment on a couple of my decorations. "I really don't like that there." "Where'd you get that?" "You might want to replace that. It really doesn't go anymore."

This always amazes me. Can't they see the historical family richness in these items? Don't they know that the patchwork tree skirt has glorious history? Even though the fabric is no longer "in style" and the colors don't really go with our new home. It really doesn't even fit the tree anymore. But it is beautiful - to me. I made it myself with the same fabric I used to make dresses for myself and Colleen. They were long and very Seventies. She would fall in hers when she ran after Dan. Mine was maternity because I was 8 ½ months pregnant. Ah, yes, it may not "go" anymore, but it is a *lovely* tree skirt.

Don't they know that the cross-stitched Jesus, Mary and Joseph on the mantle were made on the way to New York to see my Grandma, who is now dead? Don't they know the trip took eight hours with little kids in the car? And that this was in the pre-mini-van days, no DVD player, no perks. Don't they know that I saw a Jesus, Mary, and Joseph like them at a church bazaar, but couldn't afford them? They were $15 and I had to come up with another way to have them. So, I found three dish soap bottles, covered them and cross-stitched them into our own Holy Family. Don't they know that I was very pregnant at the time and each cross-stitch was done by hands resting on my big baby belly that housed Donna? And that as I did the cross-stitch, I could feel her moving inside.

And then there are the extremely worn and weary children's Christmas books on a table. They are not Velveteen rabbits but they sure look like them. Very worn, but worn by use, worn by love. Beat up and beautiful.

Oh, we have lovely decorations too - Shiny, sparkly, the right colors and look. But if my home catches on fire during the holidays, I won't bother to grab them. However, I might run back in and grab the worn-out things that truly mean what Christmas is all about. The old Jesus, Mary and Joseph on the mantle, the tree skirt, the very tired books.

I sort through all these boxes to decorate one more time, one more year. I look at all these decorations and wonder where I will get the energy to put them all out in all the right places. The project seems to go on and on when I am ready for it to be done. It needs to be done because I have a lot of other important things to do right now. Christmas is calling, almost shouting at me. "Hurry", it says.

Ah, but when it is done, when our home is all decorated in it's Christmas glory, to sit in the middle of it and see it, feel it, hear it, smell it – the Christmases of our past, our present and our futures. I relish and remember our family's "happy holidays". Our memories. Our traditions. Therein is the joy.

Fruitcake – A Misunderstood Treat

Rodney Dangerfield was famous for the line, "I get no respect." Which, at this time of year, reminds me of the fruitcake. Talk about not getting any respect. The poor fruitcake is not only not respected; it is maligned, demeaned and shunned. And then there are the jokes that go on and on.

If you hear someone referred to as "a real fruitcake", you can bet it's not a compliment.

Fruitcake is a funny thing. It's made up of all things most folks like – fruit, nuts, cake and booze. We like them all. But, apparently, we don't like them together because we don't like fruitcake. "We" refer to most people.

I guess I am going to just come out and be honest here. I may be alone on this. It may sound crazy but I really like fruitcake, all kinds of fruitcake. I don't even think I have ever met a fruitcake I haven't liked. The cake that is, not the people. Liking fruitcake is like rooting for University of Michigan when you graduated from Michigan State. It's rarely done.

Each year I make a great light colored fruitcake*. It doesn't make a huge amount and you cover it with rum, a nice touch. I got the recipe from my sister-in-law, Luann. I love it but my family won't touch it. I don't care. I make it anyway and eat it all myself. Actually, I often share it with my friend, Barb. She's a fruitcake lover like me and also enjoys the misunderstood treat.

I asked my daughter what she thought of fruitcake and she had a couple of good points. One, fruitcakes seem to be around forever and ever and ever, without expiring. No one eats them. They just save them and give them to someone they don't like. Then that person waits and passes the cake along to another unsuspecting victim. This goes on for years and years. There are even rumors that there is only fruitcake and it circles the globe.

The other thing my daughter commented on was how much they weigh. Some fruitcakes must weigh 30 pounds. Just think what they feel like inside our bellies.

I have a feeling other countries give fruitcakes more respect than we do here in the good ole USA. There is even a Society for the Protection and Preservation of Fruitcake. I am sure that is a worthwhile organization. I don't know anyone in it, though.

Apparently fruitcake is not a new thing. It goes back to the Crusades and was taken on pilgrimages when they searched for the Holy Grail.

Also there is a story of Ben Franklin saying his wife's fruitcake was so hard it broke someone's tooth. He suggested to George Washington that it might be used as a barricade to keep the British out.

Most people have likely heard of the fruitcake recipe where you start with a gallon of whiskey and keep sampling it as you mix up the batter. In the end, you burp, toss the batter into the trash and finish the whiskey. I've never really made that recipe.

Somewhere along the way it became part of our Christmas holiday foods. And in spite of continued rejection, it looks like it is here to stay.

If anyone out there has the courage to say that they also like fruitcake, let me know. I would be happy to email you Luann's recipe. It's a keeper even if fruitcake usually isn't.

*Recipe in chapter 15.

So Much Shopping – So Little Time

"You better watch out. You better not cry. You better not pout, I'm telling you why." I think that must have been written about holiday shoppers. Personally, I can really relate.

This week I ran into Carol at the newspaper. She perkily asked, "Have you got all your Christmas shopping done?"

I said, "Carol, I don't even have my list made yet," followed by a giant sigh.

Talking with friends yesterday, many were in the same boat as me, but one. Miss Kelly smugly told us that she has her shopping all done and it's been done for some time. We all looked at her with dismay and a big dose of irritation.

She went on further. "I also have it all wrapped. My favorite thing to do in December," she continued, "is go sit at the mall, get a cup of coffee, and watch all the shoppers rushing around."

I think I said something like, "I hate you." We laughed but I am not sure I was joking. Okay, I do really, really like her but come on, "already wrapped". It's just not right, folks. Who does that? Other than Kelly, that is.

For years I shopped early. I still shop early a little bit. In fact, I actually do have some stuff already bought. I have no idea what it is or where it is or even whom it's for. Truth be told, there are a few items I still haven't found that I bought early several years ago. Whatever.

One guy was brought up before a judge. "Why are you here?" asked the Judge.

"I did my Christmas shopping early," the guy replied.

"Why is that a problem? How early was it?"

"Before they opened the store." He was naughty. He probably won't get any presents.

My husband seems to get off the hook. I do most of the Christmas shopping. My daughters do most of his buying. Poor Dad, they think, he needs help.

Sigh. It is too late in my life to consider a sex change operation? Or would it be too drastic if my sole motivation was to avoid Christmas shopping. I suppose you would have to lie about it on the insurance forms. I don't like to lie. I don't really like to Christmas shop much anymore either.

They say Christmas is not about gifts. Tell that to kids. However, I do know two wonderful families who each have lots of children and don't "do" Christmas gifts. Wow, I wonder. How do they pull that off?

Recently one of my children shared how much they had always loved when the Sears or Penny's Christmas catalog would come. (Do they still come? Not to my house.) I used to give the catalog to them with a pen and tell them to mark everything they wanted. They would do so with glee. Looking back, they say they were surprised that they didn't get all they had marked, and yet somehow, they still had a happy Christmas.

Shopping has gotten complicated - So many choices. Even at the post office. A lady asked the clerk for 100 stamps. "What denomination?" he asked.

232

"For heaven's sake," she grumbled. "Has it come to this now? I guess I will take 50 Catholic and 50 Lutheran." Don't for one second think this shopping stuff is easy.

My dear daughter in law has offered more than once to do all my Christmas shopping for me on the Internet and she promises she can get it with free shipping. Talk about an offer you can't refuse. And yet I do. Why? I like it. In spite of the stress, in spite of the rushing, in spite of the frustrations, in spite of the exhaustion, it is still fun. I plan to go for it, get 'er done. And I intend to follow that ole Christmas promise, "Yule be happy".

Remembering Santa

Santa Claus is coming to town. If you stop for a minute and think about it, what does that mean to you? What memories do you have of Santa? Are they near and dear?

My most vivid memory of Santa is when I was about 8. It was Christmas Eve and I was sound asleep. I felt a kiss on my cheek and opened my eyes and saw Santa in his red suit ducking out the bedroom window. I suppose some would say I dreamt it. I suppose others might say I imagined it. What they can't make me do is not believe it. It was and is as real as one can imagine and I intend to treasure it within me for the rest of my days.

I asked others about their special Santa memories. Sue remembers terrible angst over worrying about Santa. Their chimney was connected directly to their incinerator. Every Christmas Eve she prayed no one would incinerate the garbage. That's a lot of worry for a little tot.

Patti remembers her engineer son, Ryan, getting out a measuring tape to measure the opening of the chimney to be sure Santa could fit through - The beginning of his future occupation.

Her son, Trevor, exclaimed when he was little, that he 'knew there was a real Santa because he knew his dad wouldn't ever spend that much money on his presents. He wouldn't even buy him a sucker after dinner and it was only ten cents'.

Linda's daughter came home one Christmas Eve and exclaimed, "He's been here. See the reindeer tracks?" Who can doubt such childish sureness and who would want to?

When we lived in Spain, there was no Santa. The 3 Kings come with gifts January 6th. December 25th is a religious holiday. It has always amazed me that their children get off school like ours do. And then they wait all that time and get their gifts the day or so before they go back to school. Who planned that?

Gisela is from Germany. St. Nick reins there, not Santa. Perhaps Santa doesn't speak Spanish or German. St. Nick comes on December 5th. His bag of goodies is carried by Knecht Ruprecht. On Christmas Eve the children would have to wait upstairs until they heard a bell. Then they would follow angel hair down the stairs to the tree decorated with real candles and sparklers. They would have to sing carols before they got to open their presents, which were brought by the Christ child.

My grandson, Danny, just turned 5. His mom told him they were going to visit Santa this week. He smiled and asked, "Do we tell him what we want for Christmas?"

She replied, "Sure, what will you tell him?"

"It's a secret."

"You're not going to tell me?"

"You'll find out when I open it."

Oh, no!

Alison, a friend in San Diego, wrote me that one Christmas she asked Santa for a checkbook. She thought she could get everything she wanted with her own checkbook. She got one, too, and took it to the neighbors to "buy" things that her house didn't have, like Oreos.

Sue is a college professor. The other day she was leaving the administration building on campus as a gentleman was entering. "He had the most luxurious white beard that extended to his mid chest. I couldn't help myself," she said. "I made eye contact with him and said, 'I have been very good this year.' He looked directly back at me and said, 'I know that you have been', and nodded. I was tickled by the interaction and a smile comes to my face every time I think about it. I do not know who the fellow was nor have I seen him again. Which makes it all the more magical! What if . . . could it really be . . .of course not. But I wonder."

I was always prepared with the answer I would give to my children, if they ever came to me doubting the reality of Santa. I would say - he is real. He is the spirit of Christmas in everyone. And yes, I believe, Santa lives.

Let me close with one of my favorite quotes. I found it on a sign, years ago.

First you believe in Santa Claus and then you don't believe in Santa Claus and then you are Santa Claus.

Merry Christmas dear readers! May you each take a moment to relish your personal Santa memories. HO, HO, HO, BELIEVE!

Peace – The Majesty and Promise

I remember when I was a child and my mother was beside herself with frustration. She would look at us and say, "Would you kids just give me a little peace and quiet." I was young. I wasn't sure why that was so coveted but I understood that it must be something precious.

When my four children were in different schools, with individual hectic schedules, I remember how hard it was to juggle my work, my family and my life. At one point I went to Holland to a weekend silent retreat. Silence was the magical draw. I needed to regroup, to get some R and R. I needed peace.

Shortly after I was married, the V for peace sign was popular. It seemed it was everywhere. Our tots learned to give it. You saw it on T.V. It didn't even need words to convey the message. People wanted the war to end. Our world was clamoring for peace.

It seemed as if pop culture moved from that to, "Peace, Bro!" This became a greeting and a note of farewell. It started ethnic but became everyone's sign.

And then there's the famous line, "Peace on you." No, I'm just kidding. I think I saw that in a bad movie once.

My cousin, Bobby worked with the Ottawa County police department. He was hit and killed by a drunk driver some years ago. At his funeral they sang, *Peace is flowing like a River.* It was years before I could hear that song in church without crying. It was also years before his family found peace with his death.

In my church, and others, there is the time when folks share a sign of peace with those around them. People look each other in the eye, usually smile, shake hands and say, "Peace be with you." We don't necessarily know them. We wish them peace anyway.

This is Christmas week. Families and friends gather for the biggest holiday we have. It is such a big holiday even stores close. "I'll be home for Christmas" becomes a mission statement. We gather together to share gifts, food, love . . . and, hopefully, some peace.

Last Christmas my daughter-in-law, Drea, gave us each a book by Maya Angelou, the great American poet and writer. It is a teeny book called,

Amazing Peace, A Christmas Poem. I am going to close with some of Maya's profound words. I will paraphrase them.

* * * * *

"We worry. God, are you there? Into this climate, Christmas enters, with lights of joy, bells of hope, songs of forgiveness.

The world is encouraged to come away from strife, to come the way of friendship. This is the Glad Season.

Hope is born again in the faces of children and rides on the shoulders of our aged.

In our joy, we think we hear a whisper. At first it is too soft. We listen carefully as it gathers strength. We hear a sweetness. The word is Peace.

It is loud now. Louder than bombs. We tremble at the sound. We are thrilled by its presence. It is what we have hungered for. Not just the absence of war, but true Peace - A harmony of spirit, a comfort of courtesies. Security for our beloveds and their beloveds.

We clap hands and welcome the Peace of Christmas. We beckon this good season to wait awhile with us. We, Baptist and Buddhist, Methodist and Muslim, say come, Peace. Come and fill us and our world with your majesty.

We, the Jew and the Lutheran, the Catholic and the Congregationalist, implore you to stay awhile with us.

It is Christmas time, a halting of hate time.

We can create a language of peace to translate to ourselves and others.

At this Holy time, we shout the coming of hope, the promise of Peace.

We, Angels and Mortals, Believers and Nonbelievers, look heavenward and speak the word aloud. Peace.

We look at our world and speak the word aloud. Peace.

We look at each other, then into ourselves, and we say without shyness or apology or hesitation:

Peace, my Brother.   Peace, my Sister.   Peace, My Soul."

*****

As we enter into this holiday week, I wish you peace. And as it radiates out from each of us, perhaps we can brighten our small corners of the world. And as Sam Cooke sang, "What a wonderful world it would be." Merry Christmas.

Can We Keep Christmas?

What an interesting thing Christmas is. What a long way we have come from a baby being born in a stable to standing in line at the grocery store and other stores at 3 a.m. the day after Thanksgiving. How did we get here? I am not saying it is bad. It is just interesting.

Christmas is a wonderful time of year. Festive. Celebratory. Special music. Special clothes - Lots of La-di-dah.

We cut down trees, haul them into our homes and then decorate them. We have boxes and boxes of stuff to garnish them with.

That isn't enough, though. We decorate our entire homes. Inside. Outside. Lights. Greens. All kinds of decorations. Some lovely. Some old, worn, and very loved. They are full of our history and memories.

We fill our schedules with parties and gatherings, trying to cram social festivities into a few short weeks.

And then there are the gifts. We buy for folks we love and for some we like a lot. We buy for people we don't know. We buy when people don't need anything and we don't have a clue what to buy them. That doesn't stop us. We still buy.

We send cards and letters to people we aren't in touch with any other time of the year. We buy special stamps. Photos go into the cards. Even with the rise in the cost of stamps, we still send. It is, after all, an important way of staying in communication with friends and family - Priceless, to be exact.

And then we eat. Of course, if we are celebrating with gifts, decorations, cards and all – food has to be a part of it. And, boy, is it! Somewhere, sometime, someone must have decided that we needed to fatten up and Christmas was the time to do it. Everyone seems to be on a mission to get all the candy, cookies and treats they can tuck into their bellies. Ho, Ho, Ho.

Oh, and I nearly forgot to mention the special TV shows, movies, concerts and programs. Way too many to see or attend.

You may notice I have not mentioned the religious parts of Christmas, which really are how it all started in the first place. I am just talking about the *other* parts of the holiday season.

Did you ever think what it would be like without Christmas? December would be just another month. The 25th, just another day. No decorations. No gifts. No inside trees. No cards. No special fattening foods. No special parties or gatherings. No special shows. Just another day. What a hollow thought.

Yes, even though it's a lot of work and causes stress and busyness, we need Christmas. We want Christmas. We love Christmas.

Years ago my Grandma sent me the words of Henry Van Dyke.

"Are you willing . . .

- to forget what you have done for other people, and to remember what other people have done for you;

- to close your book of complaints against the management of the universe, and to look around you for a place where you can sow a few seeds of happiness;

- to stoop down and consider the needs and desires of little children;

- to remember the weakness and loneliness of people growing old;

- to bear in mind the things that other people have to bear in their hearts;

- to try to understand what those who live in the same home with you really want, without waiting for them to tell you;

- to trim your lamp so that it will give more light and less smoke, and to carry it in front so that your shadow will fall behind you;

-to make a grave for your ugly thoughts, and a garden for your kindly feelings, with the gate open;

- to believe that love is the strongest thing in the world – stronger than hate, stronger than evil, stronger than death – and that the blessed life which began in Bethlehem so many years ago is the image and brightness of the Eternal Love?

Then you can keep Christmas."

A pretty tough assignment, Mr. Van Dyke, but definitely something to strive for and one to put at the top of our lists.

The You're Not In Control Christmas

I thought I had all my bases covered. I thought I was in control. "Ha," said Life, "Haven't you learned anything yet?"

My lists were made. I had checked them many more times than twice. My gifts were bought, wrapped and tagged. My groceries were planned, bought and prepared. My ducks were coming home to roost about dinnertime on Christmas Eve.

At noon I noticed my mate acting weird. He was moaning, clammy, white and downright sick. No matter how much I tried to use positive thinking on him, he remained sicker than a dog. He took to his bed and we barely saw him for the next few days.

Christmas Eve went on as planned, sort of. The ducks arrived late due to snow. The evening was like a weak cup of tea. It resembles tea but isn't really tea. Someone was missing. He was upstairs feeling nasty and not nice.

The next couple days were more of the same. A few days later, my mate woke up in a kind of, "I'm a little better" state. As he arose, he noticed we had no electrical power. And that was the beginning of Phase Two of the "You're not in control" Christmas.

We began as positive thinkers. That means we went to Big Boy to wait out the power loss and have a long lingering breakfast. We returned home to the cold. We decided to go see a three-hour movie. We came home to a dark house chilled to the rafters and us chilled to the bone.

It is hard to find what you need in a totally dark house. Candles and a failing flashlight don't do the trick like they pretend to when all the lights are on.

Miserably we took what we could and should and drove to our daughter's home in Grand Rapids. Seems there were no rooms at the local inn, or so someone told us. I was thinking we were a lot like the Christ story at this point.

Day two was spent wandering stores. At least they were warm. We hung on to our positive outlook and picked up the grand boys and drove home, sure the power would come on at any second.

But alas, no power. Which means no heat; no light; no TV; no stove; no computer. Flushing the toilet becomes a worry. Drinking water gives one pause. All the while teeth are chattering and joints are yelling.

This night the Mexican Restaurant got us. I felt sorry for them. The children were wild as were the adults. Add to that sorry state of affairs a marguerita and some vino.

It was nearly 9 p.m. and surely the power wasn't coming on. We were all set to return to Grand Rapids, our positive thinking dimmed.

But one last drive by. A flicker here. A flicker there. A call saying, "THE EAGLE HAS LANDED. WE HAVE POWER!"

You think as an adult you still get excited about Christmas. You think you don't get that excited about heat and light. You are wrong. Ecstasy just begins to touch our joy.

Driving home, there were rows of power trucks at Big Boy. We went in. It was empty except for a lone group in the back, the power rangers. They looked at us kind of odd, but often folks do. They weren't even from Michigan but from Indiana and Kentucky and had come just to help restore the tens of thousands of power failures in west Michigan. We thanked them for everyone.

As drove further, nine more power trucks passed us leaving our area. We neared our house and saw the Christmas lights and tree had been lit. Lamps were glowing. The furnace was humming. Joy. Our chills remained but we knew they weren't long lasting. We were positive thinkers after all.

When we all tucked in last night with extra blankets and clothes, we also had extra joy at being restored to our normalcy, for being together, and for the Christmas adventures we had just shared. They had not been planned or were on our lists but they were okay just the same.

Sometimes life nudges to remind us who is in charge and what is really important. Snuggling in and thinking it over, I realized the power of positive thinking may not always work, but it always remains better than the alternative. I closed my eyes, nestled into my covers and sighed, "Thank you, Lord, and to all a good night."

Some Say Love

All You Need Is Love

He said, "You know what we should do?"

I said, "No", thinking he was going to suggest a movie.

"Get married."

I was stunned. I said, "I'll have to think about it." I thought for ten seconds and said, "Okay."

The wedding was August 19th, forty years ago. As I write this, I almost choke. How can it be? As the cliché says, "Where does the time go?"

My daughter, Cara, said, "Wow, 40 years is a *really long* time to even *know* someone, let alone be married to them." I agreed.

As I think back over it, I am amazed so many of us share these long happy marriages. I mean, it isn't like we really had a clue as to the seriousness of what we were getting in to.

Bill Cosby says, "For two people to live together in a marriage, day after day, is unquestionably the one miracle the Vatican has overlooked." I think he might be right.

When you take a trip with others, or have folks come visit and stay with you, or spend a long car ride with people – relationships can really be taxed. Doesn't the adage say, "Company is like fish? After three days they all stink." Something like that. The message being how really hard it is to get along for extended time periods; no matter how much you like the people.

I think of the naivety of newlyweds, for better or worse, for richer or poorer, till death do us part. Those are just words. Spoken with love and commitment but likely not with the harsh reality of what they really mean.

So much of marriage is communication, attraction, appreciation of the other person. Add to that common values, shared faith, trust and the magic potion of shared humor.

Recently we saw Jeff Daniels, the famous Michigan actor, in concert. He wrote and sang his own music, all based on witty experiences he has had. His wife and two children were near us, enjoying his performance. His wife, especially, was truly delighted with his shtick. Afterwards, I told her how much I had enjoyed watching her. I shared that I had always joked that my husband married me because I was the one who kept laughing at all his jokes. Obviously, she was the same way.

Erma Bombeck used to say that marriage was laughing at the same joke you have heard 5492 times and listening to the same story you have heard 6095 times. I sure have to agree. I still think my husband's stories and jokes are funny, though I have to admit when I hear him begin the one about the dentist in Guatemala; I begin to cringe a bit. I'm not saying it isn't a great story. It is just that I have heard it a lot. I am sure he feels the exact same way about some of mine.

Looking back over forty years, you go through a lot together. Raising children, which is the greatest joy and the greatest anxiety of all. Illnesses, surgeries, lots and lots of deaths, including parents. Moves, different cities, different homes. Jobs, schooling, getting degrees. Dealing with finances, dealing with friendships, traveling together. Encouraging each other. Believing in each other. Helping each other to grow physically, mentally, spiritually.

This sounds like work, but most things that are wonderful are work. Rarely do good things come easy. It doesn't mean it is hard, but just like caring for any other valuable item; marriage needs care, maintenance and attention.

"A successful marriage requires falling in love many times, always with the same person," says Mignon McLaughlin. What a sweet journey.

Marriage is having a witness to our lives, the good, the bad, and the mundane. It is waiting together for test results, fear in both your hearts.

It is joy beyond belief as children are born. It is taking out the trash, doing the laundry, making one more dinner, watching a TV show you both like. And these things become your shared history that no one else can ever know or understand. This is what the true union of marriage is, your memories.

Gloria Steinem said, "Being married is like having somebody permanently in your corner." I love that thought. And in that corner, you each protect each other, care for each other, encourage each other, and love each other. What a wonderful summary.

Perhaps Love

John Denver and Placido Domingo sang, "Perhaps Love is like a resting place, a shelter from the storm. It invites you to come closer. It wants to show you more." At this point in my life, it seems love certainly is more than what I used to think it was. Valentine's Day brings to mind romantic love but love is so much broader and, thus, so much more wonderful. Don't get me wrong. I like romantic love. I mean I love it. It "fills up my senses" to further quote John Denver. But love fills our lives in so many other ways.

We can love many of our friends. The other day a girlfriend of mine called from Florida and chatted with my husband. When he hung up, he said, "Clearly we have come to a new place in life, when other women are telling me they love me and it is okay!" And it is. At this point many of us realize how precious our relationships and friendships are and how fragile and fleeting our lives are. We have long rich histories together. As friends we grew up together, experienced getting married together, raised families together. We have gone through births, deaths, illnesses, divorce, moves, career changes – all the things that make friendships deep and rich and full of love. Yes, we have many friends we love, both men and women. And it is good to tell them.

Love isn't easy. Sometimes along life's journey we love someone but it isn't lasting. Perhaps they hurt us deeply and we need to let them go.

For me, when this has happened, it is always very painful, but it is part of the journey of love and life. Hopefully it doesn't happen often because it can make people afraid to love again. But we must. We need love. It is as simple as that.

Love may be magical but it isn't magic. It takes work. It takes time. It takes caring.

Love is a two way street with both people caring about the other and sharing along the way. When only one person cares it is like one hand clapping, an empty sound, hollow. Love needs communication. I feel it is necessary for love to have trust, affirmation, encouragement, forgiveness. Love needs listening. It needs growth. And for me, it also needs big doses of humor, laughter and fun. I feel blessed to be married to a wild and crazy guy, to have very fun children and grandboys. That is the icing on my cake.

Love doesn't stop when someone dies. It goes on in a spiritual dimension that lifts us up. It stays rooted in our memories, our feelings. It warms our heart as we continue our life.
The memory of a loved one is like a wonderful hug, precious and dear.

Valentine's Day. Love. Spouses, children, family, friends, pets – so many to love, so little time. Yes, love is more than romantic and that is one of the joys of life.

Elisabeth Kubler-Ross was a preeminent writer on death and dying. She reminded us to tend to our loved ones. She once said, "I have been with thousands of dying people and in the end, they never talk to me of their things or their jobs – it is always of their relationships and what they were or what they wish they had been."

As we celebrate Valentine's Day this week, may we be filled with joy and peace over all the loving relationships we have. May we be grateful for the richness they bring to our lives and what we bring to theirs.

"And even if we lose ourselves and don't know what to do, the memory of love will see us through."

The Dance

One day this week my friend and I were meeting our daughters for dinner. We are prayer partners and have been praying together for twenty years or so. We decided to get to the restaurant early, do our praying together and then meet the girls. So, when we get there at 4:00, the restaurant isn't open yet so we go into the bar. We each ordered a glass of wine and told the waiter we didn't need anything else. We were just there to pray, after all. Don't judge us.

Now the reason I am writing this was not how odd it was for us to be praying in a bar. The reason I'm writing is what the other people in the bar were doing.

When we arrived, we noticed there were only two couples in the bar. Did I mention this was an out of the way place?

The couples seemed strange right away. First of all, they were deeply looking at each other with full attention. That ain't right.

Couple number one, the man was doing all the talking. The woman laughed at something he said once and he leaned over and ran his hand over her upper back, only for a moment, while looking deep into her eyes. In fact, his eyes never left her face.

So, right away my friend and I knew. "They're not married . . . at least to each other."

The other couple, she did all the talking. She was using her hands a lot as she talked and would often touch his knee. He listened to her intently. He never once, not even for a second, not even with a fast glance – looked at the big T.V. hanging above them with a sports game on. "Oh, yeah," we agreed, "They're for sure not married either."

My friend commented, "That's the dance. I remember that."

It is so different when you see married couples out together. They are usually talking with the kids. First, one is on the phone, then the other.

Then they hang up and talk *about* the kids. Or they are silent. Or the woman is talking her heart out and the guy is listening - Sort of. But he is often looking at other people in the place, "people watching" he calls it. And then there is the game on the T.V. He just needs to catch the score. Who's playing? Does it matter? Not really, but he has to have the score anyway.

Oh, yeah, married couples out in bars are a very different deal all together. And then there is the reality of married couples at home. The music may still be playing but that ole dance has stopped.

In its place - flannel oversized pajamas; wearing big ole sox to bed; dogs sleeping between you; watching the news during dinner; taking each other for colonoscopies. Do I need to go on?

Somewhere along the way, the idea of meeting for an intimate chat in a secluded bar in the late afternoon – well, that just fades away. I'm not saying that's a bad thing. I mean I have been happily married for 40 plus years. I think my mate would say the same thing. But that "dance" is certainly not life as we know it these days.

Perhaps Dr. Karl Bowman was right when he said, "Love is an obsessive delusion that is cured by marriage."

But if we're lucky the beat goes on, even though the dance doesn't. Love has many dimensions.

Love is a Verb

We all have rules. One of my rules is I don't go out on Sunday night. I want to be home on Sunday night. I want to snuggle in, watch some TV, regroup and plan my week. Like comfort food, Sunday night is comfort night. That is my rule and I hold it sacred. Most of the time, that is.

Last Sunday I broke it. I hated doing so. It didn't feel comfortable. I felt stressed, hated going, but what a reward. I went with my daughter to Grand Rapids to see Clint Black in concert. For anyone who doesn't know Clint Black, he is a country singer who was popular in the 90s. He has the most pure, wonderful voice and it is classic country. I love his voice. Plus he has always seemed to be a sweetheart of a guy and cute as a bug. After a minute on stage, we agreed that those perceptions were true. His voice lifted us and all the way home I kept thinking how lucky I was to see and hear him. And how glad I was that I had broken my rule.

Perhaps you have rules too. Are they flexible? Sometimes great things await us if we allow ourselves to have flexibility with what we do and don't do, even though it may not be easy to let ourselves go.

One of Clint's songs says, "Love isn't something that we have, it's something that we do." I got thinking about that – love as a verb, not a noun.

When people date, they think about falling in love, as if it is a noun. But it is so much more than a noun and it is the verb part that makes love come alive, the action.

Love has so many facets: lovers, children, family, parents, friends, pets. We love a lot. We even love our work, if we are lucky.

My friend, Joan, has horses. State champion horses, actually. For many years I have watched her quietly get up early and work very hard to care for those horses. To me, that sounds like tough work. To Joan it is the verb of love.

I have a friend who for months now has not been her usual perky self. She has been distant, quiet. The verb of love meant visiting her and spending time talking with her until she was able to share about her depression. This led to hope and help. We have shared many, many years of joy and fun together. I love her. Sometimes love is laughing, but sometimes it is reaching out, listening and encouraging.

I watch people I know and care about as they care for their ill loved ones. Some no longer know them. They still care for them with love. Some can't do much or anything for themselves. They still care for them with love. Love is definitely a verb.

We love our children when they are wonderful and when they are not. Sometimes the verb of love is worry. Sometimes it is prayer. Sometimes it is getting up in the middle of the night to listen or tend to them.

The verb of love is active when we call our parents or older relatives. It is there when we visit them, tend to them.

I think love is also verbal. It is saying, "I love you". No one ever hears that too much.

At this point in my life, I have begun to tell people, other than my family, that I love them. Why? Because I do, and I want them to hear it.

As Clint sang, "There's no request too big or small. We give ourselves. We give our all. Love isn't someplace that we fall – It's something that we do."

May the love in your life be both verbs and verbal and may you receive all that you give.

How About Some Reverse Polygamy

With all the media attention of polygamists lately, I got thinking…What about reverse polygamy?

I emailed some ladies and asked their thoughts. Many comments I couldn't print no matter how much I agreed with and appreciated them.

Laurel sent this. "I read that husbands only do 30% of the housework. So if I had multiple mates, I could get closer to them doing 100%. Not bad."

D.C. said, "I would like one to shop with, one to decorate with, one to hang out with and one to la-di-dah with." I didn't ask her what "la-di-dah" meant. I think I can guess.

A couple gals got into specifics. They clearly had given it some thought and had come up with a plan.

Gayle said, "I would like one mate to be a gardener, one for house maintenance, one to help raise the children, and one to support the entire estate. I would also like one to match socks, one with a more feminine side to chat about décor, one to be a masseuse. I would also need one to be a big conversationalist for when I really want to talk things over."

She wasn't done yet. "I would never beat any of them and would treat them with total respect. As I would only go to bed with one a night, the others would be free to stay up and play cards or watch sports. Yes, I can see it now. I could be a very happy camper. I think I would spend a lot of time out on my swing enjoying coffee laced with Bailey's Irish Cream."

Clearly one of the most insightful comments came from Mary. "I believe that when men think of polygamy, they think about just one thing and the women are not wearing clothes. When I think about polygamy, all of my men are dressed. One of them is wearing a handyman's tool belt; one of them is wearing a chef's hat, one of them, the accountant, has on a three-piece suit and has a calculator in his hand. The gardener is dressed in denim tight jeans and carries a trowel. The car mechanic wears a greasy jumpsuit, and that's all right. And then there's the one with the vacuum in one hand and the feather duster in the other. You get my point." I did.

As I read about Polygamy, it seems the men want lots and lots of children as they feel it helps you get to Heaven. I notice they are not the ones raising and caring for all those children. I also read that the men go to town and visit with people. The women stay home and see no one outside of the compound. That doesn't sound like fun to me. Perhaps polygamy isn't about fun for everyone, just for the men.

Lest you think Polygamy isn't very real. It is more real than you think. I know - I watch *Big Love*. That and I read current statistics say there are

30,000 to 100,000 practicing polygamists in the United States.

Personally, when I thought of reverse Polygamy, I thought I would like one mate to do the grilling, one to be the chief chef and grocery shopper, another to be the baker. I suppose one would have to be the kitchen cleaner upper. Then with all that eating, I would likely need one to be a personal trainer. I know I would need one to manage my clutter. That could really help me out. I do so poorly with that on my own.

I would need one for the yard, one for housekeeping, one to walk the dog, one to maintain my schedule. Oh, and one would be the assigned errand doer. That would be wonderful. Errands often take up my day and I get no credit or satisfaction for them. It would be a treat to have a separate mate to handle all those low level tasks. As I think of jobs for all these mates to do, the list is endless. It makes me wonder how I do it all with just one ole mate and myself.

I suppose that magical thing called love enters into the picture. Perhaps it is love that makes the world go round, after all, and not how many mates we have. After giving it some unserious thought, I think myself and all the ladies who shared their reverse polygamist thoughts with me are quite glad to have only one mate. Neither polygamy nor reverse polygamy seem like a very good way to go. There must be better ways to get to heaven.

America, America

Why Can't We All Just Get Along?

His name was Dan. He was bright, patriotic and kind - A proud Marine on his way to Viet Nam.

We were all newlyweds saying our farewells. He pulled me aside. "If I don't come back, please take care of Kathy." I assured him I would, but that he needn't worry because he was coming back.

Kathy and I were pregnant with our first babies. Kathy had a boy. Dan got to see a photo of his newborn son. Kathy was to meet him in Hawaii when the baby would be three months. The world was good.

Dan was Captain of his platoon. He led them on a raid. Dan and most of them were killed. The world stopped.

I remember getting the call. A heavy fog settled into our brains. Sometimes it is nearly impossible for reality to seep in. Sometimes it is better when it seeps slowly. It would be too much all at once.

It took weeks for him to get home. His coffin was glassed over. No one could recognize him as him. His funeral ended up being the day she was to have met him in Hawaii.

Kathy renamed her son Daniel. We had our son and named him Daniel.

Life went on. Kathy remarried another wonderful man and had a large family and a happy life. Her Danny grew up. Our Danny grew up.

When our children were old enough, we took them to Washington, D.C. to visit the Viet Nam Memorial. We took paper and pen and found his name, Daniel J. Jaskiewicz. We carefully etched it, brought it home and mounted it on our wall. It still hangs in our home.

Ours was by no means the only loss of the war. There were many, so many. It scars you and you are never the same. We shouldn't be the same. We should remember.

Recently I read a book called, *March*, about the father from the book *Little Women*. It is his tale of being in the Civil War.

What struck me the most were some comments his wife made near the end of the story. Mr. March had been injured. She visited him in a hospital in Washington, D.C. The streets were not paved. The Washington Monument was being built and there were comments that it would probably never get done. Horses were everywhere. Medicine was scarce. Patient care was rough.

As Mrs. March wandered around the horrific sights, she said. "I was angry at myself, for not having the courage to stand against the crying up of this war and say, No. Not this way. You cannot right injustice by injustice. You must not defame God by preaching he wills young men to kill one another. For what God could possibly will what I see here? There are Confederates lying in this hospital. There is union at last, a United States of pain. Did God will the lad in the next ward to be shot, or to run a steel blade through the farmhand who now lies next to him?"

"But I said none of this a year ago, when it might have mattered. It was easy then to convince one's conscience that the war would be over in ninety days, as the president said: to reason that the price paid in blood would justify the great good we were so sure we would obtain. To lift the heel of cruel oppression from the necks of the suffering. Ninety days of war seemed a fair payment. What a corrupt accounting it was. I still believe that removing the stain of slavery is worth some suffering – but whose? If our forefathers make the world awry, must our children be the ones who pay to right it?"

I read this and was sad. I write this and am sad. It is Memorial Day and we honor the fallen heroes and with them, our friend, Dan. It is amazing that so many years later we are still sad as we remember. It is also amazing that Mrs. March said such profound things more than a hundred years ago.

Every morning now I hear the news, listing casualties. The more things change, the more things stay the same.

Recently we were chatting with our friend, Jerry. He was in the Gulf War and also in Iraq. He is bright, patriotic and kind. He said, with the pain of experience on his face, "Why can't we all just get along?" And I wonder...

This Wise Old Woman

She's mad as hell and she's not taking it anymore. She's sick of people taking advantage of her, taking her for granted. It's never about her. It's always about them.

They believe she's bottomless and always want more from her.

She gets hot, steams. She gets depressed, dark, stormy. When gloomy she gushes. Pushed to the edge, she crackles, pops. At times she snaps.

She's been known to blow her top. You don't want to be in her way when she let's go. And she's also been known to get violent, very, very violent.

Why, she wonders, don't they care for me as I do for them? They are bright. They know better. I warned them. I'm tired, so very tired. I just can't do it all alone anymore.

She cries a river and then some. She howls and wails. She's clearly over the edge, beside herself.

She's been known to be cool, chilly, to freeze people out. At times she shows no warmth at all. Sometimes her anger is so heavy that she'll strike out with vehement hits that break those she loves. She'll lash out and destroy their things. She's had it.

Yes, it's obvious we've angered her. We've pushed her to the limit. She resents our selfishness, our not caring and our foolish behavior.

Looking back, she was always so strong, so invincible. If we try we can remember when she was gentle, unscathed. We could almost always count on her to routinely be the same with us. Not so anymore.

We still love her. We really do. We are grateful for all she does. When we take time to think about it, we are very, very appreciative. We realize we're not much without her.

She's a beautiful woman and her beauty is breathtaking, boundless even. She wears color well. She's lovely really, just lovely.

When in a good mood, her brightness can light up a room, perhaps even a corner of the world. She sparkles. She's dewy.

Her movements can be gentle, natural, and graceful, like the rhythm of the wind.

Some people are now showing concern for her well-being, but others scoff at them. They don't see anything wrong. They claim, "She's fine. This is a big to do over nothing. This is just the way she's always been."

It's really not our fault "Not me," as my grandson, Louie, says. It's clearly those other folks. It must be their fault. They are responsible.

We do love her. We may take her for granted but we don't mean anything bad by that. We live in our own personal la-la-lands of life. We are just so busy. Gotta do this. Gotta do that. No time for this. No time for that. No time for her.

Yes, we really do love her. We just don't show it very well. We haven't taken her seriously. We're sorry, so very sorry. We didn't mean to hurt her. We didn't think what we did bothered her.

All of a sudden we realize how desperately we need her and love her and want her.

"Please don't give up on us," we beg. "It can't be too late. We can change. We will change. Please be patient with us. Please forgive us. We need you. Oh, how we need you."

Who is she? Why you know her well, of course. She's a mother, a mom, a grandmother, a nana, a great grandmother even. She's wise, loving, beautiful, resourceful. She's always there.

She's our Mother Earth, of course.

The Lion Sleeps Tonight

I stumbled out of bed and my husband said, "Ted Kennedy died." Sometimes emotion surprises us. When we think we should feel things, we don't necessarily feel them as we expect. And then sometimes when we don't expect it, they overwhelm us.

I quickly turned on the T.V. and watched. He had just died and the news was brand new. As I watched, my heart sank, tears flowed, and I thought to myself how surprised I was that all this emotion was within me about this man. I wouldn't have expected it.

I grew up in a small community that hated Catholics. Unless you have been on the raw end of prejudice, it is hard to imagine the way it feels. The scars from it last a lifetime no matter how hard you work at erasing them.

I was in high school when John F. Kennedy became President. I felt pride and joy that "one of us" had made it to an esteemed position. It gave all of us worth.

I remember vividly sitting at a dinner table while Americans passed by his coffin in the rotunda. The man whose table I was at said, "I don't know why they are making such a big deal. He was just a blank, blank Catholic." I still regret that I sat in silence and didn't reply to that hateful comment. But I was just a girl. I didn't know what to do. I am sure these things tied me to the Kennedy family.

The Kennedy's had a lot of imperfections. Just like the rest of us.

I loved the matriarch. Rose was such a strong faithful Irish woman. What wonderful gifts she gave to the world in her children.

Bobby was my hero. His vision was one of positive steps for mankind, all mankind.

I think what I have admired most about the Kennedys is their true caring for the underdog. They epitomized their mother's lesson, "To those to whom much has been given, much is expected."

I loved Teddy for taking care of the enormous brood of family he was left with. He never missed their events and was a father figure for all of them. In a life of many achievements, that was one of his greatest successes.

Recently we watched a documentary about Ted Kennedy. I was surprised at how he had, right from the beginning, fought for health care. When his father died, he said, "My father was able to have the best health care for the several years he was ill because we could afford it, but what about the person who can't afford it?"

When his teenage son had cancer and his leg was amputated, he said, "My son has been able to have the very best health care because we could afford it, but what about the person who can't afford it?"

Health care was not a new issue for Ted Kennedy. It was a lifetime mission he truly cared about. What so ever you do to the least of my brothers . . .

I remember my friend Gary went to Washington, D.C. years ago and heard Ted Kennedy speak. Gary had little respect for Teddy due to Chappaquiddick. After he heard Kennedy speak, Gary, who has the gift of oratory himself, said, "Hearing his enthusiasm, fervor, and dedication to provide justice and opportunity for all peoples, convinced me that he was too strong a champion for humanity to dismiss him because of one, albeit serious, personal mistake. I felt so moved when he finished, I think I would have followed him to hell and back".

This morning one of my friends, a staunch Republican, said, "Ted Kennedy wasn't just a democrat. He crossed the line." Meaning he was out for America, not just party affiliations. I thought this was high praise, even more so because it came from her.

I feel for the Kennedy family who has just lost Eunice, the founder of Special Olympics, and now their beloved Uncle Teddy. I feel for America. This family gave us so much: the peace corp., great civil rights progress, men on the moon, and on and on - Even their lives.

Talking with my friend, Hilda Sorvari, this morning, we shared how this is the end of Camelot. This is the end of that era. And, she said, "This was our era."

It has been quite a ride with the Kennedy Clan. John's rise to the top. His death. Bobby's rise. His death. John Jr.'s promise. His death. The parents. The siblings. The children. The spouses. The politics. The accents. The touch football. The faith.

The lion of the senate is no more. Uncle Teddy is no more. What he shared at Bobby's funeral rings true for him as well. "He need not be idealized or enlarged in death beyond what he was in life but to be remembered as a good and decent man, who saw wrong and tried to right it, saw suffering and tried to heal it."

In France there is a statue of Jesus with no hands. Where the hands should be is a sign that simply reads, "I have no hands but yours." The torch has been passed. Will we, all Americans, have the courage, intelligence and spirit to take it in our hands and continue the mission?

"Each evening, from December to December, before you drift to sleep upon your cot, think back on all the tales that you remember of Camelot. Ask every person if he's heard the story, and tell it strong and clear if he has not, that once there was a fleeting wisp of glory called Camelot. Don't let it be forgot that once there was a spot for one brief shining moment that was known as Camelot."

"May the angels welcome him to paradise…"

I Could've Had a Baby

Years ago, I ordered a chair for our living room. It took ten months before it arrived. I remember complaining to them, "I could have had a baby in this time."

Well, I am no longer of childbearing years. However, if I was, I could conceive and carry that baby through the first trimester, through the second trimester, through almost all of the third trimester, and then deliver a just slightly premature infant in the time it is going to take before we vote for President in November.

A pregnancy is a long, long time. If you don't think so, ask any woman who has accomplished this task - A long, long time. One goes through a lot in nine months. Ups and downs, nausea and aches, exhaustion and food cravings are but a sampling. These may be similar to things we will all go through as we await Election Day.

In a pregnancy, one wonders, "What will this baby be like?" As we watch the unbelievably long campaigns, we wonder, "What will this candidate be like as President?"

Is there really a baby in there? Is there really a President in there?

Will this baby change our lives? Will this new President change our lives?

I am *into* this election. I have watched more debates, listened to more CNN, NPR, and read more articles on this campaign than ever before in my life. But, I wonder. Can they sustain our interest for another 9 months? We are a fickle bunch. We are of instant feedback. We get bored more than quickly. It is quite amazing we have all been excited and interested this long. Another 9 months? I am not sure how they can keep our attention.

Imagine this. Right now we have snow up to our eyeballs. One day, not soon, they say, we will have spring. It will come, it really will. And... spring will go.

Summer will come. And summer will race by, as it usually does.

And then, one day, a long, long time from now, summer will leave us and kids will return to school. People will walk across Mackinac Bridge. Leaves will fall. The air will get crisp again. But, we will still not have gotten to Election Day. Oh, no, baby cakes.

We will have to go through the entire pumpkin and apple season. A gazillion people will have gone to orchards. Halloween will have come and gone.

And then, later yet, trick or treat candy will be on closeout sales. You can bet by November, Christmas songs will already be on the radio and Christmas displays will be in full regalia in the malls. Winter coats will be out. Mittens, hats and boots will be at the ready. Turkeys will be on the covers of magazines. And then, and only then, will we wander off to the election booths to decide our Presidential election.

Doesn't it all seem unbelievably far away? If so, that's because it is. Especially when most of us have likely already made up our minds who we want to vote for.

How will we make it? How does this go again?

Oh, yeah, I remember. Next it will get dirty. There will be lots of nasty ads. No matter who the final candidates are, they will likely do all they can to demean, debase and destroy their opponent. Ah, and that is how they will reel us in for the long haul. They will give us a new dose of reality TV.

Personally, I hate reality shows. I prefer unreality. Give me a dose of sex, violence and mystery. I can take that. It doesn't scare me. But reality, puh...leese. Do we have to prolong this agony? Couldn't we just vote now and spare ourselves the interminable wait?

High Hopes

It was a sunny day in April, 1968. My sister-in-law, Julie, and I stood together in downtown Grand Rapids watching a vibrant man speak. We were a few feet away. He wore a white shirt, sleeves rolled up. He had everyone captivated with his words, charm, sincerity and vision. He was running for President of the United States and we were on his bandwagon.

America was in the midst of a nasty war. Our country was in turmoil. Race riots and rebellion were everywhere. We needed Hope and he offered it.

About six weeks later, I was at Michigan State University. It was finals week. In the middle of the night I got up and heard the tragic news that our Hope had been assassinated as he won the California primary. He was, of course, Bobby Kennedy.

A couple days ago my husband and I watched the film, *Bobby*. It did not have an actor portray him but cleverly used real footage and tape to have the real Bobby Kennedy in all his shots. It brought back all the Hope he had given - All the Hope that had been shot away.

Fast forward forty years. And it did go fast. I sit here tonight. CNN has been showing the New Hampshire primary for hours. I like most of the candidates in both parties. Although a couple, not so much. But most of them I like, not that I would choose all of them for President.

As I watch CNN, our country is in the midst of a nasty war. Our country is in turmoil. Jobs gone. Health care a mess. World relations at a low point.

I see several speeches. Some better than others. But one reminds me.

He talks about unity in government, not division. He seems to understand that parties are so divisive that they are hurting America rather than helping it, that parties have lost sight of the real goal which is that it is more important to be an American for America than to be a Democrat or a Republican for their party.

He talks about hope. He tells us, "There has never been anything false about hope. Something is happening in America. We are not as divided as our politics suggest. We are one people. We are one nation. There is a spirit of America, a spirit of Americans that says, 'Yes, we can, heal our nation, yes, we can . . . "

I remember back to Bobby Kennedy saying, "That which unites us is, must be, stronger than that which divides us. We can concentrate on what unites us, and secure the future for all our children; or we can concentrate on what divides us and fail our duty through argument and resentment and waste."

I have hope. I want America to heal. I can't help but be inspired by this true voice ringing on the TV tonight, "Yes, we can heal our nation. We are one people. We are one nation."

Hope is unseen, but it is felt, and it feels good. We need it. It has been too long.

As I go to turn off my computer, I remember one last quote by Bobby. But I also remember that it was the last thing Teddy Kennedy said in his eulogy at his brother Bobby's funeral.

"There are those who look at things the way they are, and ask why . . . I dream of things that never were and ask why not?"

And I go to bed tonight with renewed hope. And I think to myself, "Why not? Something is happening in America. Yes, we can."

I'm Too Old To Be President

I'm tired. I don't think I should be. Been there?

We just drove back from Chicago. I use that verb loosely as my part of the driving was reading old Newsweek magazines. We listened to a few tunes, chatted a bit, and even made a couple stops on the way. Now we're home and I'm exhausted.

All this reminds me of a question I have about one of our political candidates for President. Now I am not talking politics here. I am not talking Republicans or Democrats. I am just talking the A word, age.

I like him. I admire him. I read his book. I have used him as an example in my talks for at least fifteen years. However, I am not sure, but I am thinking he might be too old to be our next president. What do I base this on? Myself – and a lot of my tired friends who will remain nameless and blameless.

I am more than a decade younger than him. I have always had a lot of energy. I think friends and family would say I do too much. And yet I often find myself too tired too often. I can still do what I used to do but now it takes longer, plus it also takes a few days to recover. Sometimes I need more than a few days.

The grandsons come to visit. They leave. I am exhausted.

I go on a work trip. I need a few naps to regenerate.

I used to stay up until 3 a.m. and my world would hardly blink. Now it takes a couple weeks to replenish my bad self.

I go to the mall, look at it and think, "It's just not worth it. I don't need anything that bad." I grab a latte and go home. My friends and I discuss the energy shopping takes and how it just has lost its glow. So have we, I'm afraid.

I asked several people if they think he is too old to be President. Most looked at me weirdly and said, "No, not at all." One, who is his age, said, "You have to remember, Maureen, he won't be doing laundry, meals, shopping, cleaning, yard work, errands, etc. He will *just* be being the President." Her words might as well have said, 'Piece of Cake'.

Perhaps that is the problem with my life. Perhaps it is the regular stuff that wears me out. Perhaps I need more things done for me to conserve my energy for the more important things, like meetings and big honkin' decisions.

I asked my husband what he thought of this candidate's age. He said, "Have you seen his Mother?" Apparently she is 96 and stumping the political trails with him. Both of them seem to be teeming with energy.

As I end this, I still feel tired. I don't know how he will do it. In fact, I look at each of the political candidates and think all of them will need a year or so to rest after this grueling year of campaigning. I sure would.

Peace, Hope, Truth and War

While visiting our daughter last week in Boston, we happened upon a Peace March. There were a variety of marchers - Quakers for peace, Veterans for peace, Surfers for peace. We noticed several MSU T-shirts. Go Green, I thought.

Signs were thought provoking. "This is what democracy looks like." "If you want peace, work for justice." "Build bridges not walls." "Give peace a chance."

One person was dressed like a cow. His sign read, "No war, no whey."

There was a group of Raging Grannies singing. They are part of a national organization. They held signs and sang for peace. One song was to the tune of *Over There*. The words were, "and we won't shut up till it's over, over there."

Many signs urged "support our troops". I believe that is a universal American value. Everyone supports the troops, wants them safe and is grateful to them.

The march was surrounded by rows of military boots, one pair for each U.S. soldier killed in Iraq. Each was tagged with their name and pertinent information. There was also a moving wall inscribed with the names of all those U.S. soldiers killed to date in the Iraq War. Each one was someone's child; someone's loved one, someone's hero. We have lost thousands and the Iraqis have lost hundreds of thousands.

Years ago, at the height of the Viet Nam war, my husband and I went to a party in Spain. When we got there, a man from North Viet Nam was also there. It was unnerving. I remember looking at him, trying to see what kind of person he was, fear in my heart.

Our images of Iraqis are individual, likely colored by media and politics.

Yesterday I had surgery. My doctor is top in his field in Western Michigan. All of my encounters with him have found him to be gentle, quiet, kind and brilliant. He has been here since the early 70's. I assumed he was Lebanese or something similar. When I asked him where he was from, he quietly said, "Baghdad, Iraq, the place you are at war with."

I had not met anyone from Iraq before. I would have liked to talk with him about it more, but by then it was time for me to take the anesthetic and him to take the knife. In spite of the war and our nationalities, he was on my side.

I think when we think of war, we forget about the actual people. It is too much for us to take in. It is easier for us to go about our day. How else can we survive?

According to the American Friends Service Committee, there was more than $1 trillion spent in the first four years of this war. I can't wrap my brain around one trillion dollars. I am so old that I still think $100 is a lot of money. They also said that one day of the Iraq war equals 720 million dollars.

Whether one agrees with these statistics or not, that is a lot of dinero, bro. As we look around and see so many things being cut and so many needs going unmet, one wonders. Political speeches. Statistics. Facts. Confusion. The truth?

When I was a preschooler, I lived with my great grandparents. My great grandpa used to sing, "Glory, Glory, Hallelujah. Glory, Glory, Halleluiah. Glory, Glory, Halleluiah, the truth is marching on." And so it is, if we can find it. War. Peace. Money. The facts, ma'am, nothing but the facts.

A person in the peace march wore a sign in Spanish, "Todos somos esperanzo." We all are hope. Blanche, our friend, has recently been quoted, "I see hope." I want to see hope too. I want to believe in hope when I look into the big blue eyes of my little grandsons.

Where do we go from here?

Elie Wiesel, the famous writer and holocaust survivor, said, "Mankind must remember that peace is not God's gift to his creatures; it is our gift to each other." The truth is marching on.

Patriotism is Alive and Well

I am a proud American. Aren't we all? All we need do is take note around us.

A couple weeks ago I stood at the National Prayer Day celebration. It was full of people of all ages. It was very pro America and very pro God. Children came to the microphone and sang, "I'm Proud to be an American" as the crowd sang along. I was not the only one who had tears in my eyes as we experienced the powerful blend of patriotism and faith. To watch the children standing in their plaid uniforms singing their heart out about America, all from their heart, was extremely touching. Patriotism.

Last week we went to a Detroit Tigers game. The Tigers lost, but to be there in that beautiful stadium, full of people of all ages, singing the national anthem, was worth the drive. It was touching and heart warming. Patriotism lives. Let's play ball.

Monday we went to a friend's funeral in Illinois. As he was a former marine, the final part was the military honors. The firing of the guns followed by the mournful taps and then the careful folding of the American flag and giving it to the family. As a sidebar, this family had another funeral two days later for one of their nephews who was killed in Iraq last week. Patriotism.

Recently I was one of a group of women who went to see Barack Obama in Grand Rapids. The audience of 12,000 was all ages and economic levels. A soldier home from Iraq in dress uniform and on crutches with a major injury came out to lead the crowd as they put their hands on their hearts and all said the Pledge of Allegiance. It was very powerful to experience that in such a huge group. Patriotism.

And now, tonight - We've come a long way, baby …. Boomers. We have lived through the race riots in Detroit in the sixties. We have lived through the race riots in Grand Rapids the same summer. We have lived through Rosa Parks getting on the bus. To us she is not just a park. We have lived through Martin Luther King's dream. We have lived through many demonstrations for equality. And now here we are. June, 2008. This is the moment. A half black man is the democratic candidate for President of the United States. What a great historical moment for America. We all had a dream and it was of equality and this is the moment. How can we be anything but proud of our country? Whether we are Republican, Democrat or Independent, this is a wonderful moment in our country. Yes, we have come a long way and I am proud. Patriotism.

Yes, God blesses America and God loves all the children of the world. Red and yellow, black and white. God loves all the children of the world. Patriotism.

Proud To Be An American

A few years ago Bette Midler sang a popular song, *From a Distance*. The refrain sang, "God is watching us. God is watching us."

America today is in a new place, a place I am proud to see. I have two little grandsons who will never remember when you had to be white to be President. That will be something they will only read about in history books.

My friend, Kean, said this morning, "It is our generation that rose the current generation of young voters to not be racist." I hadn't thought of it that way. As Representative John Lewis said last night, "Some gave their life for this moment. Some gave their blood."

I am so proud to be here today and see our country rise to this moment of greatness.

I heard an 84 year old woman on National Public Radio yesterday. She was born in a cotton field. She said, "Racism still lives in the hearts of many. They hate me just because I am black. I don't know why. I'm beautiful."

Right here in our county there have been comments using the "N" word. People hatefully spit it out. This is sad, but it is more than that. It is intolerable.

I believe we are called upon to not just listen when we hear words like that, but to speak up and say something.

A few years ago a local businessman I know told me a joke which mocked gay people. I listened and when he finished I said to him, "You should never repeat that." I felt if I didn't speak up, I was part of it. I did not want to be part of it.

Silence can be golden but it can also be agreement.

This is a new day. Machiavelli said, "There is nothing more difficult to take in hand, more perilous to conduct or more uncertain in its success than to take the lead in the introduction of a new order of things."

Last night John McCain gave an eloquent and gracious concession speech. It was from his heart and rang of the old John McCain. He encouraged all Americans to come together and work together with our new president.

My cousin, Deirdre, lives in Connecticut. I saw her recently and she said she visualizes Barack Obama surrounded by angels protecting him. I loved that. I have done it many times each day since and have shared it with others to do. I now share the concept with you. May we all see Barack surrounded by angels for protection, and also, for guidance. May they guide him on this perilous and critical journey.

As we come to this new day, as we come to this new dawning in our country, may we each look into our hearts and say, in the words of St. Francis of Assisi. "Lord, make me an instrument of your peace: where there is hatred let me sow love; where there is injury, pardon; where there is doubt, faith; where there is despair, hope; where there is darkness light; where there is sadness joy."

And may we look to the future with open hearts and open minds. May we each be willing to change and to let go of prejudices and fear and believe in the hope unseen. And may we each believe in our hearts that yes, we can heal America. Yes, we can become better. And, yes, we can be a part of this greatness. "God is watching us. God is watching us."

For Your Reading Pleasure

For Your Reading Pleasure '09

My friend, Laurel, says she is going to write her life story. The title will be, "The Only Place You Take Me is for Granted". It sounds quite titillating, but until this happens, here is a list of books you may want to read over the summer and year.

Harriette, Gisela, Paul and Dolores and Laura all suggested *The Guernsey Literary and Potato Peel Pie Society* by Shaffer and Barrows. As goofy as this title sounds, people rave about it and say it is a charming, delightful historical novel. I'm in.

Ladies recommended their favorite chick reads. *Annie Freeman's Fabulous Traveling Funeral* by Kris Radish. Kean - *While My Sister Sleeps* by Barbara Delinsky. My cousin, Diane, said *Dewey, The Small-Town Library Cat Who touched the World* by Vicke Myron is a wonderful book. Laura gives us *A Friday Night Knitting Club* and the sequel *Knit Two* by Kate Jacobs, also the *Yada Yada Prayer Group* by Neta Jackson. She said they are great easy reads. Gisela suggests *Bonesetter's Daughter* by Amy Tan. *Sing Them Home* by Stephanie Kallos comes from Mary who just loaned me *No! I Don't Want to Join a Book Club* by Virginia Ironside. She and Linda said they laughed out loud as they read it. The subtitle is 'Diary of a Sixtieth Year' – wonder why she thought of me.

Maureen suggests, *The Soloist* by Steve Lopez. Beth urges us to read *Yellow Star* by Jennifer Roy. My daughter, Colleen, recommends *The Girl Who Stopped Swimming* by Joshilyn Jackson as a great beach book. Jodie felt *The Middle Place* by Kelly Corrigan was a fast, easy read and said she called others to read parts out loud so they could laugh together over it.

Bonnie said the spiritual story, *The Shack*, by William Paul Young, was good for discussion. I got some good stuff out of it.

I just finished a personal favorite of all time, *The Book Thief* by Marcus Zusak. The writing style and descriptions were as good as any I have ever read and the story pulls you right in. My husband and daughter, Donna, also loved it as did Connie and Hilda.

My daughter-in-law, Drea, just read *Columbine* and said it was hard to put down. It is highly reviewed and compared to *In Cold Blood* by Truman Capote, a book I will never forget.

Mary said for light fun the *#1 Ladies' Detective Agency* series is delightful. It is by Alexander McCall Smith and currently an HBO series. Darci and I really enjoyed *Whistling In The Dark* by Lesley Kagen.

Patti suggests the *Fancy Nancy* series for reading to young children. I found them delightful.

Holly said *Stealing Buddha's Dinner* by Bich Minh Nguyen is a fun read many of us will relate to as the author grew up in Grand Rapids.

Carol felt the award winning *The Florist's Daughter* by Patricia Hampl was mesmerizing and beautifully done. Harriette suggested *Consider This, Senora* by Harriet Doerr and said the writing is exceptional. Arleta's book club in Steamboat Springs enjoyed *Still Alice* by Lisa Genova and thought it a great read.

Nancy said *Thunderstruck* by Eric Larson is a suspenseful, action packed true story.

Gerry recommends *The Secret History* by Donna Tartt. I liked it and one of my favorite sentences came from it. "A spider of anxiety crawled up my spine."

My son, Dan, is reading the latest Stephen King, *Just After Sunset* and raving about it. Don said the latest John Grisham, *The Associate* is a good fast read.

If you want to stay or get hip, read *Twilight* by Stephanie Meyer, the first in a series of vampire books that fill the best seller lists. Though not very into vampires, I found it a decent read. And, now I'm hip. Well, maybe not, but I did read it.

Two non-fiction ones I got lots out of were *The Screwtape Letters* by C.S. Lewis and *Faith Club* by Idliby, Oliver and Warner. Gary says if you want to enrich your life read *The Art of Being Human* by Janaro and Altshuler.

Let me throw out a couple more that are on my table waiting for me. Each came highly recommended: *Loving Frank* by Nancy Horan, about Frank Lloyd Wright; *People of the Book* by Geraldine Brooks, my daughter loved this one; *The Double Bind* by Chris Bohjalian; and *True Fires* by our last years One Book author, Susan Carol McCarthy. Of course, the book I have to read next was given to me by Phyllis, *Coping with Your Husband's Retirement*. Gulp.

Here's hoping you get some good reading out of the above book suggestions. Remember what Mark Twain said, "The man who doesn't read good books has no advantage over the man who can't read them." Enjoy.

For Your Reading Pleasure '08

Memorial Weekend is over. School years are ending. Get ready to kick back and relax for summer. I checked with several readers and have come up with a new batch of books you may want to read as you relax in the sunshine.

Tom just reread *Pillars of the Earth* by Ken Follett and claims, "It is still one of my favorites. The new sequel, *World without End*, is also very good." Tom, along with Marty and most readers I know, recommend, *A Thousand Splendid Suns* by Khaled Hosseini. We loved *Kite Runner* and this one is even better.

Barb just finished *Mistaken Identity*, the true story of the Taylor University accident victims by Newell Cerak, Susie and Don VanRyn. "I thought I really knew what happened but this was a very heartwarming tale."

Julie raved about *Luncheon of the Boating Party* by Susan Vreeland. "It's a historical novel about Renoir's masterpiece, a delight, very French. It discusses Impressionism, Degas, Monet, the Prussian war, etc."

Mo is excited over *A Long Way Gone: Memoirs of a Boy Soldier*, by Ishmael Beah.

Many are excited with Eckhart Tolle's *A New Earth / Awakening to your Life's Purpose*.

Linda enjoyed *Sin in the Second City* about Chicago after the world's fair by Karen Abbott; *The Liar's Diary* by Patry Francis, described as riveting; and *After This* by Alice McDermott, a novel that covers the span from World War II to Nixon and all the colorful events in between.

Connie and Katie both recommend *A Girl Named Zippy* by Haven Kimmel, a light memoir of a girl growing up in Indiana. I enjoyed it and laughed out loud at times. Connie also loved *The Other Boleyn Girl* by Philippa Gregory. It is lots better than the movie.

Gisela has been shouting from the rooftops about *The Good German* by Joseph Kanon. She read it and immediately read it again. She hated the movie and said it didn't even relate to the book.

Don and Donna were both engrossed with *Miracle in the Andes* by Nando Parrado, the true story of the crash in the Andes Mountains where people were left for dead for 72 days. This is the first thing written by one of the survivors and it got 4 stars in reviews.

Mary enjoyed *Snow Flower and the Secret Fan* by Lisa See, a story of women in China.

Julie highly recommends *90 Minutes in Heaven* by Don Piper, a true story of a man who died for 90 minutes and came back to life. Julie raved about it so much I gave it as Christmas gifts even though I haven't read it yet.

Many people have suggested *Three Cups of Tea* a true story by Greg Mortenson and David Oliver Relin about a man's mission to promote peace, one school at a time.

Several women I know have enjoyed *Eat, Pray, Love* by Elizabeth Gilbert.

My husband liked John Grisham's, *The Appeal*. Jodi Picoult's *Change of Heart*, came out as #1 on the New York Times Best Sellers List. I really liked it.

The Sledding Hill by Chris Crutcher is one to try. I had a friend from Ohio call and tell me, "Go get all Crutcher's books. They're fabulous."

While in Chicago, I noticed an ad about *The Long Goodbye*, a mystery by Raymond Chandler, written in 1953.

Michigan Reads, a statewide One Book program, is reading *The Nick Adams Stories* by Ernest Hemingway, featuring a lot of Michigan.

Don't miss *Lay that Trumpet in our Hands* by Susan Carol McCarthy. Dotti called me a few minutes ago and said she had just finished it on CD and loved it. I said, "It is good." And she replied, "No, it is way better than that. It is magnificent. It is tremendous." I hope you read it and feel the same way she did.

Ahh, there you go – several good books, sunshine and thee. Enjoy.

For Your Reading Pleasure '07

For most people, summer is different than the rest of the year. There is all that promise of what we will do, see, and get done. Part of that promise is reading some good books.

As I am in a few book clubs, I thought I would share some of our favorites as ideas for good summer reads. These come with the endorsements of me, my family and my reading buds.

Jodi Picoult has *Nineteen Minutes* and *My Sister's Keeper*, both fast, excellent reads.

Khaled Hosseini wrote two fantastic books – *Kite Runner* and *A Thousand Splendid Suns*.

Other famous authors have changed their pattern and come out with non-fiction, both to high acclaim. John Grisham has *The Innocent Man* and Scott Turow has *Ordinary Heroes*.

If you like historical fiction, *1000 White Women* by Jim Fergus and *March* by Geraldine Brooks are wonderful stories. I loved them both!

Some oldies but goodies that I just read or reread and found phenomenal - *Cry, the Beloved Country* by Alan Patton and *To Kill A Mockingbird* by Harper Lee.

If you like historical romance, everyone I have talked to loved *The Other Boleyn Girl* by Philippa Gregory. The sequel received four stars, *The Boleyn Inheritance*. Fast paced, romance, history.

Some fantastic non-fiction. *Devil in the White City* by Erik Larson, a superb book on Chicago. My son said this is his "favorite non-fiction of all time". Quite a comment as he is a voracious reader. *Ghost Soldiers* by Hampton Sides is unforgettable, as is *Night* by Elie Wiesel. *Left to Tell* by Immaculee Ilibagiza and *Glass Castle* by Jeannette Walls are quick memoirs that shake your boots with their reality.

Just darn good novels – *The Girl with the Pearl Earring* by Tracy Chevalier, *The Memory Keeper's Daughter* by Kim Edwards, *The Time Traveler's Wife* by Audrey Niffenegger, *East of Eden* by John Steinbeck, and *The Poisonwood Bible* by Barbara Kingsolver

Quick and suspenseful – *House of Sand and Fog* by Andre Dubus and *Montana, 1948* by Larry Watson.

Light and delightful – *The Curious Incident of the Dog in the Nighttime* by Mark Haddon, *The Secret Life of Bees* by Sue Monk Kidd, and *Broken for You* by Stephanie Kallos.

If you are looking for motivational, *The Secret* by Rhonda Byrne, can offer you some ideas.

If you want pure raucous fun, and I often do, listen to the numbered series by Janet Evanovich. You can read them, but I love to listen to their fun New Jersey accents and characters that just come alive on audio. Begin with *One for the Money* and proceed through the numbers until you get to her latest. Carl Hiassen is another delight. *Skinny Dip* and *Nature Girl* are two fun ones to start with. Both of these authors make you laugh out loud with their colorful characters and fun shenanigans.

Water for Elephants by Sara Gruen is fast paced, suspenseful, educational, and has a surprise ending. It is just a great story and one that both men and women can enjoy.

Abe Lincoln once said, "The things I want to know are in books; my best friend is the man who'll get me a book I ain't read." I hope you find one or two books here that you haven't read and that you really enjoy them. Happy summer reading, friends.

Relevant Recipes

The Best You Can Buy

I have a few recipes that are so good that once I made them, I never tried another. I felt it just couldn't get any better. For instance, I made a *macaroni and cheese in the seventies and it still remains the best we have found. I would serve it to the Queen. That may be hard to do, though, because I don't know her and I don't think she is coming to my house for dinner in this lifetime.

In the last few years I have found some products that are so good that I make a decision, then and there, to never try another brand or to make my own. I couldn't do it better so why bother. Life is too short as it is. I decided it might be a good idea to share some of these treasures with you.

In the frozen bread section you'll find La Brea French baguettes. They are small loaves and take ten minutes to bake - Hot, crusty, kind of like sour dough. Yumm. I love to make bread and I love to eat homemade bread, but none are any better than this. I first had these at a dinner party and thought, for sure, that the hostess had slaved baking them. What a delightful surprise to find out they came out of a plastic bag all ready to bake. They are often a regular on our dinner table.

Key lime pie can be an ordeal to make. Once I tried Edward's frozen, I decided to never make homemade key lime again. I recently was asked to take dessert to a gathering of gourmet cooks. The stakes were high. I took Edward's frozen key lime pie, topped it with fresh raspberries and voila. I noticed everyone cleaned their plates and a couple strangers came over and asked for a piece. That Edward knows what he's doin'. Oh, and I nearly forgot to tell ya, you can buy single servings. I'll bet, though, that one serving won't be enough. It is so good my daughter-in-law asks for it as her birthday cake.

Sangria is the national drink of Spain. There are many recipes out there but I have not tried or tasted one that tastes authentic. Real Sangria comes in bottles or a nice bright orange box with a spout. It tastes authentic and wonderful. Add some lemon, orange and lime slices and you've really got something. How do you say ahhhh in Spanish?

Today a couple of my friends and I confessed to each other that we never make our own oil and vinegar salad dressing. Why would you when Paul Newman has done it for you? Paul's oil and vinegar is perfecto and the raspberry walnut vinaigrette is equally superb. And the money for Paul's products goes to charity. Way cool!

Connie told me that Paul Newman's Own Lemonade is the best she's tasted. It comes in a paper milk type carton - Just what you need on a hot day.

She said this thought process also works for other things. She has a stainless steel refrigerator which shows every mark and is difficult to keep clean. She quit buying cleaning products for it and now uses a solution of 1/3 vinegar and 2/3 water which she puts in a spritz bottle. How smart is she? And green too. Actually this was an idea from her husband who got the idea when he worked in the kitchen at Michigan State University. There was a lot of stainless steel to clean and this was the solution - Even more meaning to Go Green.

Remember the old line about reinventing the wheel? I guess that is what this is all about. When certain items are so great, why reinvent that ole wheel? Better to just enjoy and be grateful.

*Recipe in this chapter.

6-Hour Oven Stew

3 pounds cut stew beef, trimmed

1 bag carrots, cut (I use the ones ready to eat.)

5 pounds potatoes, cut (peeled or not)

Fresh mushrooms, sliced (could do canned or omit)

1 ½ lg. onion, cut into pieces

4 cans tomato soup, undiluted

4 cans French onion soup, undiluted

4 cup rose or red wine (any cheap kind –
the red makes it richer, I prefer the rose)

Seal VERY tight with foil and bake in a roaster.
Bake 350 for one hour then 250 for 5 hours.

Add bag peas the last half hour.

(This is the recipe as Nancy Fox gave it to me. You can't go wrong.
I usually double it in my turkey roaster and it fills it.
You could add anything else you want. You can see that measurements
are loose. No matter what – it turns out yummy.)

Stew in a Pumpkin

3 pounds stew beef	3 Tbl. oil, divided
1 cup water	3 large potatoes, cubed
8 medium carrots, sliced	1 lg. green pepper, chopped
8 oz. fresh or canned mushrooms, drained	1 ½ c. frozen peas
4 cloves garlic	1 medium onion, chopped
2 tsp. salt	½ tsp. pepper
2 tsp. beef bullion, instant	28 oz. can crushed tomatoes

12 – 14 pound pumpkin (Be sure it will fit in your oven. You can use foil for the top – you can also bake the top alongside of the pumpkin)

Adjust amount of ingredients for pumpkin and guests. Adjust water & bullion for desired consistency.

Brown beef in 2 Tbl. of oil in heavy pot. Add rest of ingredients except remaining oil and pumpkin. Simmer, covered for 2 hrs.

Wash pumpkin. Cut 6" – 8" hole for top. Clean out.

Preheat oven to 325 degrees.

After 2 hours of simmering, put stew in the pumpkin & place in a shallow pan, like a cookie sheet. Brush outside of pumpkin with the rest of the oil. Put pumpkin top back on top of the pumpkin or use foil.

Bake 325 for 2 hours or till pumpkin is tender. Do not overcook!

Serve with a bit of pumpkin in each dish.

Makes 8 servings. Takes 5 hours.

(I got this recipe from my friend, Sharon Cooper.)

Blueberry Cobbler

Filling:

6 cups blueberries
½ cup sugar
1 T and 1 t. cornstarch
1 tsp. lemon juice
¼ tsp. coarse salt
Mix all together and put into 8 x 8 pan.

Topping:

¾ cup flour
½ cup rolled oats
½ tsp. baking powder
½ tsp. salt
6 Tbl. unsalted butter (softened)
1/3 cup sugar

Cream together softened butter and sugar.
Slowly add rest of ingredients.
Bake at 350 degrees for about 50 minutes.
Put loose foil over the top if it starts to get too brown.
Once mixed, put small amounts in your hand and put over blueberry mixture.

(I got this recipe from my daughter, Donna.
Someone told me Martha Stewart did it on T.V.)

Yummy Chicken Casserole

¾ cup chopped onion
½ cup chopped celery
1 Tbl. chopped green onion tops
¼ cup chicken broth
10 ½ oz. can cream of chicken soup
1 cup dairy sour cream

3 cups cooked, cubed chicken
4 oz. can sliced mushrooms, drained
3 slices crisp crumbled bacon, if desired
1 tsp. salt
1 tsp. Worcestershire sauce
1/8 tsp. pepper
¼ c. shredded cheddar cheese

Preheat oven 350 degrees

Combine onions, celery and chicken broth in saucepan; simmer 20 minutes.
Combine in 2 qt. casserole – soup, sour cream, chicken, mushrooms, bacon, salt,
Worcestershire sauce, pepper and cooked vegetables. Mix well. Drop biscuits
by tablespoonfuls onto casserole. Bake at 350 for 40 – 45 minutes until golden
brown. Sprinkle with cheese. Return to oven until the cheese begins to melt.

Biscuits:

1 cup flour
2 tsp. baking powder
½ tsp. salt
2 eggs, slightly beaten
½ cup milk

1 Tbl. chopped green pepper
1 Tbl. dried red pepper flakes or chopped pimiento
1 cup shredded cheddar cheese

Combine in mixing bowl – flour, baking powder and salt.
Add eggs, milk, peppers and cheese. Mix just until blended.

Serves 6 – 8.

(This recipe was a Pillsbury Bake-Off Third Prize Winner.)

Warm Apple-Buttermilk Custard Pie

(The key to both a flaky piecrust and crisp strudel is to keep them as cold as possible before putting them into the oven.)

Crust:
½ (15 oz.) pkg. refrigerated pie dough

Cooking spray

Streusel:
1/3 cup all purpose flour
½ tsp. cinnamon

1/3 cup packed brown sugar
2 ½ Tbl. chilled butter,
cut into small pieces

Filling:
5 cups sliced peeled granny smith apples
(about 2 pounds)
2 Tbl. all purpose flour
3 large eggs
1 tsp. vanilla

1 cup granulated sugar, divided
½ tsp. cinnamon
¼ tsp. salt
1 ¾ cup buttermilk

Preheat oven to 325

For crust – roll dough into a 14" circle, fit into 9" deep dish pie plate coated w/ cooking spray. Fold edges under, flute. Place pie in refrigerator until ready to use. (I have used an 11 x 7 pan and it filled it to the brim)

Streusel: Spoon 1/3 cup flour into a dry measuring cup, level with a knife. Combine 1/3 cup flour, brown sugar and ½ tsp. cinnamon. Into a medium bowl Cut in butter with a pastry blender or 2 knives until like coarse meal. Put in refrigerator.

Filling: Heat in a large nonstick skillet coated with Pam over medium heat – add sliced apples, ¼ cup sugar, 1/2 tsp. cinnamon. Cook 10 minutes or until apples are tender, stirring occasionally. Spoon apple mixture into crust.

Combine remaining ¾ cup sugar, 2 Tbl. flour, salt and eggs, stirring with a whisk. Stir in buttermilk and vanilla. Pour over apple mixture.

Bake 325 degrees for 30 minutes. Reduce to 300 degrees. (Do not remove pie from oven.) Sprinkle streusel over pie Bake 300 degrees for 40 min or 'til set. Let stand 1 hour before serving

(This recipe was a Pillsbury Bake Off Champion.)

Pineapple Zucchini Bread

3 eggs
1 cup vegetable oil
2 cups sugar
2 tsp. vanilla
2 cups shredded zucchini
¾ tsp. nutmeg
1 cup raisins

3 cups flour
2 tsp. baking soda
1 tsp. salt
¼ tsp. baking powder
1 ½ tsp. cinnamon
1 can (8 ¼ oz) crushed pineapple, well drained
1 cup chopped walnuts

In mixing bowl – beat eggs, oil, sugar, and vanilla – till thick. Stir in flour, soda, salt, baking powder, cinnamon and nutmeg.

Add zucchini, pineapple, raisins and walnuts. Blend well.

Pour into 2 greased bread loaf pans (5 x 9).

Bake 350 degrees for one hour or till toothpick comes out clean.

Makes 2 loaves.

(This recipe came from my friend, Sharon Pridgeon.)

Baked Apple Donuts

Combine: 3 cups flour
1/8 tsp. salt
1 tsp. nutmeg
4 tsp. baking powder
1 cup sugar.

<u>Cut in:</u> 2/3 cup shortening.

<u>Add</u> – 2 eggs, beaten
½ cup milk
1 cup apple, peeled and grated.

<u>Mix</u> just to moisten.

Put in muffin pans ½ full.

Bake 350 degrees, 20-25 minutes.

Remove while hot.

<u>Dip</u> in melted butter.
Then roll in mixture of 1 cup sugar and 2 Tbl. cinnamon.

(This recipe came from my mother-in-law, Florence Burns.
My daughter, Colleen, won a newspaper cooking contest with it.)

Apricot Slush

Boil 9 cups of water - steep and squeeze with 4 green tea bags.

Add - 1 large frozen orange juice and 1 large frozen lemonade.

Stir in 2 cups sugar and a Fifth of apricot brandy.

Freeze.

To serve: mix in a glass ½ frozen mixture and ½ Fresca, 7-Up or the like.

(This recipe came from Molly Jorgensen.)

From Chapter 7: "Goofin' Goofballs"

Cream of Asparagus Soup

1 T. vegetable oil
½ cup onion, chopped
4 cup chicken broth
¼ cup butter
¼ cup flour
½ t. salt
¼ t. pepper
3 cups milk or half and half

5 cups asparagus, cut into 1" pieces
1 ½ t. lemon juice
¼ t. tarragon
reserved asparagus tips to garnish

Heat oil in large saucepan and sauté onion over medium heat until soft but not brown, about 5 minutes. Add chicken stock, asparagus and seasonings. Simmer over medium heat until vegetables are tender. When vegetables are soft, blend in food processor or blender until mixture is smooth. Do small amounts at a time.

Melt butter in a heavy 8 qt. pot over low heat. Slowly blend in flour, salt and pepper. Cook, stirring to form a smooth paste, just until mixture starts to turn golden. Add milk slowly, stirring constantly. Cook until mixture thickens. Add asparagus puree and cook, stirring, until heated through. Serve immediately. Garnish, if desired.

Serves 6.

(This recipe came from Simply Classics – The Junior League of Seattle.)

Crusted Lamb Chop

4 servings
Grilling method: direct/medium heat

1 rack of lamb (8 bones) about 1 ½ pound
Kosher salt
4 large cloves garlic, cut in half
3 T. Dijon mustard

1 Tbl. Herbs de Provence
fresh ground pepper
¼ cup chopped fresh parsley
ground salt

1. Prepare charcoal fire or preheat gas grill.

2. Pat the lamb dry with paper towels. Cut the rack into 4 double chop portions and spread them out on a sheet of waxed paper. Sprinkle both sides with salt. Using half a clove per side, rub the garlic all over the meat. Discard garlic and set meat aside.

3. In a small bowl, mix the mustard and herbs and pepper. Spread this mixture over both sides of the lamb chops.

4. Place the lamb in the center of the cooking grate over direct medium heat, bone side down. Cover and grill 8 – 10 minutes with out turning. During the last 2 to 3 minutes of cooking time, sear both sides of the lamb over the heat to add grill marks.

5. Remove the lamb to a clean platter, and let it sit for 5 minutes before serving on a bed of parsley with the bones interlocking. Sprinkle with ground salt. (The bones make their own rack, holding the chops away from the cooking grates.)

This recipe comes from the wife of my dentist.

Corned Beef Glazed

3 pound corned beef
1 cup dark orange marmalade or light will work
4 Tbl. prepared Dijon style mustard
4 Tbl. brown sugar

Put corned beef in a large pot and cover with boiling water. Bring to boil on low heat, cover partially and simmer as slowly as possible for about 3 hours or till very tender when tested with a fork. **(I put mine in crock pot and cook for 7-11 hours. I also add potatoes, carrots, onion and cabbage - whatever amounts you want – I fill the crock pot.)**

When done – preheat oven to 350.
Mix marmalade, mustard and sugar in bowl.
Remove meat and drain, put on baking dish, pour marmalade mixture over it, coat thoroughly – Bake for 30 min or until glaze is crisp and brown. (I have also broiled this when in a hurry.) Serve hot or at room temp.
I keep veggies warm and serve all together on one plate, hot.

I usually get a bigger corned beef and follow same glaze recipe. You can't go wrong with this recipe. As long as your beef ends up tender.

(This recipe originally came from the Silver Palate Cookbook. I've adjusted it.)

Irish Whiskey Bread Pudding with Caramel Whiskey Sauce

For Pudding:
¼ cup butter, melted
½ cup raisins
¼ cup Irish whiskey
1 cup sugar
12 oz. can evaporated milk

10 oz. French bread baquette,
cut into one-inch thick slices
1¾ cup milk
1 Tbl. Vanilla
2 large eggs, lightly beaten

Cooking Spray
1 Tbl. Sugar   1 tsp. cinnamon

- Preheat oven to 350. Brush melted butter on one side of French bread slices, placing bread buttered sides up on baking sheet. Bake 10 min. or until lightly toasted. Cut bread into ½ "cubes, set aside.

- While bread is toasting, combine raisins and whiskey in bowl and cover. Let stand 10 min. or till soft – don't drain.

- Combine milk, sugar, vanilla, evaporated milk and eggs in lg. bowl, stir well with a whisk. Add bread cubes and raisin mixture, pressing gently to moisten, let stand for 15 minutes.

- Spoon bread mixture into 13x9 baking dish coated w/ cooking spray. Combine 1Tbl. sugar and cinnamon and sprinkle over pudding. Bake 350 for 35 minutes or until pudding is set.

Serve warm with caramel whiskey sauce. Yield – 12 svgs. You may substitute ¼ apple juice for Irish whiskey, if desired.

Caramel Whiskey Sauce
1½ cups sugar
¼ cup butter
¼ cup Irish whiskey

2/3 cup water
2 oz. cream cheese
¼ cup milk

Combine sugar and water in a small heavy saucepan over medium-high heat. Cook until sugar dissolves, stirring constantly.

Cook for an additional 15 minutes or until golden – do not stir. Remove from heat. Carefully add butter and cream cheese, stirring constantly with a whisk – the mixture will be hot and bubble vigorously.

Cool slightly and stir in the whiskey and milk. Yield 1 ½ cups, serving size 2 Tbl.

You can substitute 1Tbl imitation rum extract and 3 Tbl. water for the Irish whiskey, if desired.

Don't let these directions scare you. This is worth the effort and not hard to make
(This recipe is used on Norwegian Cruise Lines. I got it from a magazine.)

Luann's Fruitcake

4 cups walnut halves.
1 ½ cup pitted dates, halved
1 ½ cup whole candied cherries
1 ½ cup candied pineapple chunks
¾ cups diced candied orange peel
1 cup + 2 Tbl. flour
1 cup + 1 Tbl. sugar
¾ t. baking powder
1 tsp. salt
4 eggs
1 T. vanilla
1 tsp. rum flavor
¼ cup brandy or dry sherry, optional

In large bowl, combine walnuts, dates, cherries, pineapple, and orange peel.
Add flour, sugar, baking powder and salt. Mix well.

In small bowl, beat eggs with vanilla and rum flavorings.
Pour over fruit mixture. Stir until well mixed.
Turn into paper lined and greased 9 x 13 pan. Spread evenly.

Bake on bottom rack of oven at 275 degrees for about 1 ½ hours
or until it tests done.

Remove from oven. Let stand ½ hour in pan. Remove from pan and cool
thoroughly. If desired, sprinkle evenly with brandy or sherry. Cut crosswise
into four even strips. Wrap each in foil and store in cool place or freeze.
Makes 4 small fruitcakes.

(I got this recipe from my sister-in-law, Luann Potts.)

Homemade Macaroni and Cheese

Cook 1 ½ c. elbow macaroni, drain

Melt 3 Tbl. butter
Stir in 3 T flour.
Add 2 cups milk (whole is best but skim works).
Cook and stir till thick.
Add 2 cups sharp cheddar cheese, shredded.

Add ½ tsp. salt (I add more) and pepper to taste,
¼ cup minced onion (I cook up some raw onion on the side, in a little butter – I add quite a bit of onion as we like it in it – we think it is what makes the dish so good.)

Mix sauce and pasta.
Put in 1 ½ qt casserole dish.

Bake 45 minutes, 350 degrees.
Makes 6-8 servings.

(I got this recipe from an old high school friend, Glenda.)

Other books by Maureen Burns:

RUN WITH YOUR DREAMS

Over 100,000 copies sold internationally!

"...one of the most powerful tools I've read to change your life for the better." – Og Mandino

"There is no greater gift to bestow than to encourage people to follow and develop their positive dreams. This book does just that ... for everyone. Read ... and be inspired!" – Dr. Robert Schuler, Minister Crystal Cathedral, California

FORGIVENESS

Featured in Reader's Digest and McCall's magazines.

"Wonderful! Very moving, simple and direct – a firewooks finale." – Norm Nickle, Therapist, Washington

"Without a doubt, Maureen's best! A timeless master. Vital." Rudy Bengston, Businesswoman. Arizona

"This book is an invaluable tool for forgiving others and forgiving yourself." – Jim Doughty, Therapist, Tennessee

GETTING IN TOUCH . . . INTIMACY

A book about people, love and caring. Vital message. Easy format. Practical ways to enhance relationships in your life – with yourself, mate, children, family and friends.

"Excellent! Made me re-evaluate my life." – J. H.

"A wonderful gift for everyone you love – including yourself!"

CARA'S STORY

By Maureen A. Burns and Cara M. Burns
Illustrations by Mary B. Stek

Foreword by:
Elisabeth Kubler-Ross, M.D.

COPING WITH LIFE, DEATH, AND LOSS
A TRUE STORY

Featured across the United States and Canada in major newspapers, T.V. and National Public Radio.

A book for children written by Maureen and her daughter, Cara, when Cara was eight years old.

"I recommend this book . . . it is very valuable." – Elisabeth Kubler-Ross, M.D.

"Book about life, death, called hit." – Lansing State Journal

". . . moving beyond words . . ." – Teacher and Mother

To Order Books and Tapes:

Run With Your Dreams – book $10

Cara's Story – book $10

Forgiveness / A Gift You Give Yourself – book $15

Getting in Touch / Intimacy – book $10

Looking and Laughing at Life – book $12

Maureen Burns on Humor – C.D. or tape $10 for C.D. / $5 for tape

Maureen Burns on Motivation – C.D. or tape $10 for C.D. / $5 for tape

Maureen Burns Presents: Forgiveness –
    C.D. or tape $10 for C.D. / $5 for tape

Maureen Burns Presents: Stress Busters –
    C.D. or tape $10 for C.D. / $5 for tape

Maureen Burns Presents: Change Happens –
    C.D. or tape $10 for C.D. / $5 for tape

Email maureenburns@maureenburns.com or call 616-754-7036 to order.
Visit our website at www.maureenburns.com

Maureen Burns is an international professional speaker, author of five books and a weekly columnist. She has four grown children, two adorable grandsons and lives in Greenville, Michigan, with her husband and gifted dog. Visit Maureen's website at www.maureenburns.com.